7-29-74

The
Man's Cookbook

Also by the author:

THE INSTANT GOURMET

THE
MAN'S COOKBOOK

F. A. Roszel

SOUTH BRUNSWICK AND NEW YORK:
A. S. BARNES AND COMPANY
LONDON: THOMAS YOSELOFF LTD

© 1974 by A. S. Barnes and Co., Inc.

A. S. Barnes and Co., Inc.
Cranbury, New Jersey 08512

Thomas Yoseloff Ltd
108 New Bond Street
London W1Y OQX, England

Library of Congress Cataloging in Publication Data

Roszel, F   A
    The man's cookbook.

    1. Cookery, International. I. Title.
TX652.R674   641.5   73-122
ISBN 0-498-01317-0

Contents

1824880

SOME USEFUL AMERICAN, ENGLISH
AND METRIC EQUIVALENT MEASURES

U. S. Liquid Measures	*Metric*
1 gallon	3.785 liters
1 quart	.946 liters
1 fluid ounce	29.573 mililiters

U. S. Dry Measures	*Metric*
1 quart	1.101 liters
1 pint	.550 liters
1 teaspoon	4.9 cubic centimeters
1 tablespoon	14.8 cubic centimeters
1 cup	236.6 cubic centimeters

U. S.	*English*
1.032 dry quarts	1 quart
1.201 liquid quarts	1 quart
1.201 gallons	1 gallon

1 English pint	20 fluid ounces
1 American pint	16 fluid ounces
1 American cup	8 fluid ounces
8 American tablespoons	4 fluid ounces
1 American tablespoon	½ fluid ounce
3 American teaspoons	½ fluid ounce
1 English tablespoon	⅔ to 1 fluid ounce (approx.)
1 English tablespoon	4 teaspoons

The American measuring tablespoon holds ¼ oz. flour

Preface

In spite of my obviously light-hearted approach, I admit that the preparation of outstanding food is a serious business. There is, however, no reason to approach the kitchen in other than the best of spirits. (That's the cooking wine, friend.)

The secrets of the truly great chefs are related to time, temperature, and sequence of adding ingredients in the cooking process, as well as the cunning use of herbs, spices, and wines to enhance flavor and titillate the taste buds. If you are squeamish about using alcoholic beverages in your cooking, you are not a gourmet, you're a Puritan. In that case you may dash off and spread your snowy cloth on Plymouth Rock, while I get on with making happy things for the initiate.

The recipes I use have been carefully chosen and tested for the best results in taste. I have also taken into account the problems of the busy host-chef who must entertain guests on short notice. I have supplied short-cuts to gourmet meals for the minor miracle of, "Dinner in just a few minutes, folks."

Whether you use the long or the short routes to being the hero of the kitchen and the lion of the party, you will find these recipes will help you make a friend(s). Stick closely to the important directions as to time, temperature, and ingredients. If you follow these priceless gems of the culinary art carefully, you'll be a popular host. Should you overtrain on the cooking wines, you may flip out and fall flat on your Escoffier, and become famous for the production of meals that taste like stewed blotting paper.

Depending on the ends you have in view, it may at times be advisable to take a little more time in the preparation of a meal. "Just help yourself to some more wine, honey. I'll be just a few more minutes in the kitchen." This may result in a somewhat delayed dinner, but in such a situation, who thinks of time?

Of course, in the event that you are entertaining your boss, the opening gambit is different. In that case, you prepare your gourmet items the night before, and just pop them into the oven, so you'll have plenty of time to hoist a few with your personal slave driver, while giving him your views on the problems in the old jute mill. He'll admire your efficiency, and will maybe be softened up enough for you to approach him about the raise you've been angling for.

I certainly have no intention of recommending that you learn to cook like grandma did. Don't let your nostalgic memories fool you. At that age you could digest a nail, and your hunger was an awesome thing. Your grandmother lacked many of our advantages of today: our tenderizers and spices, our wines and herbs, our transport and communication. Due to these factors it is regrettably true that some of grandma's cookbooks were about as digestible as some of grandma's cooking, and the baking soda was a postprandial institution.

Our aim is to help you entertain with brilliant cookery that will enhance your reputation, make your guests happy, and still leave you with time and energy for the more important diversions. If you are the lucky host who has a lady friend with kitchen skills, this will lighten your burden when entertaining a group. However, should you forget the old adage about flogging a willing horse, you may find that you've thrown a hook into your other avocation.

Very few people agree as to the selection and use of wines in cookery, or as to what wine to serve with what dish. As a general rule, serve dry wines before the meal and sweeter wines after eating. A sweet aperitif wine or a bitter wine will dull the taste buds. In wine cookery, the standard rule of white wines with white meats and fish, and red wines with red meats, does not necessarily apply. If you are fond of a particular wine in your glass, it usually follows that you will also like the flavor in your cooking, and that a wine taste you dislike will be no more pleasurable in your favorite dish. Adventurers have more fun than hidebound traditionalists, anyway, so let your spirits rove free while you experiment. The selection of wines as to quality and cost is another indeterminate area. I have a friend who is considered an excellent host, who often serves good domestic wines with a considerable flair. It must be remembered that women young enough to be in the exciting bracket are seldom connoisseurs of wine, and that taste and atmosphere is more important to them than vintage, cost, and origin.

My friend to whom I referred goes in for atmosphere. He has a few of those wicker serving baskets for wine, and a few old wine bottles. I have seen him decant a bottle of good domestic wine into an old Clos Veugeot bottle, wrap it in a snowy cloth, and put it into the wicker basket, then serve it with appropriate verbal tributes such as, "Can't compromise with quality, darling. For you, only the best is good enough." Should you, however, be serving a boss or client, who is portly, red-faced and rheumy eyed, be more careful to serve a highly rated vintage wine. You may find that he has long been supporting two vineyards in France, and that he can name the wine and the vintage by the bouquet alone.

If you are a long-time gourmet host-chef, it is likely that your figure may have taken on a certain rotundity through the years. Some male counterpart of Twiggy may make some snide remark to the effect that you are much too heavy for your height. Explain to him that this is not so; what you are is too short for your weight and you just can't seem to grow any taller. While he is figuring this one out, you can escape to enjoy your obesity, unimpeded.

Introduction

This aid to convivial gourmets is aimed at those free souls who are dedicated to the entertainment of business associates, together with their wives or mistresses, clients and the women of their choice, mistresses (ours or theirs), and sometimes maybe, just friends.

In presenting these gems of culinary art from around the world, I assume that my most interested readers will be those free-swinging singles who are involved in entertaining people, and in the enjoyment of the resulting dividends.

These forays into the gourmet world of spicy capers are for the palate-tickling, soul-satisfying interludes where man gets closest to whatever heaven he believes in—via the shortest route—his, or her, appetite.

In presenting my suggestions for dining and entertaining, I make no apology for collaboration with that seductive quartet:

candles,

wine,

Hi-fi,

and Simmons.

1

It's Cocktail Time

Assuming that you have hidden the Wedgewood, and checked your insurance policies, you may consider the entertainment of the local aborigines in a bash called a cocktail party. This is the kind of togetherness that could start World War III. These peripatetic house wreckers are dedicated to damaging as much furniture and as many reputations as possible in the shortest time. Ideally, a cocktail room should be hewn out of solid rock, with stainproof, breakproof furniture weighing four hundred pounds per piece. Failing the ownership of such a room, you may be able to save some of the finish on furniture by covering the tops solidly with ash trays. Even so, some potted arsonist will be ingenious enough to find a gap and burn hell out of your Louis XIV breakfront. I've always thought that credenzas and cocktail tables should be topped with firebrick slabs. If you have a Bokhara, I hope you hid it. The only rug that could come unscathed out of a cocktail party is one of those indoor-outdoor rugs that resist weather, horse hooves, and farm tractor cleats. The comic who grinds out cigarette butts on your pet Bokhara may be frustrated, but you'll be happier. You'd think that craftsmen clever enough to weave a beautiful Oriental rug could also teach it to scream!

It is wise to remember that men and women are different. (Okay, okay, I'll drink to the difference!) However, what I meant is that men and women differ greatly in their eating

and drinking habits. Women like long, mixed drinks, and
dainty little hors d'oeuvres, while convivially minded men
like more lusty fare. If you are pitching a mixed party you
can conserve the liquor, control the decibels, and curb the
lease-busters by serving tasty, hearty snacks. Your guests will
not arise the next morning with a gargantuan skull due to
gastric imbalance from ingesting too many drinks and far
too many little marinated horrors. They will be grateful
that you sent them home healthy and happy, rather than
having put them into orbit.

Regarding drinks, I build the party around one main
drink, very successfully. For instance I may make rum blos-
soms the day before the party, and store them in the refrigerator in a large pitcher. Then if you put the nicely frosted
pitcher on ice in a large bucket, everyone will be duly im-
pressed. This presentation is worth its weight in guilders.

I will now lay out for you, chapter and verse, all the rules
for producing party goodies that may elevate you to saint-
hood, in your time.

MELTON-MOWBRAY PIE

This is the famous and lusty old English meat pie, eaten and
loved by all the visiting pub crawlers, as well as the local
gourmets. History is not clear as to the origin, whether Melton
invented the crust and Mowbray the filling, or perhaps it is
a breeding line, and the pie is by Melton out of Mowbray.
Perhaps it is not a pedigreed pie, and it may be that Melton
had an oven deep in the woods outside a village called Mowbray. Whatever the origin of the name, the product has been
famous for many years.
I will not attempt to give you the old recipe for the crust,
as its long and tedious preparation might keep you away
from earning your living in the slave shop for a whole day.

What
1 pig's foot
1 onion
1 stalk celery, with leaves
1 carrot
1 bay leaf
1½ lbs. lean pork, diced ½ inch
Pastry for 2, two-crust pies
2 tbsp. bacon fat, or oil
½ cup seasoned flour

How
Cover pig's foot, onion, celery, carrot, and bay leaf with water. Boil slowly, covered, for three hours. Stock should be reduced to ¾ pint. Shake diced pork in seasoned flour, and brown in the fat or oil. Roll out pastry about ¼ inch thick and line a deep, 1-quart baking dish, saving enough for the cover. Moisten meat with ½ cup of the stock, and press firmly into the pie shell. Cover with pastry and flute the edges. Make a ½-inch hole in the center of the cover. Bake at 300 degrees for 2½ hours. Make a thick gravy with the seasoned flour and the balance of the stock. When pie is removed from oven, pour full of gravy. Keep the gravy hot, and fill the pie again as it cools and shrinks. This pie jells firmly when cold, and is eaten cold.

Note
Some chefs prefer to put a few hard-boiled eggs in the middle of the pie. This is a matter of individual taste.

BEEF AND KIDNEY PIE

This dish is referred to as Vintage B & K pie in London. Usually served cold for lunch. Also made into small pies for an entree at dinner.

What

1 beef kidney, diced about ½ inch
1 lb. round steak, or flank steak, diced ½ inch
1 cup kidney fat, diced fine
3 onions, chopped
3 cups hot water
1 tsp. salt
½ tsp. pepper
1 tsp. dry mustard
½ cup flour, browned lightly
½ cup cold water

How

Melt the kidney fat until crisp. Add the diced meats and brown over high heat, two minutes. Add the onions and continue to brown. Pour the hot water and seasonings over the meat and bring to a boil. Cover and cook over low heat about two hours, until meat is tender. Mix the flour and cold water and add to meat. Cook until well thickened.

Line an earthenware or Corningware deep pie dish with pastry, and pour in the meat mixture. Top with crust, cut vents to let steam out, and bake one hour at 375 degrees. Serves six to eight.

Pastry:

What

¼ cup water
½ cup lard
2 cups all-purpose flour
½ tsp. salt
½ tsp. savory
¼ tsp. sage
½ tsp. baking powder

How

Sift dry ingredients together until well mixed. Bring water to boil and add lard. Remove from heat and stir until creamy and smooth. Stir in dry ingredients and mix well. Shape into a ball, wrap in waxed paper, and refrigerate for an hour. Roll out thin.

TOURTIERE

This is not a misspelling of the word torture. This is a lusty and taste-tempting meat pie, traditionally French. It may, in fact, be partly responsible for the virility attributed to thousands of Frenchmen. I take no responsibility for what happens in the bedrooms of France, but I can recommend this dish for hearty satisfaction.

What

½ lb. beef, minced
¼ lb. lean pork, minced
¼ lb. smoked bacon, minced
1 medium onion, chopped
1 garlic clove, minced
¾ tsp. salt
½ tsp. savory
½ tsp. celery powder
¼ tsp. ground cloves
¾ cup water
½ cup fine bread crumbs
2 tbsp. Burgundy

How

Place all ingredients except breadcrumbs and wine in a saucepan and boil twenty minutes. Remove from heat, add the wine and half the crumbs. If fat is not all absorbed, add the balance of the crumbs. Cool, and pour into pastry-lined pie pan. Cover with crust. Bake at 400 degrees until golden brown.

Pastry:
Bring ¼ cup of water to a boil and add ½ cup lard. Melt lard and remove from heat and stir until smooth and creamy. In a large bowl sift together 2 cups all-purpose flour, ½ tsp. salt, ½ tsp. savory, ¼ tsp. sage, and ½ tbsp. baking powder. Stir in the lard-water mix, and mix well. Shape into a ball. Wrap in waxed paper and refrigerate for an hour. Then roll out for the crust.

BEEF ROLLS SUISSE—For guests you love!

What
8 cube steaks—about 4 inches square
2 tbsp. peanut oil
½ tsp. garlic salt
½ tsp. salt
¼ tsp. pepper
8 slices natural Swiss cheese
8 thin slices back bacon
1 egg, beaten with 2 tbsp. water
¼ tsp. thyme
¼ tsp. oregano
1 cup fine, dry, bread crumbs
1 can condensed mushroom soup
½ cup red Burgundy

How
In hot pan, quickly saute cube steaks in oil, about ½ minute on each side. Remove and cool. Season, and roll up with cheese and bacon slices. Fasten with picks. Add balance of seasonings to bread crumbs and mix. Dip rolls in beaten egg, then in crumbs. Put in baking dish. Pour in mushroom soup and wine. Bake 45 minutes at 350 degrees. Serves 4 or 8.

SWISS ONION CAKE

I picked this gem up in Geneva, where they served it both hot and cold. It's a popular snack at any time.

What
For the pastry:
1½ cups sifted all-purpose flour
1 tsp sugar
½ tsp. salt
½ cup butter
3 tbsp. milk
The filling:
6 slices bacon
3 cups chopped onion
2 beaten eggs
1 beaten egg yolk
½ tsp. M.S.G.
1 tbsp. all-purpose flour
½ tsp. salt
Dash of white pepper
1 tbsp. parsley or chive flakes

How
Sift dry ingredients into bowl. Cut in butter. Add milk, 1 tbsp. at a time, just until flour is moistened. Gather into a ball. Pat ⅔ of dough into bottom of an 8″ x 1½″ round cake pan. Bake at 425 degrees until lightly browned. Cool on rack. Turn oven down to 325 degrees. Fry bacon crisp, drain, and crumble. Cook onion in bacon fat until tender. Drain off fat, and mix onions with balance of ingredients, except parsley or chive flakes. Return cooled cake to pan. Pat remaining dough around edges of pan. Pour in filling. Bake at 325 degrees about 25 minutes. Let stand to set, about ten minutes, then cut in wedges, to serve. Excellent as an appetizer.

OYSTERS HOWARD HUGHES

The serving of Oysters Rockefeller has long been a tradition at the party intime. The difficulty with this status symbol is that the sauce is always made with spinach. People who are truthful seldom admit to a real liking for spinach. It's doubtful if even the oyster would admit liking spinach, so it's a lousy way to treat an inoffensive oyster. I have replaced the spinach with watercress, which makes a richer, more tasty sauce, so much so, in fact, that I call my dish Oysters Howard Hughes, rather than Rockefeller.

What
1 dozen oysters on deep side of shell
1 cup chopped watercress
2 tbsp. parsley
4 tbsp. chopped celery
4 tbsp. chopped green pepper
1 clove garlic
2 green onions, with tops
1/4 tsp. dried thyme
1/4 tsp. salt
1/4 tsp. black pepper
4 tbsp. butter
1 tbsp. lemon juice
2 oz. white wine
1/2 oz. brandy

How
Fill deep pie pans two thirds full with salt. (Coarse salt if available). This will keep oysters from tipping and spilling sauce and juice, and will keep them hot at the table. Arrange six oysters in each pan. Make sauce by running watercress, onions, parsley, celery, green pepper, and garlic through the fine blade of meat grinder. Put the ground mixture in saucepan with the butter, salt, pepper, and thyme, and

simmer slowly for thirty minutes. Add wine and brandy
and cook five minutes. Stir in lemon juice. Put 1 tbsp. of
puree in each oyster. Broil under medium hot broiler for
ten minutes and serve hot.

Caution!
If you are the timid type, remember the reputation of
oysters for potency. Serve only to a lady whom you trust. I
would not want the responsibility for an attack on your virtue!

SHRIMP RAREBIT

When I make this dish, I hollow out Vienna rolls, cut in
half, or thick slices of French bread, hollowed out to make
patty shells. I then butter, and toast them under the grill.

Filling:
What
1 — 7 oz. can drained shrimp
½ cup diced green pepper
¼ cup butter or margarine
⅔ cup flour
2 cups milk
4 oz. grated, old cheddar cheese, soaked in 2 tbsp. dry
      white wine
1 tsp. Worcestershire sauce
½ tsp. dry mustard
¼ tsp. paprika
Dash of freshly ground black pepper
6 patty shells, bought, or prepared as above

How
Saute green pepper in butter until tender. Stir in flour
until well blended. Stir in milk and stir-cook until smooth.
Add cheese, Worcestershire, mustard, paprika, and pepper.

Stir until cheese melts. Taste and correct for salt, but remember that canned shrimp are rather salty. Add shrimp
and heat to serving temperature. Fill hot patty shells with
the shrimp, sprinkle a little paprika on the top, and serve.

L O B O Y S T E R

If you like to go first class in dining, and hang the expense,
this dish will light up your horizon on the darkest day.

What
1 lobster—about 2 lbs.
Juice of one garlic clove
2 tbsp. butter
2 tbsp. flour
18 fresh oysters
½ pint whipping cream
½ tsp. paprika
¼ tsp. white pepper
½ cup medium sherry

How
Boil lobster in salted water for ten minutes. Shell, and cut
meat into bite-sized pieces. Saute in the butter and garlic
juice, for five minutes, stirring and turning. Remove from
pan and stir in flour, until smooth. Add oyster liquor and
cream, and stir-cook until thickened. Add sherry and seasonings, then the lobster and oysters. Simmer until the edges
of the oysters curl. Serve in patty shells or on toast points
to anyone you wish to put in a mellow mood.
Serves up to four.

B A R   H A R B O R   T A R T S

With all the emporia that make the name Bar Harbor for
real, you might look deep into your martini and exclaim,

"All this and Bar Harbor tarts too." Before your thoughts go too far afield, we hasten to explain that these are highly edible tarts, with a goodness your guests will remember long after the platters are cleaned.

What
1 cup crab flakes
¼ lb. grated mild cheddar
1 cup sliced mushrooms
2 tbsp. lemon juice
1 tbsp. flour
¼ tsp. mace
½ tsp. salt
⅛ tsp. pepper
3 eggs
2 tbsp. grated Parmesan
Paprika
Pastry for 2-crust pie, or 10 patty shells

How
Line tart tins with thin pastry. Put in each a layer of mushrooms, a layer of crab, and a layer of grated cheddar cheese. Sprinkle on lemon juice. Beat eggs with seasonings, flour, and cream. Pour evenly into tins. Bake 25 minutes in a preheated 375 degree oven.

Caution!
Set one aside for yourself. Your guests will not leave one for you! You can also use clams—baby or diced— in this dish.

DANISH SANDWICHES

The open-faced Danish sandwich is a natural at a cocktail party for fast preparation and attractive appearance. Since bread is the foundation, you can use a variety of breads, such as pumpernickel, whole wheat, swartbrod, toasted French, cheese bread, corn bread, and other varieties of party breads. Having buttered the foundation slice, you have a choice of basic meats, alone or in combination, for the piece de resistance of the sandwich. The thinly sliced meats are put on with one third of the slice rolled, usually with three of these overlapping rolls per sandwich. They can be garnished with tomato slices, gherkin fans, cucumber, green pepper, or onion slices. Egg slices, sieved egg yolk, diced jellied bouillon, and a variety of cheeses are also used, either as garnish or part of the melange.

The true art in making these sandwiches lies in the artistic sense of the host or hostess. Color and taste combinations are infinite. Variations such as curry mayonnaise, chive mayonnaise, horseradish cream, devilled ham, change or accent the tastes of the more solid parts of the concoction. Just let yourself go, and prove your individuality.

Try Some of These
Sliced pepperoni with mozzarella cheese and green pepper rings.
Camembert cheese with Mandarin orange slices.
Corned beef with cucumber slices and onion rings.
Tuna fish on lettuce with horseradish cream, watercress, and a twisted lemon slice.
Ham slice with pineapple slice and chive cream cheese.
Salami with slices of head cheese, and chive cream cheese.
Pork roll slices filled with horseradish cream, and with stuffed olives.
Danish Blue cheese with shredded carrot and black olive slices.

With the above as an example, you can let your imagination rove free, and be a hero to your guests.

TUNA MUSHROOMS

What
24 medium mushrooms

2 tbsp. parsley flakes
24 apricot halves
1/4 tsp. black pepper
1/4 cup wine vinegar
1/4 cup soy sauce
1/3 cup sugar
1/4 cup dry sherry
2 tbsp. chopped onion
1 can tuna—6 or 7 oz.

How
Bring liquid ingredients to boil with sugar. Pour over mushroom caps and marinate 5 hours. Drain, reserving 1/2 cup marinade. Finely chop mushroom stems and heat in the marinade to a slow boil. Boil 3 minutes. Strain off and reserve marinade. Mix mushroom stems with pepper, parsley, and tuna. Stuff mushroom caps and top with apricot half.

SHRIMP TOAST

What
2 cans shrimp—5 1/2 oz. each
4 links cooked pork sausage
1 tbsp. Parmesan cheese
2 tbsp. minced onion
1 tbsp. soy sauce
1 egg, beaten
1/4 cup fine cracker crumbs
8 slices bread

How
Chop shrimp and sausage finely. Mix with other ingredients, except bread and Parmesan cheese. Toast one side of bread under broiler, very fast. Remove and spread opposite side with mixture. Sprinkle with Parmesan and toast under broiler. Cut into triangles and serve with a lemon wedge.

QUICHE CANADIENNE

For cocktail parties in French Canada, they whop up a dish called Quiche Canadienne. The filling is used either in pie shells, or in tart shells, and makes a delicious change from all the little bores on sticks, and smeared on limp toast.

What
Pastry for 9-inch pie shell, or 24 small tart shells
6 strips bacon, fried and crumbled
¾ cup grated old cheddar cheese, plus 2 tbsps.
1 tbsp. flour
3 eggs, well beaten
¾ cup light cream
¼ tsp. salt, and dash of pepper
1 tsp. instant onion

How
Line pie plate or tart tins with pastry, and bake in a 425 degree oven for 12–15 minutes. Place bacon in bottom of shell. Dredge ¾ cup of cheese with the flour and sprinkle evenly on top of bacon. Combine eggs, cream, and seasonings and pour in. Sprinkle with remaining cheese, sprinkle with paprika, and bake at 350 degrees until custard is set—30–35 minutes. Serves six, or twelve cocktail snacks.

Note
This dish is versatile. You can vary the cheese, use tuna, salmon, ham in the filling. Wedges of smoked meat can be used in topping, and for men, small slices of blue cheese can be added as topping—for a zingier flavor.

SAUSAGE RUSSE

Sometimes, for a cocktail party, a hot dish will cool the fast drinkers and restore balance. To serve 8, you need 8 ramekins or other small ovenproof dishes. This dish doesn't take long to make, and can be made ahead and reheated.

What
16 links of pork sausage
8 servings of instant mashed potato
1 can brown gravy
¼ cup dairy sour cream
1 cup grated old cheddar
1 tsp. Kitchen Bouquet or Bovril
2 tbsp. grated Parmesan
1 tbsp. paprika

How
Saute sausages until browned lightly all over. Prepare potatoes as directed on package. Divide into greased ramekins. Top with 2 sausages each. Heat gravy, stir in sour cream and cheddar cheese, and pour evenly over sausage. Sprinkle with Parmesan and paprika. Reheat and serve. Serves 8.

Occasionally your guests will be hungrier, or there will be more of them than you expected, or late stayers will expect something more substantial to eat. In such a case, you can have in the refrigerator, all ready to heat quickly in a casserole:

SWEET-SOUR BEANS AND FRANKS

What
2 #2 cans red kidney beans
6 frankfurters
⅓ cup granulated sugar
1½ tbsp. cornstarch
¼ cup water
⅓ cup cider vinegar
1 tsp. basil flakes

How

In saucepan, heat sugar, water, cornstarch, liquid from beans, vinegar, basil. Boil 10 minutes, stirring. Slice franks and stir in with beans. Cook 5 minutes. Remove from heat, cool, and refrigerate.

Next day, if required, turn into a casserole and heat.

Serves 8 smorgasborders or 4 hungry late stayers.

HUNTER'S LOAF

Here is an excellent cold buffet snack that keeps well and is also inspirational fare at a picnic.

What

1 large loaf French bread
¾ lb. ground lean beef
½ lb. ground pork
1 cup chopped onion
4 oz. tomato sauce
1 envelope plain gelatin
½ tsp. garlic powder
1 tsp. salt
½ tsp. black pepper
¼ tsp. hot paprika or cayenne
1 tsp. oregano flakes
2 eggs, beaten with
4 tbsp. milk
2 tbsp. potato flour or cornstarch
1 cup soft bread crumbs

How

Saute pork in pan until lightly browned, with onion. Add beef and brown lightly. Soften gelatin in tomato sauce, and add with seasonings. Remove from heat and cool slightly and mash meats together. When cool, stir in beaten eggs,

combined with milk and cornstarch. Stir in bread crumbs.
Remove inside from French loaf, from one end, and stuff
with the mixture. Return end to loaf, and fasten with picks.
Bake at 350 degrees for 1 hour, brushing occasionally with
milk. Cool and slice as desired.

New Orleans has some winning ways with crab. This dish
will inject some real gourmet expertise into your bash.

CRABMEAT DIJON

What
1 lb. flaked crabmeat
2 cloves garlic
¼ lb. butter
8 mushroom caps
6 green onions, with tops, sliced
1 green pepper, chopped
1 cup milk
1 tbsp. flour
1 tbsp. parsley flakes
½ cup medium sherry
4 tbsp. Parmesan cheese
8 rounds of toast
1 cup bread crumbs
1 tsp. Dijon mustard
Salt and pepper

How
Slice garlic and brown in the butter. Discard garlic. Add
mushroom caps and saute 3 minutes. Remove and set aside.
Add green pepper and onions. Stir-cook 5 minutes. Add flour
and mix well. Stir in milk and parsley and stir-cook until
smooth and thickened. Mix in crabmeat, sherry, and bread
crumbs. Season to taste, cool enough to handle and form

into 8 balls. Put toast rounds on a cookie sheet. Put 1 ball
on each round, sprinkle with Parmesan cheese. Spread Dijon
mustard on mushroom caps and put one on each ball. Brown
lightly under broiler. 8 canapes or 4 snacks.

CRAB AU DIABLE

What
12 slices bacon
1 lb. crabmeat
¾ tsp. dry mustard
½ tsp. paprika
½ tsp. celery salt
¼ tsp. garlic powder
¼ tsp. Tabasco sauce
½ cup chili sauce
1 tsp. wine vinegar
1 cup mayonnaise
½ cup cracker crumbs
2 tbsp. cream

How
Divide crabmeat into six ramekins. Fry bacon and crumble
evenly on top of crabmeat. Mix balance of ingredients
thoroughly and divide on top of bacon and crabmeat. Glaze
lightly under broiler.

ARE YOU FONDUE A CHAFING DISH?

A chafing dish and/or a fondue pot is a swank and easy
way to feed a group.

You'll be thrilled to learn that some variation of the
chafing dish or fondue pot has been around for about a
thousand years—give or take a hundred or two. The ancient
Chinese who were not too busy procreating sat around large

earthen pots of boiling oil and cooked chunks of passing animals. Sometimes their meals were a bit irregular, due to the unpredictable travel schedules of the animals. The happy faces, reflected in the cooking oil, were the Chinese version of modern TV. When they needed an oil change, they dumped the boiling oil over the wall on the heads of their visiting enemies.

When you are having a party, the chafing dish keeps the guests busy, and panders to the inquisitor submerged in the more elemental souls. Watching the look of fiendish glee on the ugly pans of some of your guests as they skewer pieces of meat on a long, lethal fork, and immerse them in the hot oil, you can be sure that, on the couch, they'd admit to symbolically deep-frying a love rival or business associate in the said oil. Anyway, the chafing dish gives the creeps something to do besides boring you with their golf scores, or inciting your jealousy by recounting their successes with the wench in the next office.   1824880

For tools at this kind of clambake, you need a solid chafing dish stand with a good Sterno or alcohol burner to keep the fat or bouillon at a constant heat.

Should your guests have slanted eyes, or even think they have, give these poseurs chopsticks that have been presoaked in water. This prevents their becoming a funeral pyre before Nature has a chance to catch up with them.

If the party is mixed you will need several sauces. Men like more highly flavored sauces than do women.

A few ramekins that you can use to keep sauces hot in the oven until serving are useful.

So . . . happy chafing, and if your guests drink faster than they dip, hide the forks. Dueling you don't need.

So . . . let's go on with the adjuncts to less painful partying.

WHOLE PEA SOUP (ERBENZUPPE)

A full-bodied, flavorful pea soup, made with a master's touch, is sheer gustatorial delight. This one is made the Penn-Dutch way. I have seen a three-quart tureen disappear in an hour at a buffet party.

What
For the stock:
1½ lbs. smoked pork hock
2 beef soup bones
1 lb. chicken neck or backs
2 carrots
2 stalks celery, with leaves
1 medium onion
2 bay leaves
½ tsp. pepper corns
1½ tsp. salt
3 whole cloves
1 clove garlic

For the soup:
1 lb. whole dry peas
½ tsp. baking soda
1 finely diced carrot
½ cup diced onion
½ cup finely diced celery
¼ tsp. thyme
¼ tsp. rosemary

How
Soak the peas in water to cover, with the baking soda, for five hours. Put all the ingredients for the stock in three quarts of water in a covered soup pot. Simmer three hours, keeping the stock built up to 2½ quarts by adding water when required. Strain off the stock and save it. Flake the meat off the bones, and hold it aside. Wash the peas well, after draining, and add them to the strained stock. Cook them in the stock until the skins begin to flake off. Add

the vegetables and seasonings, with the flaked meat. Cook twenty minutes, and serve. You should have three quarts of soup and a lot of happy gourmets. Even nongourmets will admit to liking this Erbenzuppe. Serves about fifteen, without seconds.

FONDUE ALPINO

In this elastic dish you can use anything from chunks of uncooked Polish sausage (kielbasa) to beef tenderloin. Small spicy meat balls, pork tenderloin, cubes of firm Swiss cheese, chunks of chicken breast, are the common ones.

The tenderloins and chicken breasts should be cut into chunks, then flattened and recut into serving size dipping pieces. Fill the fondue pot with about 2 inches of cooking oil (peanut oil is good), and bring to a bubble. Add a slice of raw potato to prevent splattering.

It is usual to serve a chunky salad and crusty bread with the meal. Give everyone a plate to work on, and have the sauces handy so they can put a selection of their favorites on their plates. Dipping dishes are not very satisfactory for sauces, as they become diluted with oil from the pot.

Some people like their meat chunks marinated in various marinades for an hour or two before the eating starts. One good marinade for pork tenderloin goes like this:

Crush one clove of garlic into a paste with one tsp. salt. Add to one cup soy sauce, with ¼ tsp. ground ginger, 1 tsp. sugar and ½ tsp. M.S.G. Mix with the sliced meat in a bowl and marinate 24 hours in the refrigerator. Bring to room temperature before serving. Should be well drained before dipping into the oil to avoid spattering.

Other marinades include French dressing with oregano and garlic, and such marinades as a clove of garlic crushed into a tablespoon of dry red wine vinegar, 1 cup of red wine, ½ cup dry white wine, 2 tbsp. lemon juice, 1 tsp. dry mustard. The possibilities for the inventiveness of a free-roving spirit are infinite in the making of marinades. It is wise to remember that the function of a marinade should be to accent, rather than to submerge flavor. As to dipping sauces, the variety goes on and on into the far distance. Should you happen to have a blender, the variety of sauces and the texture of them are certainly enhanced.

FONDUE EMMENTALER

Since the Swiss serve kirsch both in this fondue and on the side, you can end up both well nourished and comfortably stoned. Prosit!

What
1 clove garlic
2 cups grated or chopped Swiss cheese (Tilsit or Emmentaler is best)
3 tbsp. flour
½ tsp. dry mustard
2 cups dry white wine
A dash of nutmeg
1 tsp. salt
¼ tsp. white pepper
½ cup kirsch, or light rum
Large loaf crusty French bread, cubed 1½ inches

How
Split garlic clove and rub inside the fondue pot or chafing dish. Pour wine and seasonings into pot and bring slowly to a bubble, but do NOT boil. Mix cheese, flour, and mustard thoroughly, and add slowly to wine, stirring steadily, until smooth and thick. Reduce heat and stir in kirsch. Keep hot, and dip the bread cubes at will. Happy kirsching!

CRAB FONDUE

What
10 oz. sharp cheddar cheese spread
16 oz. cream cheese
1/2 tsp. Worcestershire sauce
2/3 cup milk
1 1/2 cups crabmeat
French bread cubes

How
Over low heat, combine cheeses, milk, and Worcestershire sauce. Stir until smooth and well mixed. Fold in flaked crabmeat. Hold hot, and dip in French bread cubes.

QUICK'N EASY FONDUE

There's a fast, easy way to cheat a little on preparation time, and yet serve an appetizing fondue.

What
1 10 oz. can cheddar cheese soup, undiluted
1/4 cup grated cheddar cheese
1 tbsp. grated Parmesan cheese
2 tbsp. dry red wine
1/4 cup apple juice
1/4 tsp. garlic powder
2 egg yolks, beaten

How
In the chafing dish, heat soup, garlic powder, and cheese, stirring until cheese is melted. Add some of the hot mixture to the egg yolks, stirring in a little at a time. Return to main dish, and stir in wine and apple juice. If you wish, this may be made ahead of time and kept in a double boiler until ready to transfer to chafing dish or fondue pot.

WELSH RAREBIT

This dish is sometimes called Welsh rabbit, but the only hops in the dish are in the beer!

What
1½ tbsp. butter
¼ tsp. salt
3 cups strong cheddar cheese
Pinch of cayenne
1 tsp. Worcestershire sauce
2 egg yolks, beaten
½ tsp. dry mustard
¼ cup ale
4 slices toast, buttered and oven dried

How
Make in the top of a double boiler, over hot but not fast-boiling water. Grate the cheese. Melt butter in the top of double boiler, and stir-cook until cheese is melted. Add the Worcestershire sauce, mustard, salt, and cayenne, and stir. Add egg yolks slowly, stirring well while adding. Slowly stir in the ale. Stir-cook until smooth and velvety. Use as dip, or serve over the toast. This is a very versatile rarebit. Although some Englishmen would be horrified at a departure from tradition, you can add many other types of cheese, such as bleu, Roquefort, or Swiss Tilsit, to change the flavor of the dish. The Swiss make it with Tilsit, flavored with kirsch, instead of ale.

SAUCE DIAVOLO

Is certainly one of the good sauces, for dipping.

What
1 cup white wine
2 tbsp. tomato sauce

2 green onions chopped fine
1 pinch cayenne
1 garlic clove, finely minced
1/4 tsp. salt
1 beef bouillon cube
1/2 cup white wine
1/2 tsp. parsley flakes
1/2 tsp. cornstarch
1/2 tsp. dry mustard

How
Place 1 cup wine, green onions, and garlic in a saucepan. Simmer until wine is reduced by half. Add beef concentrate cube, and the cayenne. Stir until dissolved. Add the tomato sauce, salt, mustard, and the cornstarch dissolved in the 1/2 cup wine. Stir until thickened.

FONDUE DIP

This is an inspirational cheese dip, especially for an after sports party in the winter. Great for dipping hot French fries speared on a fork.

What
1/4 cup butter
2 tbsp. flour
1 tsp. salt
1/4 tsp. garlic powder
1 1/2 cups milk
1/4 cup dry white wine
2 packages frozen French fries
1 lb. old cheddar or Swiss cheese, grated
1/2 tsp. grated nutmeg

How
In a saucepan melt half the butter. Stir in flour, half the salt,

and the garlic powder. Add milk slowly and stir-cook until thick and smooth. Add wine and cheese, stirring well until cheese is melted. Spread French fries on a baking sheet. Dot with remaining butter, sprinkle with nutmeg and remaining salt. Heat about 20 minutes in 400 degree oven, turning once to brown. If you run out of French fries, cubes of French bread may be used, buttered and toasted in the oven.

HAPPY NIBBLES

Here are some tricks in preparing French bread sticks, for the fondue or chafing dish party.

Cut the French loaf diagonally into slices about two inches thick, cutting almost through to the bottom crust. For variety spread each slice with different spreads or sauces as below.

Start with one cup of softened butter for each spread, or one half cup for smaller groups. For ½ cup butter, add any of the following mixes and work well into the butter.

——1 tbsp. chives and 1 tsp. curry powder

——½ cup crumbled bleu cheese and 1 tsp. chopped chives

——¼ cup peanut oil, ¼ tsp. garlic powder, ¼ tsp. oregano, ¼ tsp. rosemary

——2 cups grated old cheddar cheese and 2 tbsp. sherry

QUICK STROGANOFF

What
1½ lbs. thinly sliced beef tenderloin
3 tbsp. butter
½ cup canned tomatoes
1 can mushroom soup
1 tbsp. instant onion
¼ tsp. garlic powder
¼ tsp. pepper

½ tsp. salt
½ tsp. oregano flakes
3 tbsp. flour
1 cup sour cream
2 tbsp. red wine

How
Cut beef into thin strips and brown in butter. Cover and cook slowly 20 minutes. Put balance of ingredients into blender and blend until smooth. Pour over beef and cook 15 minutes on low heat. Serve with sauteed mushroom caps and small boiled potatoes. Serves 6.

PANCAKES

Pancakes are always a delightful addition to a chafing dish or fondue party. They are delightful covered with fondues, or other spreadables or pourables.

GREEN CORN PANCAKE

These can only be made when green corn is available, but are well worth the trouble of waiting.
Grate or press out the pulp of young corn to make 2 cups. Add ¼ cup milk, and one egg and one extra yolk, well beaten. Add 1 cup flour, sifted with 1 tsp. baking powder, 1 tsp. sugar, and 1 tsp. salt. Add ½ tsp. of fresh ground pepper, and a heaping tbsp. of soft butter. Beat leftover white of egg and fold in. Bake on lightly greased griddle. Just short of Heaven!

EASTERN SHORE OYSTER PANCAKES

Breakfast for the gods, and good for mortals at any time.
To make the batter—sift together 2½ cups flour, ½ tsp.

salt, 2 tbsp. sugar, 1 tsp. baking soda. Stir in 1½ cups sour milk, and ½ cup oyster liquor, 1 tbsp. melted butter, and 1 egg, well beaten. Heat griddle or heavy skillet. Grease with a piece of salt pork before starting and between each batch. Put two spoonfuls of batter on the griddle, and immediately drop in 3 small oysters. Bake as any other pancake, but do not overcook. These are great, served with coleslaw and bacon.

ADIRONDACK FLAPJACK

These are big ones, and fill large, hungry cavities with satisfaction.

For eight, seven-inch flapjacks, sift together 2 cups flour, 2 tsp. baking powder, ½ tsp. salt, and 1 tbsp. white sugar. Separate whites from yolks of four eggs. Beat yolks well and add 2 cups milk. Pour into the flour mixture and beat to a smooth batter. Beat the whites of the eggs until stiff. Fold into the batter. Fry in large cakes on a hot griddle, and butter each flapjack. Serve with fondue or any of the creamed meat or seafood mixtures from the chafing dish.

BLUEBERRY PANCAKES

It's a little like gilding the lily, to add anything to these great golden flapjacks, but to the Adirondack batter you can add fresh blueberries, or drained canned blueberries, for a deliciously different pancake to serve with small sausages or bacon.

POTATO PANCAKES

For a dozen guests, or three Irish lumberjacks. The potato pancake may have originated in Ireland, or maybe back to the days of the Incas, who found this kind of cookery well adapted to cooking on a hot rock. They are appetizing wrapped around a sausage for finger eating, or in the conventional manner with bacon and syrup. Also delicious spread with maple sugar and rolled.

What
¼ cup butter
2 tbsp. sugar
3 eggs, beaten
¾ quart flour
1½ tsp. baking powder
1 tsp. salt
1½ cups grated raw potato
¾ quart milk

How
Cream butter and sugar together. Add eggs and sifted dry ingredients. Fold in grated potato and milk. Cook as with any pancake, on a greased griddle.

CREPES SUZETTE

Somebody will surely say, "Can you make Crepes Suzette?" Well, you can—with this easy recipe that strips the veil of mystery off this culinary secret, and enshrines you with Larousse.

What
2 cups flour
3 eggs
2¼ cups milk
½ tsp. salt
2 tsp. sugar
2 tsp. kirsch liqueur

How

Put all ingredients in blender, and blend 15 seconds. Set in refrigerator for 10 to 20 hours. Fry in butter in small, thin cakes when ready to serve.

CREPES SUZETTE SAUCE

What

3 tbsp. sweet butter (unsalted)
6 lumps sugar
1 orange
Juice of half an orange (strained)
½ cup granulated sugar
1 lemon
2 tbsp. light rum
¼ cup Benedictine
¼ cup Grand Marnier

How

Cream the butter. Rub four lumps of sugar over the peel of the orange until well impregnated with the oil of orange. Rub 2 lumps over lemon peel until well impregnated. (Don't get frightened over all this impregnation. It is not contagious.) Crush lumps of sugar into the orange juice. Work into creamed butter. Work in well for a smooth mixture.

Heat in chafing dish, and when butter foams, lay in the crepes, one by one. Turn over, then fold into quarters. Sprinkle well with granulated sugar, and pour over the combined rum and liqueurs. Let simmer a few seconds—then tilt pan and ignite the sauce. When flames die down, serve the crepes, two per serving, spooning a little sauce over each.

Hail to the Chef!

So . . . now you have all the dishes and liquids for a successful cocktail party, laughingly called a fête worse than death. If you can eat, drink, and be wary, and make your guests feel at home when you wish they were, you've achieved the thick skin required for a cool host. However wonderful your dishes may be, some guest with the abrasive personality of a file will be unable to find the exact thing to tickle his goofy palate, and will grumble that the least you could have done would have been to serve roast tufted puffin, or fricassed baby penguin. If you can smile, while hoping that he will go home and electrocute himself on his own electric carving knife, you are a diplomat of the highest order.

Cocktail parties are beset with problems, most of the besetters being guests. Should you find that your pet jokes are falling flat, serve more potent drinks. This will shortly improve your wit, and the laughter will be balm to your injured soul. If old adages become a little distorted, and you find men making passes at gals who drain glasses, don't let it unseat your reason. The gambit is to keep your cool, and your own gal from draining too many glasses.

2
Party Drinks and Punches

When you are serving drinks, and want to go first class in the fame department, these zingers could make your reputation. The first one is a lovely that should be treated with love and respect, for reasons that will become more evident after the third one. It's called

MOLOTOV JULEP

Start with a tall 12 oz. or 14 oz. glass. Conventionally, mash fresh mint leaves in 4 oz. of water. Add 2 oz. of Bourbon and stir well. Add 1 tsp. powdered sugar, and stir. Fill glass with cracked ice almost to brim. Pour 2 oz. of light Jamaica rum over the ice. This julep is a light, refreshing sipper, and the addition of the rum seems to sweeten the bourbon so well that my guests have asked me what kind of wonderful old bourbon I was serving. This is a twosie. Any more at your own risk.

THE SNEAKER

This one is sheer alcoholic poetry. Combine one part each of white rum, gold rum, Jamaica, and Demerara. This should equal one pint. Add 1 pint of pineapple juice, and

2 tbsp. of powdered sugar. Shake up this witch's brew, and put away in the refrigerator to marry well. The longer it sits, the better it tastes. Serve in tall highball glasses with four ice cubes in each.

BLITHE SPIRIT

This'n is a doozy. Should be called Hail and Farewell. It's made with 2 oz. light rum, 4 oz. pineapple juice, and 2 oz. champagne. Smo-o-oth.

RUM BLOSSOM

What
20 oz. light rum
20 oz. dark rum
4 20 oz. cans unsweetened pineapple juice
6 oz. lemon juice
½ cup sugar
¼ tsp. Angostura bitters
2 oz. lime juice

How
Mix and let marry a day or two. Serve over cracked ice. Timber-r-r-r. Three of these will stir up a seismograph.

CANAVERAL PUNCH

So named because the fifth drink starts the countdown for an orbital trip!

What
3 pints Porter

3 pints Ale
½ pint brandy
1 pint sherry
½ cup powdered sugar
3 lemons, sliced thin
2 jiggers orange curacas
2 bottles cold champagne
1 block ice

How
Combine all ingredients except champagne. Stir well and add block of ice. Add champagne . . . zero, ignition, and off to the stars!

CHAMPAGNE SEDUCTION

What
1 block ice
½ lb. powdered sugar
2 jiggers brandy
2 jiggers Curacao
2 jiggers Maraschino
3 jiggers lemon juice
¼ tsp. Angostura bitters
4 thin slices orange
4 twists of lemon peel
3 bottles of champagne

How
Combine ingredients in punch bowl in order given. After the first hour, guests who cannot count their toes are cut off!

CHAMPAGNE TOREADOR

In good Spanish tradition, the host can claim an ear from the first guest who gets smashed.

What
1 large punch bowl
1 block of ice
Juice of 2 oranges
Juice of 2 lemons
½ cup sugar
4 oz. light rum
4 oz. dark rum
1 cup pineapple juice
2 bottles cold champagne
Red and green maraschino cherries

How
Combine ingredients in the order shown. You can gauge the success of the party by counting the cherries before and after!

CHAMPAGNE PUNCH

What
1½ cups sugar
Juice of 6 lemons
1 can pineapple tid-bits
3 pints ice water
1 pint fresh-frozen strawberries
1 quart champagne
1 bottle (about 25 oz.) white wine

How
Mix and chill all ingredients except wines. Add ice and wine just before serving. Makes about 140 oz. Very popular with the ladies. Warming but not stunning.

ITALIAN STINGER

The unique flavored Galliano makes this a different and

exciting drink. Shake together with cracked ice, 1 oz. Galliano, and 1¼ oz. brandy. Serve over the rocks in an old-fashioned glass.

ALPINE SCREWDRIVER

Start with a large old-fashioned glass, or highball glass with two ice cubes. Pour 1 oz. light rum, and ¾ oz. Galliano over the ice and fill with orange juice. Guaranteed to tame the most stubborn screw.

ITALIAN HEATHER

Made with 2 oz. Scotch and ¼ oz. Galliano, mixed in an old-fashioned glass with two ice cubes, and a twist of lemon.

PINK LADY PUNCH

What
1 cup sugar
½ cup lemon juice
2 cups raspberry syrup
2 cups water
2 quarts pineapple juice (4 20 oz. cans)
2 quarts soda water
40 oz. gin (or rum)

How
Boil sugar and water five minutes. Cool and add raspberry syrup, lemon, and pineapple juice. Chill and add carbonated water just before serving. Add liquor and serve.

CONTINENTAL PUNCH

What

1 quart pineapple juice
1 cup grape juice
1 cup pitted cherries
2 oranges, peeled and sectioned
1 quart rum (I use the light rum, but suit yourself)
2 cups pinapple tid-bits
2 cups fresh strawberries
1 pint soda water
1 dozen sprigs of mint

How

Combine all ingredients and put in punch bowl with a block of ice. Spread some of the strawberries, cherries and orange sections on the ice, with the sprigs of mint for decoration. If I am serving women, I add a bottle of lime rickey to improve flavor and cut the orbital thrust.

3

Tête-à-tête

Tête-à-tête dining, if properly organized, can result in some very interesting developments. I imply no criticism of any skills you may have gained by experience, in giving you my recommendations for guiding you and guarding you against the disappointments inherent in the use of faulty techniques. Tête-à-tête implies an intimate situation, and requires privacy, and a competent host-chef, together with a lady friend, or even a mistress, and an atmosphere of romance and mystery. One of the best arguments for a bachelor becoming a chef is that this skill makes his pad a logical spot to bring his favorites of the fair sex for dining, and any other diversions that may occur as a dividend. Whatever her motive for joining you there, she can always defend herself to her conscience for whatever may have happened by saying that she only went there to dine, and was kept up until the "oui" hours of the morning! Another fine reason for the possession of cheffing skill is that the most beautiful and exciting wench you know may be a beautiful dancer, a brilliant conversationalist, and adept at horizontal sports (like swimming), yet may have flunked Home Ec. at school. She may be fluent in three languages and fluid in four dimensions, yet put her in a kitchen and she could burn the water and louse up shredded wheat. Last, but not least, by dining at home, you avoid those dinner checks of gastronomical proportions.

We all know that tête-à-tête means head to head, in French. Sometimes under certain influences, this sort of thing can get out of hand and take in more anatomy than the term implies. To discussion of these fortuitous accidents, I turn a deaf ear. It is recognized that candlelight, soft music, seductive drinks, and the proximity of reclining furniture may have certain train effects, for which this department takes no responsibility. I restrain myself to suggesting artful cookery that lulls the diners into a sense of well-being. No criticism of other diversions beyond dining is implied. When setting the scene, and leading up to the inevitable (I meant dining, whatever you may have thought), it is wise to control the liquid openers to the game. Remember, wine makes the dish, but don't let her overtrain. And those liquid lightning bolts, the eleven-to-one Martinis, can spoil the real odds— your pick of the field may not even make the finish line.

When preparing the diner-à-deux, don't get carried away into proving your culinary skills with too many or too heavy dishes. Sad to relate, heavy eating makes people sluggish, and dulls their responses to the more exciting nuances of life. So, keep the dishes small, tasty, and few in number. Serve leisurely, with appropriate wines. Cool wine has never been known to chill a warm guest, and has even been credited with warming a cool one!

Appetites for drinks, food, and other things, should be attended to in the order of their becoming evident. Should this result in a late dinner—well time is relative to the accomplishment therein.

In the following recipes I have tried to select those which are amenable to small-quantity preparation, and which do not require prolonged hovering over the range. The natives might become restless, or worse.

I insert here a word of caution to girls dining tête-à-tête.

Do not forget that it is fun to be a party girl, if you took your pills, like a good girl.

CRAB BISQUE

Since it is bad manners to keep a luscious guest waiting, here's a delicious bisque you can make the night before your diner-à-deux. Just heat it in the top of a double boiler.

What
1 can (5½ oz.) Crabmeat
2 tbsp. butter
½ cup chicken stock
1 tbsp. minced green onion
⅛ tsp. white pepper
Salt, if required
¼ tsp. paprika
1 tsp. parsley flakes
1 cup heavy cream
1 tbsp. dry sherry

How
Drain crab and add juice to chicken stock. Flake crab and pick out any shell or tendons. Saute onions in butter until soft. Add crab and toss gently 1 minute. Add chicken stock, pepper, parsley, and paprika. Bring to boil. Add cream and bring just to boil. Taste for seasoning. Just before serving, stir in sherry. If made the day before, do not add sherry until reheating. Reheat slowly in top of double boiler.

Here we go with one of the products that made Victor Borge famous. These are the kind of chicks you stuff while you are waiting to stuff the chick you're entertaining with the ones you have already stuffed. Is that clear?

ROCK CORNISH HEN

What

2 small Rock Cornish hens
Stuffing:
2 cups soft breadcrumbs
½ cup dried apricots, chopped
1 tbsp. chopped parsley
¼ tsp. salt
¼ tsp. M.S.G.
¼ tsp. black pepper
¼ tsp. thyme
¼ tsp. rosemary
1 orange
2 tbsp. butter
2 tbsp. chopped onion
½ cup chopped celery
Basting Sauce:
¼ cup butter, melted
2 ozs. white wine
¼ cup orange juice
½ tsp. garlic salt

How

Brush each hen with cooking oil. Combine peeled and
sectioned orange with balance of stuffing ingredients. Stuff
hens and place balance of stuffing in a small covered casserole
to be baked aside from the hens. Place hens on a rack in
a shallow baking dish, and bake about one hour at 325
degrees until lightly browned. Bake the dressing at the same
time. Baste the hens a few times in the last half hour of
cooking. Serve on a bed of hot dressing from the casserole.

Once in a while, while you are working, I will bring
you a gem or two of wisdom to ponder while you guard your
bachelorhood. Are you ready? Mink may not buy love, but
it puts you in a handy bargaining position.

CHICKEN PIE

What

1 disjointed chicken (about 2 lbs.)
1 stalk celery with leaves
1 carrot
1 onion
1 bay leaf
½ tsp. salt
6 peppercorns
4 tbsp. butter
4 tbsp. flour
¼ tsp. salt
1 tbsp. white wine
¼ tsp. thyme
Pastry for one-crust pie

How

Put 3 cups water in large saucepan. Add chicken, celery, onion, carrot, bay leaf, salt, and peppercorns. Bring to boil and cover. Cook slowly until meat is ready to fall off bones, likely about 1 hour. Remove chicken from stock, and cool slightly, until meat can be removed from bones. Cut meat into bite-sized chunks. Strain off stock, and save. Arrange pieces of meat in baking dish, alternating white and dark meat. Melt butter and stir in flour. Move pan aside and let stand until butter is well absorbed into flour. Return to heat, and add 2 cups stock, and seasonings. Cook slowly, stirring, until thick and creamy. Pour enough over chicken to cover. Put on pastry, make air holes, and bake at 450 deg. until sauce bubbles through air holes and crust is golden. Serve hot with tossed salad.

LITTLE FILETS NAPOLITANI

What

1 lb. beef tenderloin, cut ¼ inch thick

2 tbsp. butter
3 slices prosciutto, chopped
2 tbsp. dried mushrooms
1 tbsp. parsley flakes
Juice of ½ lemon
½ cup beef broth, or consomme
Salt and pepper

How
Soak mushrooms in warmed broth until soft. Drain, reserve broth. Chop mushrooms fine. Melt butter in skillet. Sprinkle in prosciutto, mushrooms, and parsley. Put meat slices on top and press down. Brown lightly on medium heat. Turn gently so some of chopped mixture sticks to each slice. Brown lightly, sprinkle with lemon juice, and add 3 tbsp. of broth. Cover and cook 3 minutes. Serve with pan-sauce poured over steaks. Serves 2.

CHATEAUBRIAND FOR TWO

Chateaubriand is a thick beef filet, cut from the thickest part of the filet, on the diagonal. 1 lb. to 1¼ lb. serves two. Rub steak well with salt, pepper, and softened butter. Broil 3 inches under broiler, turning often to brown and not burn. 10 to 12 minutes for rare, 13 to 16 minutes for medium. Anyone who asks for Chateaubriand well done should be served broiled seal flipper, fricasseed whale steak, or other plebeian food. Cut the steak into thinnish slices and serve with sauce Bearnaise. (See Sauce section.)

MUSHROOM OYSTERS

Should your paramour be a discerning diner, this dish will send her winging to the heights.

What
8 large mushroom caps (save stems for other uses)
8 large or 16 small oysters

How
Season the inside of the mushroom caps lightly with salt and pepper, brush with melted butter, and saute the round tops of the caps in butter for five minutes. Now sit caps hollow side up in a baking pan. Put 1/4 tsp. of soft butter and 1/4 tsp. of cream in each. Drop in the oysters, and sprinkle with a touch of cayenne. Broil 3 inches under broiler until edges of oysters start to curl (about 5 minutes). Sprinkle with lemon juice and serve. For extra flavor, a little Parmesan cheese sprinkled over each in the last minute of broiling.

ABALONE STEAKS SANTA MONICA

What
3/4 lb. abalone steaks
1/4 tsp. salt
1/4 tsp. paprika
2 tbsp. melted butter
1 tbsp. mayonnaise
1 tsp. minced parsley
2 tsp. lemon juice

How
Steaks should be 1/2 inch thick and pounded soft with wooden steak pounder. Mix salt, paprika, and lemon juice. Marinate steaks 15 minutes, turning once. Preheat broiler to 400 degrees. Broil steaks 2 inches below heat 5 minutes. Turn, spread with mayonnaise, broil 10 minutes to golden color. Serve with minced parsley and lemon wedges.

LOBSTER AU CHAMPAGNE

Champagne should make the lobster happy, and who doesn't love to dine on happy lobster?

What
1½ cups cooked lobster meat
¼ cup butter
¼ cup minced onions
¼ cup minced celery
2 tbsp. parsley flakes
4 beaten egg yolks
1½ cups whipping cream
1 tsp. salt
¼ tsp. fresh black pepper
6 oz. champagne
1 tbsp. Parmesan, grated

How
Melt butter in saucepan. Add onions, celery, and parsley. Simmer until celery is soft. Beat egg yolks into half the cream, and stream into pan, stirring steadily. Add lobster, cream, salt, and pepper. When thick and smooth, stir in champagne well, and serve with croutons or toast points, sprinkling Parmesan on top, or serve in shaker on the side.

DEVILLED CLAMS

Save the Mephisto influence for later capers.

What
6 large clams and juice
2 tbsp. Sauterne
1 tbsp. chopped chives
1 tbsp. minced onion

2 tbsp. green pepper flakes
3 tbsp. butter
4 tbsp. finely minced celery
1/4 tsp. Worcestershire sauce
1/2 cup cracker crumbs
Salt and pepper
1 pimento, minced

How
Drain clams. Save juice. Remove dark part of clams and discard, mince remainder. Saute with clam juice 2 minutes and remove from heat. Melt butter in another pan, add onion, celery, and pepper flakes. Saute 5 minutes. Stir in chives, pimento, Worcestershire, salt, pepper to taste, and cracker crumbs. Add clams and wine. If too dry, add small quantity of milk. Fill small ramekins, or buttered scallop shells with mixture. Bake in preheated 350 degree oven 20 minutes.

SOLE BONNE FEMME

What
4 fillets of sole
1/2 cup sliced mushrooms
4 tbsp. white wine
3 tbsp. butter
1/4 cup chopped green onions
1 tbsp. flour
1/4 tsp. salt
Pinch of white pepper
1/2 tsp. paprika

How
Saute mushrooms and onions gently in butter, salt, and wine. Add fillets and poach gently 7–8 minutes, turning

once. Remove fillets to hot platter. Mix flour with 2 tbsp. milk and stir into poaching liquid. Stir-cook until thick and smooth. Sprinkle with pepper and paprika. Spoon over fillets and reheat a few minutes before serving. Serve with hashed brown potatoes and tossed salad.

POTATOES À LA SUISSE

Bake 1 large baking potato for each serving. When done remove slice from top and scoop out center. Mash and season. Break one egg in each potato shell, season lightly, and fill with mashed potato, leaving it fluffy on top. Bake at 375 degrees for ten minutes to set egg and brown top. Serve with strips of ham or bacon. You can also mix creamed chipped beef or creamed fish with the filling, or instead of the egg.

SAUSAGE-STUFFED BAKED POTATO

Cook and scoop out potato as in Suisse. Fry about ¼ lb. of sausage meat, for two servings. Break up finely and mix with 2 tsp. of applesauce and 1 tsp. parsley. Fill into potatoes. Top with potato mashed with 1 tbsp. sour cream. Sprinkle with chives. Reheat and serve.

CRÈME ALSACE

This is a delicious light luncheon dish, cooked in individual ramekins and served with a green salad. Any left over will keep to reheat.

What
6 thin slices of bacon

¾ cup grated Swiss cheese
¼ cup grated Parmesan
¾ cup heavy cream
1 egg, well beaten
¼ tsp. salt
⅛ tsp. pepper
Pinch of nutmeg

How
Dice bacon fine. Fry until light brown and crisp. Drain on absorbent paper. Beat together the two cheeses, cream, salt, pepper, egg, and nutmeg. Fold in the bacon cubes, and pour into ramekins. Bake at 350 degrees for 25 minutes or until brown and puffy.

POTATO SALAD

Boil medium sized potatoes about 20 to 25 minutes. Do not overcook. Cool and cut in half-inch cubes. Add ½ cup grated onion for each 2 cups potatoes. Mix lightly, with just enough French dressing to coat potatoes. Refrigerate until serving time. Then, add mayonnaise to moisten well. Season with salt and pepper. Chopped chives, pickle, or parsley may be added for the festive touch.

Note
If your chick says she has nothing to wear for the tête-à-tête party, tell her that costume is okay for your kind of party.

What do you do with tomatoes? Freud knew, Kinsey found out, so where have you been? Oh well, aside from their findings, here are some other things to do with tomatoes, like making

TOMATO SURPRISE

Surprises you, not the tomato. I think.

Scoop out centers of medium tomatoes. Mix pulp with chili sauce, mayonnaise, salt and pepper, and finely chopped cucumber. Fill tomatoes with the mixture and garnish tops with a little mayonnaise, dash of paprika, and a tiny lettuce leaf. Serve on lettuce leaf.

PUFFED TOMATO SALAD

Slice off stem end of medium tomato. Gash tomato well down to center at half-inch intervals. Alternately stick thinly sliced cucumber and hard-cooked egg into the gashes. Place in lettuce cup and garnish with mayonnaise—one to a guest— 2 each to salad fanciers!

BACON SALAD

This saves arguments about calories, and has body (and soul?).

What
¼ cup diced apples
1 small head lettuce, shredded
¼ cup diced celery
¼ cup mayonnaise
1 cup diced bacon

How
Mix and let stand ten minutes, while you soft fry diced bacon. Combine everything, with a small head of lettuce, shredded, and toss lightly together.

PINEAPPLE AND CHICKEN SALAD

On each cup of lettuce, place a slice of pineapple. Cut white meat of chicken into thin slices, then into slivers. Cut celery the same way. Heap celery and chicken on pineapple. Mix equal amounts of whipped cream and mayonnaise, and heap on top of salad. Not too fattening . . . just enough.

Note

A prune is a worried old plum!

STUFFED PEPPER SALAD

What

2 large green peppers
2 tbsp. cold water
⅓ cup tomato juice
2 hard-cooked eggs
¼ tsp. salt
½ tsp. Worcestershire
1 tsp. minced parsley
1 tsp. gelatin

How

Soften gelatin in cold water and dissolve in heated tomato juice. Allow to cool. Cut stem ends off peppers, and remove seeds and membrane. Place an egg in each pepper, and fasten upright and centered with toothpicks. Add salt, Worcestershire, and parsley to gelatin mixture, and pour around eggs in peppers. Stand peppers upright in pan and refrigerate until very hard. Remove toothpicks (they are tough and lacking in flavor). Slice peppers crosswise and serve on beds of shredded lettuce. Garnish with stuffed olives, celery curls, and a little mayonnaise.

TOMATO ASPIC

What

1 pint tomato juice
¼ cup cold water
¼ tsp. salt

2 tbsp. lemon juice
2 tbsp. sugar
½ tsp. Worcestershire
Pinch cayenne
3 hard-cooked eggs
½ tsp. onion juice or onion powder
¼ cup olive oil
½ cup mayonnaise
1½ tbsp. gelatin

How

Soften gelatin in cold water, and dissolve over hot water. Add salt and sugar and stir until dissolved. Add tomato juice, lemon juice, and seasonings. Chill. When mixture begins to set, add olive oil and beat until blended. Turn into lightly oiled individual molds and chill until set. Turn out onto lettuce leaves, and garnish with hard-cooked egg halves and mayonnaise. This is more than enough for two, but it keeps well in the refrigerator.

STUFFED TOMATOES IN ASPIC

Use round molds larger than the tomatoes you are using. Make aspic jelly as in previous recipe, *without* olive oil. Pour a small amount of the jelly in each mold, and chill until set. Slice off stem end of tomato and scoop out pulp. Mix cubed cooked chicken, finely minced celery, mayonnaise, salt, and pepper. Stuff the tomatoes with the mixture. When aspic has set in bottom of molds, invert the tomatoes in the molds, and pour in the rest of the aspic. Chill until set. Serve on beds of shredded lettuce and top with mayonnaise.

TOMATOES MONACO

We didn't know they had tomatoes in Monaco, although we were apprised of Prince Rainier having imported one, who became Princess Grace! Anyway, here is a Monegasque dish, for eating.

What
2 eggs, hard-boiled
1 7 oz. can tuna
1 tsp. French mustard
2 tbsp. French dressing
Salt and pepper
4 large tomatoes

How
Scald tomatoes and peel. Scoop out centers, chop and mix with the French dressing. Slice eggs in half lengthwise, and mash yolks with tuna and the rest of the ingredients. Drain and stuff the tomatoes. Stuff the egg white halves with the same mix, and use as side garnish. Serve on lettuce leaves.

I know you are anxious to get this dining business over with, so here are a few simple and tasty desserts for dining twosome.

BABA AU RHUM

Boil for two minutes 1 cup sugar with ½ cup water. Remove from heat and add ½ tbsp. butter. Cool and add 1¼ oz. light rum. This is a buttered rum sauce that will keep a few days, if you have any left over. We hollow out the center of a sponge cupcake a little, and soak it in the sauce. Then fill the hollow with ice cream, and top with whipped cream. This is good, and the rum sauce helps to keep up spirits, while you discuss some mild healthful exercise to burn up the calories.

CHERRIES JUBILEE

(No, friends, this is not a virgin's reunion.)
For this dessert, get a can of black sweet cherries (the large Black Prince are best). Drain the cherries, and save the juice. Mix the juice with 1 tsp. cornstarch per cup, and cook until slightly thickened. Pour over the cherries, when cooled a bit. Warm a tablespoon of kirsch liqueur, flame the liqueur and pour it over the cherries, while flaming. Now, it's ready. Kirsch is a brandy liqueur made from fermented wild cherries. It is not clear whether the cherries were wild before or after being fermented M-m-m-m, I tasted it. I'll say they are wild enough after.

Note
Diamonds are a cost-of-loving bonus.

CHAMPAGNE PEACHES

Keeps the fun spirit at a peak!

What
2 fresh ripe peaches
2 tbsp. brandy
Champagne

How
Split and stone peaches. (They are stoned both before and after brandying.) Put in a bowl and sprinkle with the brandy. Refrigerate for 1 hour. Cover with chilled champagne and let stand 10 minutes. Serve liberally covered with the juices. I'll bet nobody throws out the syrup.

GINGERED PINEAPPLE

If you have a chafing dish, this is a natural. A skillet will substitute.

What

2 tbsp. butter
1 cup drained pineapple chunks
¼ cup brown sugar
2 tbsp. dark rum
1 tbsp. finely chopped candied ginger
1 pint peach (or vanilla) ice cream
¼ tsp. ground ginger

How

Melt the butter and stir-toss pineapple chunks over medium heat until lightly browned. Sprinkle on brown sugar and caramelize the pineapple lightly, stirring and turning. Add the rum and ¼ cup pineapple juice, with the ground ginger. Stir until well mixed. Spoon over the ice cream and sprinkle with candied ginger.

TREATMENT FOR FRESH BERRIES

Marinate 1 pint of raspberries with ¼ cup port and ¼ cup brandy.
Marinate ½ pint of sliced strawberries in ½ cup orange juice and ¼ cup honey.
Marinate blueberries in 2 tbsp. lemon juice, ½ tsp. lime juice, 4 tbsp. brown sugar.
Marinate melon balls in Sauterne (sweet).

4
Hors d'Oeuvres and Snacks

Polyunsaturated is not a sober parrot! Regarding hors d'oeuvres and other blubber boosters, I am glad to report that our research department is working on the invention of a snack that appeals to everyone. Currently, their thinking is about making a goody about the size of a briefcase, that looks like a baked Alaska, tastes like a chocolate eclair, and has two (count 'em) calories. Due to certain technical difficulties they have encountered, we feel that perhaps you should have a snack in the meantime, as this promises to take a little time (a lifetime?).

Too many sweet snacks are a "no-no" in the health area. What you should do is throw out those sugarloaded ickies and eat the wrapping paper. This would enable you to live longer, in case you should think of a good reason to do so.

I am going to give you the whole bit in the snack department though; canapes, bitewiches, stuffed finger rolls and other snickies that you can't get on the hard roll and rubber chicken circuit. Steady as she goes. . . .

LIVER-AND-BACON PÂTÉ

Carefully made, according to directions, this is delicious. It doesn't last at a party, because they love it. People tire of

71

the conventional things, and while it takes time to make the unusual, the host who would be known for gourmet skill will find the effort worthwhile. Pork liver is the tastiest, and also the least expensive. It does require that you put it in a bowl (sliced), and pour boiling water over it. Calves, chicken, beef liver does not require this treatment.

What
1 lb. pork liver (or any other one you fancy)
½ lb. side bacon
1 clove garlic or ¼ tsp. garlic powder
2 medium onions
⅛ tsp. sage
¼ tsp. savory
⅛ tsp. thyme
1 tbsp. cider vinegar
1 tbsp. brown sugar
3 tbsp. peanut oil
1 tsp. salt
¼ tsp. black pepper

How
Fry the bacon in the peanut oil until done but not crisp. Remove from pan. Split clove of garlic and brown in fat, with sliced onions. Discard garlic. Remove onions and reserve. Drain liver well, and fry quickly, browning on both sides, but not enough to be hard. Add seasonings to fat, also vinegar and sugar. Heat just to simmer and turn off. Grind all ingredients, starting with onions and ending with the bacon, through the medium blade of the food chopper. Add all the fat and seasonings from the pan, and mix long and thoroughly until the texture is just right. This will harden to some degree in the refrigerator. If you wish to roll it in foil and slice it, the texture will be right. If you want to spread it, it may be necessary to work in soft butter or peanut oil to soften. This pâté will keep three weeks under refrigeration, but not if your guests can get at it.

CRAB JOY IN CROUSTADES

What
1 cup cooked crab meat, shredded
2 tbsp. butter
1 tbsp. green pepper flakes
2 tbsp. flour
¼ tsp. dry mustard
1 tsp. lemon juice
¼ tsp. salt
½ tsp. Worcestershire sauce
Dash of Tabasco
1 cup cooked tomatoes, drained
1 cup grated mild cheddar cheese
1 egg, lightly beaten
¾ cup milk
1 loaf stale bread

How
Saute pepper flakes in butter two minutes. Stir in flour, mustard, lemon juice, salt, Worcestershire, and Tabasco. Add tomatoes, cheese, and egg. Scald the milk, and add the other mix to the milk. Stir-cook until thickened, and smooth. Add the crabmeat, and mix well. Make croustades as follows:

Cut the bread in slices two inches thick. Cut in quarters. Hollow out centers of cubes to make baskets or croustades. Brush with melted butter and toast in oven. Hold the crab mixture in a chafing dish or fondue pot. Serve the croustades in a basket lined with a towel (hot towel is best). Serves 8.

CHICKEN TERRAPIN

I am not sure where this dish got its name, as no kind of turtle is involved in it's preparation. May have been invented by a turtle!

What
3 eggs, hard-boiled and shelled
5 tbsp. flour
½ tsp. dry mustard
¼ tsp. pepper
3 tbsp. butter, melted
1½ cups diced cooked chicken
2 cups scalded milk
2 tbsp. pimento flakes
1 tbsp. green pepper flakes
6 ripe olives, chopped
1 tsp. lemon juice
½ tsp. salt

How
Separate egg yolks from whites. Mash yolks with butter, flour, mustard, and pepper. Scald the milk in the top of a double boiler, then add the yolk mixture. Stir-cook until thick and smooth. Add finely chopped egg whites, chicken, pimento, pepper flakes, olives, salt, and lemon juice. Serve in heated patty shells to about eight people.

CHICKEN-BACON ROLL-UP

What
12 chicken livers, halved
12 blanched toasted almonds
3 tbsp. minced onion
12 slices bacon, cut in half, crosswise
2 tbsp. butter
Salt, pepper, M.S.G.

How
Season livers with salt, pepper, and M.S.G. Cook bacon in butter until half done, not crisp. Remove and add onions and fry slowly 3 minutes. Add chicken livers, and cook,

turning, until tender. Remove and drain. Make a slit in each piece and insert almond. Wrap in bacon, secure with a pick. Broil until bacon is just crisp.

CRACKER SPREAD

For a lovely and different spread for crackers, this one has gotta have the oomph of a five-inch rocket. Put through the food chopper:

What
½ lb. old cheddar cheese
¼ lb. bleu cheese
¼ lb. cooked sausage meat
¼ tsp. onion powder
¼ tsp. garlic salt
2 tbsp. French mustard
A good pinch of black pepper

How
Work in enough dry sherry to make the mixture easily spreadable without breaking crackers.

SHRIMP LOUISIANA

Clean and break up small ⅔ cup canned shrimp. Cook 1 tbsp. chopped onion in 2 tbsp. butter. Add ¾ cup hot cooked rice and ⅔ cup cream. When hot add ½ tsp. salt, ¼ tsp. celery salt, 3 tbsp. tomato sauce, and ¼ tsp. paprika. Stir in shrimp, and reheat over low heat. Serve in croustades or patty shells. Serves four.

CRISP APPETIZERS

Fill a bowl of the required size for your party with crushed ice. Work into a mounded center. Top with radish roses, carrot sticks, celery curls, green pepper strips, cauliflowerets, turnip sticks, etc. Add olives and a few shrimp for color. Serve with:

DUNKING SAUCE

What
½ cup chili sauce
¼ cup finely cut stuffed olives
½ tsp. dry mustard
¼ tsp. salt
½ tsp. paprika
¼ tsp. black pepper
1 hard-boiled egg
1 cup mayonnaise

How
Rub egg through a sieve and mix with all other ingredients. Serve in a bowl beside the appetizers.

MUSHROOM DEVILS

What
6 hard-cooked eggs
¾ cup sliced mushrooms
¼ tsp. dry mustard
½ tsp. wine vinegar
1 tbsp. mayonnaise
¼ tsp. Worcestershire sauce
2 tsp. butter
¼ tsp. salt

How
Saute mushrooms in butter for 5 minutes. Drain on paper

towel. Split eggs lengthwise and remove yolks. Chop all mushrooms, but 12 slices, finely. Mash with balance of ingredients except whites of egg. Fill egg whites with stuffing and top with a slice of mushroom. Chill and serve on a cold plate garnished with a sprig of parsley or watercress.

CLAM PUFFIES

If you love your guests, or even like them a lot, you will take the trouble to make these.

What
1 can minced clams, drained (10 oz.)
3 oz. cream cheese
3 tbsp. melted butter
¼ tsp. garlic powder
½ tsp. Worcestershire sauce
¼ tsp. salt
1 tsp. grated lemon peel
½ tsp. lemon juice
Paprika
18 thin slices toasted sandwich bread

How
Whip butter, cheese, lemon juice, and seasonings together. Stir in balance of ingredients except bread and paprika, until well mixed. Mound on the toast and run under broiler about 4–5 inches from heat until puffy. Dust with paprika, and serve.

CELERY STUFFING

What
½ cup deviled ham

2 tbsp. sour cream
¼ cup grated sharp cheddar cheese
Paprika
½ tsp. onion flakes

How
Mix all ingredients except paprika together. Stuff the
celery and sprinkle with paprika.

GOLDEN EYE

What
½ cup shredded raw carrot
1 cup shredded Edam or Gouda cheese
¼ tsp. dry or ½ tsp. Dijon mustard
1 tsp. grated onion, or flakes
2 tbsp. mayonnaise

How
Mix grated onion, mustard, and mayonnaise. Mix well with
cheese and form into small balls. Roll in the shredded carrot.

DUTCHWICHES

A favorite sandwich in Holland.

What
3 tbsp. chopped parsley
12 square slices of pumpernickel
½ lb. thinly sliced rare roast beef
½ lb. grated Edam or Gouda cheese

How
Butter the pumpernickel. Layer on the roast beef slices.

Put a mound of grated cheese on top and sprinkle with parsley.

MUSHROOM-NUT BITS

Another goody from Holland.

What
12 slices of pumpernickel or sandwich bread
½ lb. Gouda or Edam—or cheddar
Soft butter
½ cup chopped pecans
½ cup finely crushed potato chips
1 can (10 oz.) condensed mushroom soup
¼ cup finely chopped canned pimento

How
If using sandwich bread, toast and trim off crusts. Cool, and butter. Cut into quarters. Combine soup, potato chips, pimento, and pecans. Spread thickly on bread. Press a ⅓-inch cube of cheese in center of each piece. Heat under broiler until cheese starts to melt. Guests love 'em.

ZUYDER-ZEE SPREAD

Nippy and delightful.

What
1½ cups grated Leyden cheese (I use sharp cheddar)
¼ cup bleu cheese
¼ cup mayonnaise
1 tbsp. instant onion
½ cup deviled ham
2 tbsp. snipped parsley sprigs

How

Cream bleu cheese into mayonnaise. Mix well with grated cheese, deviled ham, and onion. Mound in serving dish, and garnish with parsley sprigs. Serve with toast points, thin pumpernickel or rye bread.

DILLED SHRIMP WITH CHUTNEY

What

1½ lb. cooked, shelled, and deveined shrimp
½ cup white wine
1½ cups water
½ cup cider vinegar
½ cup sugar
2 tsp. dill flakes
1 tsp. salt
1 sliced onion (large)
1½ cup mayonnaise
⅓ cup finely chopped chutney
¼ cup heavy sweet cream

How

Bring water, sugar, vinegar, dill, salt, and onion to a boil. Pour over cooked shrimp. Marinate in refrigerator 12 to 20 hours. Combine mayonnaise, chutney, and cream, and mix well and use as a dip for shrimp.

ANCHOVY SPREAD

What

2 cans flat anchovy fillets
3 finely chopped garlic cloves
2 tbsp. dry breadcrumbs
1 tsp. water

pinch black pepper
1 tbsp. salad oil
1 tsp. wine vinegar
6 slices French bread

How
Blend anchovies with water, breadcrumbs, pepper and oil.
Add vinegar and mash in well, and mix. Brush the bread
with oil or melted butter, spread with the paste, and heat
under the broiler.

CHEESE BALLS

Make balls of cream cheese about the size of walnuts.
—Roll in poppy seeds.
—Roll in chopped nuts.
—Mix 50-50 with crabmeat and roll in grated Parmesan
cheese.
—Mix with bleu cheese and roll in paprika.
—Mix 50-50 with Oka Cheese and roll in poppy seeds.

ANCHOVY AND CUCUMBER CANAPES

What
10 slices toast
¼ cup anchovy paste
1 cup finely chopped cucumbers
¼ cup French dressing
10 stuffed olives

How
Marinate cucumber in French dressing. Trim slices of
bread and toast. Spread with anchovy paste, then with cucumber and dressing mixture, and serve with a stuffed olive
in the center.

CHICKEN LIVER CANAPE

Chop fine 1 cup cooked chicken livers, and 1 cup mushrooms, chopped and sauteed in butter for five minutes. Add 1 tsp. grated onion, and 1 tsp. dry white wine. Spread on toast or crackers.

CRAB BITS

Spread toast with Russian dressing, then with crab flakes, then dip edges in finely chopped radish.

DEVILED EGG

Cut hard-boiled eggs in half, lengthwise. Remove yolks and mash with mayonnaise, pinch of curry, chopped chives, or finely chopped olives. Pile lightly into whites and garnish with black or stuffed olive. You can also fill eggs with salmon, mixed with finely chopped pickle and a little grated onion.

FAR EAST SPREAD

Mix cream cheese with finely chopped chutney. Spread on toast quarters and top with an anchovy roll or fillet.

SARDINE CANAPE

Mash sardines with lemon juice and white wine, spread on crackers or toast, garnish with chopped olive or pimento.

LOBSTER-CHEESE CANAPE

Spread oblongs of toast with Russian dressing and cream

cheese. Sprinkle with chopped chives, and put meat from small lobster claw on top of each, or slices of lobster meat.

LADIES' SPECIAL

Mince orange sections fine. Mix with chopped chives and cream cheese and spread on toast, points or oblongs.

SWEDISH CRAB CANAPES

What
½ lb. flaked crabmeat
1 tbsp. dry sherry
½ tsp. salt
⅛ tsp. fresh black pepper
1 tsp. dill flakes
1 tbsp. butter
1 tbsp. flour
1 egg yolk
1 cup coffee cream
24 rounds of French bread, 2 inches in diameter

How
Mix crabmeat, sherry, salt, pepper, and dill in a bowl. Melt butter, remove from heat, and stir in flour. Beat egg yolk with cream, and stir or whisk well into butter-flour mixture. Stir-cook over low heat until thickened, but do not boil. Mix thoroughly with crabmeat mixture. Toast rounds of bread on one side. Mound mixture on other side of bread and brown lightly under broiler.

CRABMEAT CANAPE

What
½ lb. cooked crabmeat

2 green onions, chopped fine
2 tbsp. peanut oil
3 tbsp. white wine
3 oz. medium white sauce
1 tsp. parsley flakes
1 tsp. chive flakes

How
Saute onions in oil three minutes. Add white sauce and wine.
Simmer 5 minutes. Stir in crabmeat. Serve on toast points
with parsley and chives sprinkled on top. Snack for 8.

COCKTAIL CHEESE SPREAD

Mix in top of double boiler:
1 small can evaporated milk
½ lb. nippy process cheese, diced
¼ lb. butter, seasoned with 1 tsp. onion salt
½ tsp. garlic salt, mixed with ½ tsp. paprika
Stir over low heat until cheese is melted, and sauce is smooth.
Chill in a bowl and use as a dip, or spread.

INDIAN CANAPES

12 slices bread, cut in shapes and fried brown in butter
¾ cup potted ham
⅓ cup finely chopped chutney
¼ cup grated Parmesan cheese
Spread toast pieces with potted ham, then with chutney.
Sprinkle with Parmesan and toast lightly under broiler.

JELLIED OYSTERS

What
12 fresh oysters
1½ tbsp. lemon gelatin

1 tbsp. lemon juice
1 tbsp. minced parsley
1½ cups oyster liquor

How
Soften gelatin in a little cold water, and dissolve in hot oyster liquor. Cool slightly and add lemon juice and parsley. Pour into small molds ½ inch of gelatin, and chill until set firmly. Place an oyster in the center of each mold and chill until firmly set, after pouring in balance of gelatin. Unmold on lettuce leaf, garnish with parsley sprig and a half slice of lemon.

JELLIED CUCUMBER RELISH

What
1½ tbsp. unflavored gelatin
¼ cup cold water
1¼ cup boiling water
5 oz. vinegar
⅛ cup sugar
1½ tbsp. minced onion
1½ tbsp. chopped green pepper
1 tsp. salt
2½ cups finely chopped cucumber, drained well in colander

How
Soften gelatin in cold water and dissolve in the boiling water. Add vinegar, sugar, and salt. Cool. Add cucumbers, peppers, and onion, and mix well. Chill in wetted molds. Used with fish course, as relish, or as an appetizer.

LOBSTER CANAPE

What
¾ cup lobster paste

¾ cup butter
25 small toast rounds
8 hard-boiled eggs
13 stuffed olives

How
Cream together butter and lobster paste. Spread evenly on toast. Put thick slice of egg in center of each canape. Cut olives in half and put on center of egg slices, cut side up.

GAY FROLIC COCKTAIL

What
1 quart tomato juice
1 cup vegetable juice
1 tsp. salt
½ tsp. Worcestershire sauce
½ tsp. pepper
1 tsp. onion juice
3 oz. lemon juice

How
Combine all ingredients, shake well and chill. Serve in cocktail glasses.

ROQUEFORT CANAPES

What
25 slices toast
2 cups Roquefort cheese
1 cup cream cheese
1 tbsp. Worcestershire sauce
2 tsp. French dressing

How
Cut bread into desired shapes and brown in butter. Spread

with paste made by mixing the other ingredients. Garnish with small pieces of red and green pepper.

BAKED CANAPES

Cheese Sticks
What
25 thin strips bread
¼ cup butter
½ cup grated cheddar cheese
1 tsp. salt
¼ tsp. cayenne pepper
¼ cup minced ripe olives

How
Spread bread strips with butter. Mix salt, cayenne, and cheese and sprinkle on the bread. Brown lightly under broiler. Sprinkle with minced olives.

ANCHOVY STICKS

Preheat oven to 450 deg. Sift 3 cups flour, and cut in 1 cup butter. Rub in ½ cup anchovy paste. Add just enough water or milk to make a paste that will roll. Roll ¼ inch thick, and cut into ¼ inch sticks, 2 inches long. You can also form rings, if you wish variety. Bake five minutes on baking sheet.

CLAM 'N HAM ASPIC

What
½ cup diced clams
½ cup finely chopped ham
1 cup chicken stock or bouillon
Clam juice and enough chicken stock to make one cup

1 tbsp. spiced lemon juice
1 tbsp. chives
1 envelope gelatin (plain)
¼ tsp. thyme
¼ tsp. garlic salt
1 tbsp. tomato paste

How
Soften gelatin in the mixture of chicken stock and clam juice. Mix all other ingredients in a saucepan and bring just to a boil. Cover and let stand ten minutes to develop flavor. Reheat for a minute, and add clam gelatin mixture. Cool and pour into a wet mold. To make spiced lemon juice, simmer slowly ½ cup lemon juice with 1 tsp. pickling spice. This will keep, refrigerated, for weeks. I put one tbsp. cider vinegar with it, if keeping it for any time.

SEAFOOD NIPS

Hollow out a small red cabbage to make a bowl. Fill with Russian dressing. Arrange around it fried scallops, fried oysters, fried clams, with shrimp or tiny fried fish fillets. Put a toothpick in each fish bit. Dip 'n nip.

ZIFKAS

Don't ask what it means, or the origin. I don't know either. They are snappy and a favorite with drinkers. They are good finger pickin', and you'll need to make plenty, as they don't last too well at a party.

Mince finely 1 medium onion, 1 green pepper, and 1 clove garlic. Mix in 2 tsp. ground coriander, and 2 tsp. salt. Add and mix in ¼ tsp. each of ground cloves and ground cardamon, cinnamon, chili powder, and Tabasco. Mix very thoroughly with 1½ lb. finely ground beef and shape into balls the size of a walnut, and brown slowly all around in butter.

NOW—MIXED FILLINGS

For patty shells and finger rolls, or croustades. These big-bite canapes are popular with men. While they tend to curtail the consumption of liquor, they are cheaper than good Scotch, and avoid the necessity of moving and disposing of horizontal guests.

SAVORITA

Grind together 12 slices of fried bacon, ½ lb. nippy cheddar (or mixture of cheddar and Roquefort), 2 small onions. Mix in 1 tsp. dry mustard, 2 tbsp. mayonnaise, 2 tbsp. dry wine, and ¼ tsp. pepper. Spread on toast, or put in patty shells or finger rolls and heat in hot oven.

CHEESE IN SHERRY, FILLING

Grind together 1 lb. cheddar cheese, 1 lb. cottage cheese, ¼ lb. bleu cheese, and ¼ lb. hickory smoked cheese. (You can use hickory smoked salt instead of the cheese.) Add ¼ tsp. each of onion salt, garlic powder (or salt), black pepper. Add 2 tbsp. prepared mustard, then enough sherry to make a spreading paste.

DILL DELIGHT

Cream together ½ cup butter and ¼ cup French mustard.

Spread on thin shapes of white bread. Mix well 2 cups mashed sardines, 2 cups finely chopped dill pickle, and a dash of Tabasco. Spread on the bread, and top with slices of stuffed olives, sliced radishes, little cheese squares, or ? ? ?

CHEESE DIP

What
⅓ cup chicken stock (or milk)
2 oz. strong cheddar cheese
6 oz. cream cheese
2 oz. bleu cheese
6 oz. cottage cheese
⅛ tsp. garlic powder
¼ tsp. celery salt
Dash of Tabasco sauce

How
Blend for 20 seconds on high speed. This makes a pint of smooth, zingy dip. Excellent with potato sticks, vegetable sticks, or crackers.

BLEU CHEESE DIP

What
1 cup creamy cottage cheese
¼ medium onion
6 stalks watercress
⅓ cup cream
1 tsp. Worcestershire sauce
4 oz. bleu cheese

How
Cover and blend until smooth and creamy. Delicious dip for hot French fries or cold potato chips. Unique as a pretzel dip.

BEER CHEESE DIP

What

8 oz. cheddar cheese, cubed
8 oz. cream cheese
¾ cup beer
¼ tsp. garlic powder
⅓ cup diced dill pickle

How

Blend cream cheese with ½ cup beer on high speed for 7 seconds. Add garlic powder, balance of beer, and dill pickle. Blend for 10 seconds. Add cheddar cheese and blend 10 seconds longer.

CLAM DIP

What

6 oz. cream cheese
1 can (7½ oz.) minced clams
¼ tsp. celery salt
1 tbsp. chopped green onion top (or chive flakes)
1 tsp. chervil flakes
Dash of Tabasco

How

Drain clams and reserve ¼ cup of juice. Add the juice and half the clams to blender container, with cream cheese, onion, and seasonings. Blend 10 seconds. Add balance of clams and blend 2 seconds. Chill before serving.

CHICKEN LIVER DIP

What

½ lb. chicken livers, cut coarsely
1 hard-boiled egg, cut in eighths

¼ tsp. celery pepper
¼ tsp. thyme
½ tsp. salt
2 slices bacon, diced
2 tbsp. butter
2 tbsp. chicken fat
1 medium onion, diced

How

Saute bacon, chicken livers, and onion in butter and chicken fat for eight minutes. Put it all in the blender. Add balance of ingredients and blend 5 seconds on high speed. Make sure all ingredients have been well blended. Scrape out and chill.

INSTANT ONION DIP

What

1 pint sour cream
1 tsp. lemon juice
1 package onion soup mix

How

Blend ingredients on high speed for 10 seconds. Let chill for 2 hours to develop full flavor before serving.

HAM DIP

You may also use chicken.

What

¾ cup diced cooked ham
½ small onion
⅛ tsp. cloves

⅛ tsp. nutmeg
1 tsp. Worcestershire sauce
Dash of Tabasco
½ cup mayonnaise

How
Blend thoroughly about 20 seconds. Let sit for 2 hours to develop flavor.

HICKORY CHEESE DIP

What
6 oz. cream cheese
6 oz. diced hickory smoked cheese
⅓ cup pineapple juice
¼ tsp. Worcestershire sauce
1 tsp. tomato paste or sauce
1 clove garlic, or ¼ tsp. garlic powder
¼ tsp. salt

How
Blend cream cheese and pineapple juice. Add balance of ingredients and blend 25 seconds. Chill before serving.

BARBECUE DIP

What
1 cup creamy cottage cheese
¼ cup soft butter
½ cup chili sauce
1 tbsp. prepared horseradish
1 tbsp. lemon juice

How
Blend for 20 seconds and cool before serving.

5

Special Dishes
from Near and Far

In world traveling, I tried to collect some outstanding main dishes. Even voluptuous hostesses did not always distract me from this search, so I managed to secure a goodly selection for your delectation.

I have carefully avoided some of the favored dishes of other countries, dishes such as one hundred year old eggs, fricasseed grasshoppers, baked iguana, smoked rattlesnake, and octopus pie. While these concoctions are reputed to be high in protein, they lack something in social acceptance.

All recipes presented herewith have been kitchen tested with substitutes for ingredients not readily available in this country.

VEAU À LA SUISSE (Swiss Veal)

What
2 lb. veal loin
½ lb. smoked side bacon, sliced
¼ cup melted butter
1 clove garlic
1 tbsp. parsley flakes

4 tbsp. flour
1 tsp. salt
½ tsp. fresh black pepper
1 cup Sauterne
1 cup chicken stock or broth

How
Fry bacon crisp, and remove from pan and crumble. Drain, and discard all but 2 tbsp. fat. Split garlic, and brown in the butter and bacon fat. Discard garlic. Slice veal ½ inch thick, then slice very thin across the slices. Saute about 5 minutes, turning until white. Remove, and saute the onions until translucent. Add flour and seasonings and stir until flour absorbs the fat. Add chicken broth and wine, and stir until smooth and lightly thickened. Add veal and bacon and stir-cook over low heat for 15 minutes. Serve with parsley flakes sprinkled on each serving. Serves 6.

ROAST VENISON WITH BLEU CHEESE SAUCE

The Norwegians make this with reindeer haunch, but I've tried it with venison and it's excellent.

What
1 boneless haunch roast of venison, about 3½–4 lb.
4 tbsp. melted butter
Salt
Fresh black pepper
1½ cups beef stock or consomme
1 tbsp. flour
1 tbsp. butter
1 tbsp. red currant jelly
1 tbsp. bleu cheese
½ cup sour cream

How

While tying roast so it will hold its shape, heat oven to 475 degrees. Brush roast with the melted butter, and put on rack, in a shallow roast pan. Let it sear about 20 minutes, turning once at about 12 minutes. When meat is well browned, reduce heat to 375 degrees. Season roast and return to oven. Add beef stock to pan. Cook 1¼–1½ hours, basting every 15 minutes. Core temperature should be 155 degrees. Cover loosely and let sit in oven. Skim fat from pan juices. Mix butter and flour and stir-cook until lightly browned in a skillet, about 7 minutes. If necessary, add enough stock to pan juices to make 1 cup. Beat into the flour-butter roux. Whisk in jelly and cheese until smooth and thickened. Stir in sour cream. Serve over thin slices of venison. Serves 6 to 8.

COACHMAN'S CASSEROLE (Swedish)

What

2 pork kidneys, split in two
¾ lb. pork loin, sliced ¼ inch thick
2 tbsp. butter
2 tbsp. bacon fat
1 cup sliced onions
2 lbs. potatoes, peeled and sliced ⅛ inch
1½ cups beef stock or bouillon
1½ cups beer
½ tsp. sugar
1 bay leaf
Salt
Fresh black pepper

How

Saute onions in butter and bacon fat until soft. Remove with slotted spoon and set aside. Brown kidneys and pork slices quickly, and remove. Slice kidneys ¼ inch thick. Add beer, stock, and sugar to pan and scrape browned bits into liquid. Remove pan from heat. Drain potatoes and pat dry with paper towels. Arrange layers of meat, potatoes and onions in a heavy casserole, seasoning each layer. Add bay leaf to center of top layer. Pour on liquid and bake 2 hours in center of preheated 350 degree oven. Serves 4 to 6.

SWEDISH POT ROAST (Slottsstek)

What

3½ to 4 lbs. boneless chuck
2 tbsp. butter
2 tbsp. pork or bacon fat
1 cup chopped onions
2 tbsp. white vinegar
1 tbsp. corn syrup
3 tbsp. flour
2 cups beef stock or consomme
2 bay leaves
1 dozen peppercorns, crushed in bag
Salt
6 flat anchovy fillets, washed and dried

How

Melt butter and bacon fat in skillet. Brown roast all around to seal in juices, then remove. Brown onions lightly. Remove pan from heat and stir in flour, then beef stock. Transfer to casserole and put in meat, sprinkle with salt and pepper. Add balance of ingredients, and bring to boil on top of stove. Cover and bake at 275 degree oven for 3 hours. Remove meat, hold hot, and reduce sauce to 1 cup. Serves 6 to 8.

In sunny Italy, the land of mozzarella and Chianti, they have a light touch with summer dishes, that can get you out of the heat doldrums. This dish is one you can keep in a shallow casserole in the refrigerator, and use when you are ready. Just slip the chilled and covered casserole into the trunk of your Ferrari, between the Chianti and the big crusty loaves of garlic bread. Be careful to balance the Chianti carefully with the food when imbibing, so you may enjoy the:

PORK TONNATO

What

1 lb. thinly sliced roast pork, or roast fresh ham
1 cup dry white wine
1 clove garlic, mashed
1 small onion, minced fine
1 egg
1 tsp. lemon juice
½ tsp. dry mustard
1 tsp. anchovy paste
¾ cup olive oil
4 tbsp. minced tuna
Small capers in vinegar, drained
Salt and pepper
Dash of Tabasco

How

In a small saucepan, heat wine, garlic, and onion until wine is reduced to about ¼ cup. In blender on low speed, blend egg, mustard, lemon juice, dash of Tabasco, and tuna, about 5 seconds. Dribble in the oil with blender running, until fairly thick. Add wine sauce and blend 5 seconds more. Add salt and pepper to taste. Shut off blender and stir in 3 tbsp. of capers. Spread this sauce between the slices of pork or ham, laid overlapping like shingles in the shallow casserole. Pour any leftover sauce over the top and sprinkle on top 2 more tbsp. of capers. Cover, and keep refrigerated for at least eight hours to develop flavor. Take it with you to your favorite picnic spot. Reach for the Chianti and the tossed salad, put the Tonnato on slices of garlic bread, and you're dining Ferrari class, even if you have a VW or a Datsun!

SIRLOIN MINUTE STEAK

This is part of the family jewels, and the gourmet's idea of taste from Heaven.

What
2 sirloin steaks (about 8 oz. each)
4 tbsp. Roquefort cheese
2 tablespoons cream
¼ tsp. Worcestershire sauce

How
Mash cheese with cream and Worcestershire sauce. Season steaks with salt and pepper. Spread on the cheese mix. Roll in flour, and fry slowly in butter. Serve with pan gravy and French fried potatoes; garnish with sprigs of parsley.

ROAST PORK WITH GLACE APPLES

This recipe serves 25 with 9 oz. portions. You can cut it in half if you wish.

What
1 fresh pork ham, about 12 lb.
1 tbsp. salt
2 tsp. pepper
1 cup chopped onions
1 cup chopped celery

¼ cup minced parsley
1 tsp. powdered thyme
25 small apples
2 cups raisins
2 cups chopped pineapple

How
Cut skin of ham into one inch squares, scoring right through skin. Gash the other side about ¼ inch deep, same as skin. Mix the seasonings together and rub well into ham all around. Dredge with flour and sear in 400 degree oven, all around. Reduce heat to 300 degrees and pour in one gallon of water. Cover and bake 3½ hours, basting occasionally. Thirty minutes before ham is done, surround with apples that have been cored and stuffed with raisins. Add pineapple. Finish baking, uncovered. Remove ham, cool, and bone out. Serve sliced, with an apple.

TOURNEDOS DIAVOLO ESPAGNOL

I found this little gem in a small hotel outside Madrid. Their vino de la casa was a beautiful manzanilla, pale, dry, and cold, that makes the taste buds stand to attention. The diavolo maintained the excitement very well, using amoroso liberally throughout the meal **as a** quench.

What
4 filet mignons, 4 oz. each
2 tsp. fresh ground coarse white pepper
4 tbsp. clarified butter
½ cup dry red wine
¼ cup chicken broth or bouillon
½ tsp. tarragon flakes
1 tbsp. chive flakes
1 tbsp. Worcestershire sauce
2 tbsp. unmelted butter

How

Press pepper into both sides of the steaks with the flat of a knife. Saute in clarified butter until light brown on both sides. Hold steaks in a 200 degree oven until required, on a serving platter. Pour chicken broth, wine, and seasonings into pan, and scrape browned bits into sauce. Simmer sauce until reduced by half. Swirl in unmelted butter until melted. Brush four slices French bread, toasted, with a mixture of 1/4 cup olive oil and 1 tbsp. Worcestershire sauce. Place steaks on the toast, spoon sauce over, and serve to four.

Serve with Ensalada Variada (a green mixed tossed salad with tangy garlic dressing), and hope you can get a beautiful Malaga, rich, dark, and sweet, with your café con leche. Thus fulfilled, you can proceed to the bullfights or whatever other pastime can be enjoyed on a happy stomach.

There is nothing like the contemplative mood, induced by ice fishing. For instance, while fishing through the ice (for olives) I recalled this succulent recipe for beef with olives. It is called

BEEF NAPOLITANI

What

4 strips bacon, diced
1 large onion, chopped
2 lb. beef stew meat, trimmed and cubed 1/2 inch
Flour
1/2 tsp. powdered bay leaf
1/4 tsp. thyme
1/4 tsp. oregano
1/2 tsp. salt
1/4 tsp. black pepper
1 cup Burgundy
1 can (8 oz.) tomato sauce
2 tbsp. chopped parsley, or 1 tbsp. flakes
1 cup pitted ripe olives, halved

How

Cook bacon and onion together in a heavy pot or Dutch oven, until bacon is lightly browned. Remove. Mix all seasonings with one half cup flour. Roll and toss stew meat in flour until well coated. Add to kettle and stir over high heat until browned all around. Reduce heat and return bacon and onions to pot. Add wine, tomato sauce, and ¼ cup water. Cover and simmer two hours. Stir now and then to prevent sticking and add more water if necessary to prevent gravy from becoming too thick. Add olives and parsley and simmer five minutes more before serving. Serve with buttered noodles and a tossed salad. Serves 4.

Note: I just asked my egg man for some fertile eggs. He took me aside and whispered, "Don't you know fertile eggs are the result of fowl play?" I retired in confusion.

The Danes are famous for both food and drink, and they mix them with joyous abandon. This is what you might expect from a nation that eats beer soup for breakfast. They have a dark beer, called Paskebryg, that packs an alco-wallop that can even inebriate the roots of your hair! They also make a stuffed cabbage roll with beer sauce that is really something else. It is easier to make than to pronounce, since it is called:

FYLDT HVIDKAAL MED LAGEROL SAUCE

What

1 large head of cabbage
¾ lb. ground beef (chuck)
½ cup crumbled fried lean bacon
Salt, pepper, M.S.G.
½ cup cooked rice
1 medium onion, minced fine
¼ tsp. sage

1 large onion, cut in strips finely
4 tbsp. breadcrumbs
3 tbsp. butter
1 cup canned tomatoes
2 bouillon cubes
1 cup dark beer
2 tbsp. lemon juice
2 tbsp. cider vinegar
3 tbsp. sugar
¼ tsp. allspice

How
Core cabbage. Remove 8 large outer leaves and cut off heavy part. Blanch in boiling water until pliable. Drain. Combine beef, bacon, rice, breadcrumbs, small onion, and seasoning in mixing bowl and mix thoroughly. Divide into eight equal parts. Put one part on each cabbage leaf, and roll up, tucking in sides. Lay, seam side down, in shallow baking dish. Saute large onion in butter until yellow. Drain and mash tomatoes. Add, with juice, to onions. Add beer, bouillon cubes, lemon juice, vinegar, and sugar, with allspice, and more salt and pepper to taste. Bring to a boil and pour over cabbage rolls. Simmer slowly, covered, 1 hour, in 325 degree oven. Serves 4; if you are going first class, top off the rolls with Cherry Heering and drip coffee.

CHICKEN CACCIATORE ANGELICA

Any chicken should be very happy to be a part of this.

What
6 slices bacon
1 breast of broiler
8 chicken wings
1 large onion, chopped fine

2 cloves garlic, minced
½ cup sliced celery
1 sliced green pepper
10 mushrooms, sliced
2 cups canned tomatoes
1 bay leaf
½ tsp. salt
¼ tsp. black pepper
¼ tsp. savory
¼ tsp. rosemary
Pinch of cayenne
¼ cup chopped parsley
¼ cup dry white wine
2 tbsp. oil

How
Split chicken breast, and fry with bacon, oil, and chicken wings until nicely browned. Remove meat from pan. Slice breast into fine strips, and bacon into strips about 2 inches long. Put onion, garlic, celery, and green pepper into pan and stir-fry until lightly cooked. Add mushrooms, canned tomatoes, and seasonings. Simmer ten minutes. Add the meats, parsley, and wine. Simmer slowly fifteen minutes and serve to four gourmets.

BAKED PORK CHOPS SUPREME

What
10 pork chops
1 tsp. salt
1 tsp. pepper
1 quart breadcrumbs
¼ cup chopped celery
¼ cup minced parsley
¼ cup finely chopped onion
½ cup melted butter

How

Sprinkle chops with salt and pepper, and brown in hot oven (375 degrees) on both sides. Mix crumbs, celery, parsley, onion, melted butter, and 1 quart of water. Cover chops with the mixture and bake, covered, at 325 degrees for 1 hour. Serves 5 men or 10 women.

RIB ROAST OF BEEF AU JUS

What
10 lb. beef rib
3 tbsp. salt
1 tsp. pepper
¾ cup flour
2 quarts water
¾ cup cooking oil

How

Bone beef rib. Season inside with half the seasonings. Roll and tie securely. Rub outside with remaining seasonings. Oil and dredge with flour. Sear 15 minutes in 400 degree oven, turning once. Have fat side up when finished searing. Add water, reduce heat to 300, and baste occasionally. Should take 4–4½ hours. To make gravy, strain, and skim off fat. Add a little flour mixed with water, and leave in oven fifteen minutes more. Serve with carved roast.

ROLLED RIB ROAST OF BEEF

If you purchase a rolled rib roast, prepare and roast as above.

ROAST ROUND WITH FRANCONIA POTATOES

What
5 lb. top round steak

2 tbsp. salt
1 tsp. pepper
¾ cup cooking oil
2 lb. small new potatoes
1 medium onion, chopped
1 tbsp. vinegar
2 tbsp. minced parsley

How
Season roast with salt and pepper, and dredge with flour.
Heat oven to 400 degrees. Place roast in oven and sear well,
pouring oil over seared side as you turn. Reduce oven to
300, and add 2 quarts water, and the balance of the ingredients. Roasting time about 2 hours. Baste occasionally while
roasting, about every 15 minutes. Peel, and parboil potatoes
in salted water ten minutes. Remove from water, and add to
roast pan the last 45 minutes of roasting.

PORK 'N SAUERKRAUT

This hearty dish originated in Germany, where sauerkraut
is dear to the heart. If you have never tasted sauerkraut when
married to the flavors of apple and dry white wine, you have
a new fillip for your taste buds, in this dish.

What
3 lbs. well-fleshed pork spareribs, cut 2 inches long
2 tbsp. oil
1 large onion, coarsely chopped
¾ cup apple juice
¼ cup red wine (or dry Burgundy)
1 cup dry white wine
1 tbsp. cider vinegar
2 lb. sauerkraut
2 apples, diced ½ inch

½ tsp. savory
1 bay leaf
1 tsp. salt
½ tsp. black pepper

How

If you are using freshly made sauerkraut, blanch it in boiling water, for about two minutes, and drain. Canned sauerkraut may be washed, drained, and used as is. Melt the fat in a skillet, and brown ribs well on all sides. Drain on paper towel. Cook onion in fat until golden. Drain off all but 2 tbsp. of fat. Remove pan from heat and stir in 2 tbsp. of flour. Return to heat and add apple juice, stirring and heating until smooth. Add bay leaf, salt, pepper, savory, wines, and vinegar. Now, in a deep, heavy kettle, put a layer of sauerkraut, a layer of spare ribs, and sprinkle with diced apple. Repeat until all ingredients are used. Cover tightly and simmer for 1½ hours. If in the oven, simmer at 300 degrees. Add apple juice as necessary to keep pan from going dry. With the above, serve mashed potato. Cook the potatoes with an onion, and mash together. Serves 6 very happy people.

Aside One of my pretty guests (no substitutions, please) just said to me, "Do you think maybe men are nuts? They bite a girl's neck, because she has a pretty bust." Misplaced geography?

STUFFED PEPPER SQUASH

What

2 pepper squash (about 6-inch diameter)
¼ lb. butter
1 lb. shrimp, cooked and chopped
½ lb. cooked ham, chopped
¼ cup minced onion
2 cloves garlic, minced

1 tbsp. chopped parsley
½ loaf stale white bread
1 cup bread crumbs
½ tsp. thyme
¼ tsp. powdered bay leaf
1 tsp. salt
½ tsp. pepper
2 tbsp. Parmesan cheese

How
Parboil squash until just tender. Scoop out center and mash. Soak stale bread until soft and squeeze out water. Melt butter in skillet and saute onion, garlic, and seasonings. Add balance of ingredients and mix well, stir-cooking 5 minutes. Butter bread crumbs and top mixture. Sprinkle on Parmesan and bake about 20 minutes at 375 degrees until browned. Serves 4.

I had intended to present a recipe for roast saddle of Lapland Yak, with tundra moss and lemming sauce, but couldn't find it. However, I found this one, labeled "Stolen in Rome!" This is veal at its succulent best.

SCALLOPINI AL LIMONE

What
1½ lbs. veal scallops, ⅜-inch thick
½ cup flour
1 tsp. salt
¼ tsp. pepper
1 clove garlic, slivered
½ tsp. thyme
4 tbsp. butter
3 tbsp. olive oil
½ cup beef stock or bouillon
6 thin slices of lemon
¼ cup white wine

How

Mix flour and seasonings. Dredge veal in flour and pound out to ¼ inch thick, then flour again. Melt oil with 2 tbsp. butter. Add garlic, brown lightly, then remove and discard. Saute the scallops light brown. Remove to heated platter. Pour off fat and return 2 tbsp. to pan. Add beef stock and bring to boil, scraping browned bits from pan into stock. Return veal to pan and top with lemon slices. Add wine, cover and simmer 15 minutes. Remove veal to heated platter. Reduce stock to half, swirl in the remaining 2 tbsp. butter, and pour over scallops. Serves 4 to 6.

Eating in Spain can be both an exciting and a dismaying experience. If you are accustomed to a rigid meal schedule at home, dining in Madrid will knock you for a loop. Everybody who is anybody arises late, and drinks café con leche (half coffee-half milk) and a sweet roll. Lunch is anywhere from 2 P.M. to 3:30 P.M. Dinner may be ten to eleven P.M., and is their big meal. Nightmares, anyone? However, the following is a dish of lovely memory.

TONGUE WITH CURRY SAUCE

What

1 3½ lb. smoked tongue
1½ tbsp. pickling spice
1 clove garlic
2 stalks chopped celery, with leaves
1 medium onion, quartered
1 tbsp. parsley flakes
½ cup dry red wine

How

Put all the ingredients in a large pot. Add water to cover. Bring to boil, then simmer 2 hours, until tongue is tender. Cool tongue in the cooking liquid. Remove and skin when just warm.

CURRY SAUCE

What
2 tbsp. butter
3 tbsp. flour
2 tsp. curry powder
½ tsp. salt
Pinch of black pepper
½ tsp. sugar
½ cup small sultana raisins
2 cups strained broth from tongue
¼ cup finely chopped onion

How
Saute onion and curry powder in butter, until onion is tender, about 3 minutes. Mix in flour, well. Stir in balance of ingredients and stir-cook until thickened. Add sliced tongue and serve hot with hashed-brown potatoes or brown rice. Olé!
Superb for 4 or 5.

DILLKOTT PA LAMM

Should you find yourself in Stockholm, you may wish to try this dish. Den Glydene Freden is a restaurant with excellent food and a superb cellar. Beware of too many skäls (pronounced *skoal*), as courtesy demands that you return every toast, and acquavit is a potent start for a dinner. This dish is good enough that I arranged to pilfer (liberate?) the recipe, purely in the interest of good international relations! The name translates as Lamb in Dill Sauce.

What
3 lb. lamb neck, in 2-inch chunks
2 quarts water

1½ tbsp. dill flakes
1½ tbsp. wine vinegar
¼ tsp. white pepper
12 medium potatoes
2 tsp. salt
2 tbsp. butter
2 tbsp. flour
1 egg yolk
2 tsp. sugar
1 oz. dry white wine

How

Bring water, salt and dill to a boil in a heavy kettle, add lamb chunks. When liquid boils again, cover, turn heat to "low," and cook slowly 1½ hours. Add potatoes and cook another ¾ of an hour. Drain stock off lamb. Remove lamb and potatoes from kettle. Add butter to kettle and melt, add flour and stir in. Stir in 2 cups of stock. Add balance of ingredients except egg yolk and wine, and cook, stirring until thickened. Add a little of the sauce to the beaten egg yolk, and blend well. Add wine, return to kettle and cook 3 minutes more. Add lamb and potatoes and heat slowly. Serves 6 of the aquavit and ludafisk set. It will bring them out of the aquavit orbit!

The other night while sorting souvenirs of past vacations, I found a half dozen chopsticks I had acquired on Mott Street in 'Frisco a few years ago. This led to nostalgic memories of a quaint little bistro, where I picked up the chopsticks and the recipe for their delicious Sukiyaki. Spurred by the offer of a bottle of sake, the friendly chef showed me how to make the dish. He used a wok, but assured me that a heavy skillet would do as well. Later experiments proved he was right. You may wish to try this simple Japanese route to good dining.

SUKIYAKI

What
1 lb. sirloin tip, sliced in strips ⅛ x ½ inches
¼ cup oil
1 tsp. M.S.G.
1 cup thinly sliced onions
½ lb. well-washed spinach
½ lb. mushrooms, sliced
12 green onions, with tops, sliced
1 can bamboo shoots, cut thin
2 cups sliced celery
1 can (10½ oz.) beef bouillon
⅓ cup soy sauce
3 tbsp. sugar
¼ cup sherry
4 cups hot cooked rice
1 bottle sake (optional, but yummy)
Chopsticks (optional—for mood only)

How
Heat oil over high heat in skillet. Add beef and stir-fry until browned, sprinkling with M.S.G. during cooking. Turn down heat about half and add vegetables. Stir-fry 4 minutes. Add bouillon, sherry, soy sauce, and sugar. Cover and simmer ten minutes. Serve with the hot rice, and soy sauce on the side. Serves 4. If you look in the mirror the next morning and find your eyes slightly slanted, I take no responsibility. It's the sake, not the Oriental influence of the Sukiyaki. Banzai, Sukiyakkers!

LAMB CHOPS NEW ZEALAND

What
4 loin lamb chops, 1½ inch thick
2 tsp. salt

½ tsp. rosemary
½ tsp. M.S.G.
¼ tsp. fresh black pepper
3 tbsp. dry sherry
¼ tsp. garlic powder

How
Brush chops with wine. Mix seasonings and rub into chops. Grill 4–5 inches from heat about 9 minutes per side until nicely browned. Rub in a little more seasoning after first turn, on top side.

LAMB CHOPS MAORI

Baste with this sauce, made by combining:

What
¼ cup water
¼ cup lemon juice
1 tsp. mint flakes
½ tsp. garlic powder
½ tsp. onion powder
½ tsp. powdered rosemary

CURRY SAUCE FOR LAMB

What
¾ cup peanut oil
½ cup apple juice
3 tbsp. lemon juice
3 tbsp. brown sugar
½ tsp. garlic powder
1 tbsp. curry powder
1 tsp. salt
½ tsp. M.S.G.

½ tsp. black pepper
1 dash Tabasco sauce
1 tsp. onion powder or flakes

How
Melt oil, and stir in curry powder. Add balance of ingredients and bring to a boil. Let sit 2 hours to develop flavor. Brush lamb both sides and let sit ½ hour, then barbecue, using the sauce for basting.

SCALLOPS PARISIENNE

What
1½ cups chicken stock or bouillon
1½ cups dry white wine
¼ cup sliced shallots or green onions
¼ cup chopped celery tops, with leaves
1 tsp. parsley flakes
1 bay leaf
½ tsp. coarse black pepper
2 lb. scallops, sliced ½ inch
½ lb. sliced mushrooms

Sauce

What
4 tbsp. butter
5 tbsp. flour
¾ cup milk
2 beaten egg yolks
⅓ cup heavy cream
¼ tsp. lemon juice
1tsp. salt
⅛ tsp. white pepper
¼ cup grated Swiss cheese

How

In saucepan, bring stock, wine, celery, parsley, bay leaf, and pepper to a boil. Turn down heat and simmer 20 minutes. Add scallops and mushrooms, and simmer 5 minutes, covered. Remove scallops and mushrooms to a large bowl. Boil remaining bouillon down to 1 cup. Melt the 4 tbsp. butter, remove pan from heat, and stir in flour. Let stand 5 minutes. Return to low heat and stir-cook 2 minutes. Stir or whisk in the cup of bouillon. Raise heat to medium and stir-cook until it comes to a boil and is smooth and thick. Simmer 1 minute. Mix egg yolks and cream, and add thick sauce, 2 tbsp. at a time, beating in until 4 tbsp. have been added. Return mixture to balance of cream sauce and stir in well. Stir-cook just at the boil ½ minute. Add lemon juice, salt, and pepper. Pour off any liquid from scallops and mushrooms, then mix in ⅔ of the cream sauce. Spoon the mixture into buttered scallop shells or ramekins. Top with remainder of sauce and the cheese. Heat in oven, brown lightly under broiler, and serve to 6.

OSTRICHE AL ITALIANA

In case you are worrying about how to catch an Ostrich, this simply means spicy, breaded, baked oysters.

What
2 tbsp. butter
1 cup fresh bread crumbs
1 tsp. finely minced garlic
1 tsp. lemon juice
1 tbsp. parsley flakes
2 doz. fresh or defrosted frozen oysters
3 tbsp. grated Parmesan cheese
2 tbsp. butter, cut fine
½ tsp. paprika

How

Toss crumbs in 2 tbsp. butter in skillet with garlic, until golden. Sprinkle on lemon juice and parsley, and toss until mixed. Spread ⅔ of crumbs in an 8 x 10 inch buttered baking dish. Put in oysters in one layer. Mix Parmesan and balance of crumbs, and spread on oysters. Dot with the chopped butter and sprinkle on paprika. Bake in a preheated 450 degree oven 12–15 minutes, until crumbs are golden. Serves 4 to 6.

When the month with an "R" arrives, that means the beginning of the oyster season to lovers of that succulent bivalve. The oysters have finished making their reproductive arrangements and are now ready to contribute to our amatory programs. Oysters are loaded with minerals, and essential proteins, as well as a heavy phosphorus content, conceded by the medical profession to be an aphrodisiac. For what the following Roman presentation may contribute to your enjoyment of gourmet food, I will joyously accept credit, while disclaiming all complicity in what it may add to your libidinous drives.

OYSTERS CAPRICCIO

What
36 small fresh oysters
Clam juice or broth
¼ cup butter
¼ cup finely chopped leek
¼ tsp. tarragon flakes
¼ tsp. thyme flakes
¼ cup flour
Salt, pepper, paprika
½ cup shredded old cheddar cheese
¼ cup grated Parmesan cheese

1 cup milk
½ lb. thin spaghetti
3 tbsp. very dry sherry

How

Drain the oysters and save the juice. Add enough clam juice to the oyster juice to make one cup. Combine with milk and heat, but do not boil. Cover and set aside. In another saucepan melt the butter; add leeks, tarragon, and thyme. Saute 3 minutes, stirring. Stir in flour thoroughly. Add milk and clam broth in a slow stream, stirring steadily until smooth and thickened, about 10 minutes. Stir in oysters and remove from flame. Wait 5 minutes and add wine. Season to taste with salt and pepper. Now, cook spaghetti until just al dente. Drop 2 ice cubes in the water, shake and drain. Divide into 4 individual casseroles. Make a well in the center of each and pour in the sauce. Sprinkle with both cheeses and top with paprika. Preheat oven to 375 degrees, and bake until lightly browned on top, about 20 minutes. Serve with tossed salad with an oil, lemon, and garlic dressing. Olé!

Since Holland is virtually surrounded by the ocean you would expect the Dutch to have some winning ways with seafood. This dish has distinctive flavor and nostalgic memories. Just fancy you are at a restaurant in Amsterdam called Dikker and Thijs, eating this mackerel dish, and drinking dark beer. They are specialists in seafood, and the upstairs dining room has both atmosphere and service. It was called

MAKREEL MET KNOFLOOK
(Mackerel with Garlic)

What

2 fresh mackerel, 1½ to 2 lb. each

Juice of one lemon
3 tbsp. butter
1 small bay leaf
Salt, pepper, celery salt, and chervil
1 medium onion, minced fine
1 garlic clove, minced fine
3 tbsp. instantized flour
¾ cup dark beer
¾ cup clam broth
2 tbsp. dry white wine
2 bouillon cubes
½ tsp. Worcestershire sauce

How

Have your favorite fish merchant split the fish, and remove the fins and backbone. Cut the halves in 2 lengthwise pieces. Grease a large saucepan or skillet with bacon fat. Lay the fish in, cut side up, and sprinkle with lemon juice. Add 1 cup water and ¼ tsp. salt. Cover and simmer ten minutes. Sprinkle fish with pepper and celery salt. In another saucepan, melt butter. Add bay leaf and ½ tsp. chervil. Add onion and garlic and saute until onion is golden. Remove from heat and stir in flour. Dissolve bouillon cubes in hot clam broth and add to pan, with beer, wine, and Worcestershire. Bring to a boil and simmer slowly, 5 minutes. Pour off cooking liquid from fish, and pour the sauce over the fish. Cover pan and simmer very slowly, do not boil, for 5 minutes more. Serve fish on serving dish, pouring sauce over each piece. By this time you have had enough beer, so it's time for food. Serve with hot potato salad to 4 good friends.

LOBSTER WITH RED SAUCE

What
6 lobster tails (about 6 oz. each)
3 tbsp. olive oil

3 tbsp. chopped onion
2 oz. brandy
1 cup white wine
1 tbsp. tomato paste
1 tsp. paprika
½ cup canned tomatoes
1 can (10 oz.) chicken broth
1 tbsp. butter
1 tbsp. flour
Salt and pepper, to taste

How
Saute split lobster tails in oil, meat side down, in large skillet. Cook 3 minutes, turn and cook 3 minutes more until shell is red. Add onions and cook soft. Pour on brandy and flame. Add balance of ingredients, except flour and butter. Cover and simmer ½ hour. Mix flour and butter and stir in. Stir until smooth and thick. Serve over croutons or rice. Serves 4–6.

I am sorry I can't offer you the romantic view over a small Alpine lake, that goes with

CHICKEN LUXEMBOURG

but the dish itself offers chicken at its peak of perfection.

Now, for step one in preparation, the Marinade. Mix thoroughly in a shallow pan with a cover, the following:

What
4 tbsp. light soy sauce
3 tbsp. peanut oil
1 tbsp. lemon juice
1 tsp. brown sugar
1 tsp. ground ginger
¼ tsp. garlic powder

Use a 2½ to 3 lb. broiler, split in half lengthwise, to serve two. Turn the chicken halves in the marinade a few times to coat them thoroughly. Cover and refrigerate 10 to 14 hours, turning them a few times in the interim.

Now, for the balance of ingredients:

1 tbsp. olive or peanut oil
1 onion, diced
1 clove garlic, sliced thinly
2 tbsp. cornstarch
2½ cups chicken soup
½ lb. sliced mushrooms
¼ cup chopped pimentos
½ cup slivered blanched almonds
½ tsp. tarragon flakes
2 cups cooked brown rice
¼ tsp. white pepper
½ cup apricot brandy
4 pineapple rings
1 navel orange

How

Saute mushrooms, onion, garlic, and other seasonings in oil for five minutes. Add soup and bring to a boil. Turn to simmer. Mix cornstarch with half a cup of cold water, and add to pan. Stir until smooth and thickened, about 3 minutes. Turn off heat, and cover. Brown chicken under broiler on both sides. Add to gravy and simmer 25 to 30 minutes. Add almonds, apricot brandy, and pimentos and simmer slowly 10 minutes. Mound rice on hot platter, flank with chicken halves, and garnish with pineapple rings and orange wedges. Bon appetit.

The Swiss are so famous for watches, yodeling, and Alpine skiing, that most people are not aware that the Swiss are also world famous as chefs. This little gem is one I picked up in

Geneva, where they served it both hot and cold. As a snack or as an hors d'oeuvre it is sensational.

SWISS ONION CAKE

What
For the pastry:
1½ cups sifted all-purpose flour
1 tsp. sugar
½ tsp. salt
½ cup butter
3–4 tbsp. milk
The filling:
6 slices bacon
3 cups chopped onion
2 beaten eggs
1 beaten egg yolk
½ tsp. M.S.G.
1 tbsp. all-purpose flour
½ tsp. salt
Dash of white pepper
1 tbsp. parsley or chive flakes

How
Sift dry ingredients into bowl. Cut in butter until about size of peas. Moisten with 3 tbsp. of the milk. Add just enough more to make a firm dough. Form into a ball. Pat ⅔ of the dough into the bottom of an 8 x 11½ inch round cake tin. Bake at 425 degrees until lightly browned. Cool on rack. Turn oven down to 325 degrees. Fry bacon crisp, drain, and crumble. Fry onion in bacon fat until tender. Drain off fat, and mix onions with balance of ingredients, except parsley or chives. Return cooled cake to pan, and pat remaining dough in a ring around inside edge of pan, pour in filling, and top with the chive flakes. Bake at 325

degrees about 25 minutes. Let stand about 10 minutes to set, then cut into wedges, to serve. Sometimes they top the dish with grated Parmesan, or strips of Swiss cheese, in the last 10 minutes of baking. Either way, it is a great dish after mountain climbing or after any other sport that takes your fancy.

6
Aphrodisiacs—Anyone?

Down through the ages, man has been interested in potions, concoctions, and incantations to increase virility and potency. Witch doctors, court doctors, and society doctors have all gotten rich on purported performance raisers. I have often been asked about aphrodisiac herbs, spices, and drinks. Since cooking is my bag, I couldn't answer off the cuff, but I have since done a lot of research in ancient and modern tomes on the subject. It develops that all down the years from the past, various herbs, spices, and condiments have been used in love potions. These have been credited with increasing virility and passion. Some devotees of Eros claim surprising results through the use of crushed black peppercorns, cloves, ginseng root, coriander, and chili peppers. Others believe in wild laurel leaf, sesame seed, cardamom seed, nutmeg, and other improbables. Some Indians and Far Easterners believe in curry powder as a recharge for a fading libido. The Chinese use powdered rhinoceros horn, and swear by it. I think they may be off the track a little, as the rhino is stupid, cumbersome, and not very prolific. I am not going to tell the Chinese, for fear it might make them psychotic or something.

Witch doctors have been reported to have tricks with herbs, spices, and mysterious brews, that would impel a stone statue to attempt procreation. Naturally they have made no attempt to dispel these rumors, and they have probably witched up some psychosomatic satyrs of horrifying capacities.

In parts of Africa, salt is popularly credited with the property of producing great potency. The pygmy tribes would fight to the death to secure salt. Since the guardians of the salt caravans were always bigger and fiercer than the pygmies, the pygmies lived on a mostly salt-free diet. This may account for the fact that the pygmies never went anyplace, populationwise. When some lucky warriors did return with sacks of salt, there was great rejoicing amongst the housewives, midwives, and even the hopeful virgins. After distributing the salt, the doughty warriors were allowed to invite their choice of maidens into the sack. These were called well-seasoned lovers. These diversions no doubt resulted in some very salty incidents, but that is another story.

A word of caution here; before you run out to buy a large sack of salt, I should advise you that our medics state that an excess of salt in the diet may also stiffen some supposed-to-be flexible joints, such as your knees. Nauseating, isn't it—and just when we thought we were onto a good thing.

In the not-too-distant past, in our own country, it was popularly thought that oysters and other shellfish together with hot peppers, celery, barley, porridge, and glandular meats were wonderful props for a sagging sex drive. Liquid rocket fuels such as spiced hot buttered rum produced some interesting games such as bundling, that kept the population figures rising. Even today, certain potables and spicy foods are alleged to have the ability to arouse the animal in homo sap, and to increasing the duration of his mating urge. I may explore this phase of wining and dining in another book, if I can interest enough virile, dedicated men and women to do the necessary research. At that point in time, if they are not too fatigued from their research (in depth) to report, I may have some exciting facts on animal arousal. In the meantime, I highly recommend the use of herbs, wines, and spices in food preparation, for their happy effect on your jaded taste buds. Should their use produce other more erotic fringe benefits in your case, you are on your own, and buono fortuna, as the Italiano has it.

And that, fellow fun-seekers, is what I know, suspect, or have been told, about aphrodisiacs.

7

It's Barbecue Time

Yes, it's barbecue time in Orgyville. That's the patio belonging to the nut next door. Just seeing your host resembling an aging Mephisto, with sooty eyebrows, powder-puff chef's hat, and flames from the basting sauce flickering on his satanic grin, may lead you to some horrendous reflection on your ultimate destination. This spook with the long fork usually chars the steak, whilst sampling the potables. Then he hides the evidence of cremation with a fiery sauce that convinces you he has a private pipe line into Hades, even though he claims to have invented the sauce out of sheer culinary expertise. This molten-lava sauce naturally leads to an attempt to put out the fires with whatever liquids are available. The usual result is a number of guests being slumped in odd corners with a glazed look in their shocked orbs.

Shish (kebabs?) are a current fad, maybe a hangover from the ancestral memories when your forebears skewered meat on their daggers and toasted it over the campfire. This skill now consists of skewering a lot of chunks of food, with unrelated cooking times, on a mock rapier, and serving it so that some of the chunks are overdone, and others half raw. This is considered very "in," and may not kill you right away. If you would be successful, marinate the chunks of meat well in advance, then brown in fat in a pan, before skewering. At this point, you can skewer the meat with mushrooms, green pepper, etc., with a fair chance of having a palatable presentation. Tomato should be added last, as it really won't cook properly anyway, and will be a gooey mess if overdone. Well-marinated green tomato, marinated after quartering, about four hours in salt brine, then washed and shished, or kabobbed, is not bad. I believe that shishing is from the sound of skewering, and kabobbing is the cooking. If you don't believe me, write your favorite swordsmith.

Remember that purists will not stand for marinated steak. Usually a little salt and pepper when you turn the steak is enough treatment. Some like to brush the steak before and during barbecuing with peanut oil in which a clove of garlic has been crushed. Steak sauce can be served on the side for people who hate the taste of steak, but they should be eating catfish or owl livers anyway.

STEAK TIPS

Never start with frozen, or even very cold steak, when barbecuing. You may hear things to the contrary, but don't believe 'em. Charring is not the idea, either. If you run a crematorium, don't invite guests. Ingestion of hard carbons can cause various stomach disorders, even more in the bowel. Tough cuts of meat are not suitable to this method of cooking, as they will dry out before they are tender, and char before the inside is cooked. Tougher cuts like round steak can be done in foil, where their internal moisture helps them to cook.

Short ribs are better if partially baked in the oven before barbecuing, then finished on the barbecue.

Spare ribs that you are going to stuff and cook on the spit are also better if parboiled or partly baked before barbecuing.

STUFFING FOR THE SPIT

Use any stuffing you fancy, but make sure all the ingredients in the stuffing are cooked before you cook the meat on the spit. This insures a well-cooked stuffing. Due to the method of application of the heat, the heat transfer to stuffing inside the product is not as efficient as in an oven.

Corn should be soaked in salt water, then wrapped in foil, or if you prefer, just pull out the silk and leave the husk on. Soak in salted water for about a half hour to plump the kernels and wet the husk thoroughly, so the steam will cook the kernels.

Potatoes should be washed, oiled, and wrapped in foil, before placing on the grill. Many people like to eat the skin, so well-scrubbed is a must.

Roasts such as loin of pork should be oiled, and basted often during barbecuing with an oily basting sauce such as seasoned corn, or peanut oil.

Searing a beef roast all around on the grill, then lifting onto the turnspit position will save loss of juice during the spit-roasting.

TENDERIZERS AND MARINADES

Few people agree on the use of tenderizers. If you are going to use a tough cut of steak, a tenderizer is certainly of value. Tenderizers are an enzymic extract of the fruit papaya, and the juice has long been used as a tenderizer by Southern cooks. Most tenderizers are made of nine parts of salt, or cereal, and 1 part of papain, which is the chemical designation for the papaya extract. Papain C.P. (chemically pure) is available at wholesale drug houses.

Marinades are used for both tenderizing and flavorizing. Lemon juice, wine vinegar, and wine all have some tenderizing properties, but not as great as papain. Recipes for some marinades follow. If you like marinated meats, you can try these until you find a favorite.

—Mix ½ cup dry wine with 1 cup peanut oil and a clove of garlic, crushed.

—Mix ½ cup olive oil, ¼ cup dry white wine, 1 tsp. oregano, 1 tsp. white pepper.

—Mix 1 cup vegetable oil with ½ cup lemon juice, 1 crushed garlic clove, 1 tsp. marjoram, 1 crushed chili pepper.

—Mix 1 cup dry red wine, 4 tbsp. wine vinegar, ½ cup chili sauce, ¼ cup melted butter, and 2 tbsp. bleu cheese. Melt cheese, vinegar, and butter together, and add balance of ingredients.

—Mix ½ cup lemon juice, 1 tsp. powdered cloves, 1 tbsp. black pepper, 1 cup melted butter, 1 tsp. garlic powder, ½ tsp. thyme.

Some people like the flavor of bleu cheese on steak. For those who like cheese and steak, try this. Melt ¼ lb. bleu cheese in ½ lb. melted butter, ¼ cup peanut oil, 2 tbsp. sherry.

Others like Bearnaise sauce with steak, directions for which are in the Sauces section.

INDIAN BARBECUED BEEF

What

1 cup yogurt
1 tsp. ground ginger
1 tbsp. minced onion
2 tsp. turmeric
2 tsp. salt
¼ tsp. cayenne
2 lb. sirloin, cubed 1 inch
2 green peppers, cut in squares
2 tomatoes, in wedges
¼ cup peanut oil
½ lb. mushrooms

How
Mix seasonings well into yogurt. Marinate meat for 2 hours.
Drain, and brown lightly all around in skillet. Remove and
cool slightly. Thread on skewers with mushrooms, tomatoes,
and green peppers. Broil on grill for 8–10 minutes, turning
and basting with oil. Serves 6.

TERIYAKI BEEF-KAULANI

What
2 lb. sirloin, cubed 1 inch
1 cup soy sauce
2 tsp. M.S.G.
¼ cup brown sugar
2 cloves garlic, crushed or slivered
2 tbsp. dry red wine
1 tsp. ground ginger

How
Sprinkle M.S.G. over beef. Mix balance of ingredients.
Heat to about 150 degrees. Put beef in marinade for 2 hours.
Thread on skewers and barbecue, turning until evenly
browned. Serves 6 or 8.

MEXICALI BARBECUE SAUCE

They say this one has everything. It certainly has enough
ingredients to tax the versatility of your larder. It is outstanding on chicken or spareribs.

What
1 tsp. oregano flakes
2½ tsp. paprika
1 tsp. salt
1 tsp. chili powder

½ tsp. ground cloves
1 tsp. onion salt
1 tsp. dry mustard
1 bay leaf
⅛ tsp. cayenne pepper
½ tsp. garlic powder
2 tbsp. wine vinegar
2 tbsp. tarragon vinegar
1 tbsp. chopped shallots
½ cup cider vinegar
¼ cup brown sugar
½ cup dry red wine
½ cup olive oil

How
Blend dry ingredients and add all the liquids except wine.
Simmer thirty minutes, strain and add wine.

NEW ORLEANS BARBECUE SAUCE

What
½ cup butter
½ cup vegetable oil
1 small onion, minced
3 cloves garlic, sliced thin
2 tbsp. chopped parsley
¼ tsp. pepper
1 tsp. salt
1 tsp. paprika
1 tbsp. Worcestershire Sauce
1 bay leaf
1 good pinch of each, thyme, rosemary, cumin, sage

How
Melt butter in ¼ cup oil. In balance of oil, saute onion,
garlic, and parsley, for 15 minutes. Strain off oil into butter

sauce and add seasonings. Simmer 5 minutes. Very good with any fowl.

BARBECUE SAUCE

For spareribs, franks, or hamburger.
Saute until golden, 2 thinly sliced onions, in 2 tbsp. fat.
Add, combined

What
1 tsp. dry mustard
2 tbsp. vinegar
½ bottle catsup
1 tbsp. Worcestershire
½ cup water
½ tsp. salt
¼ tsp. pepper
2 tbsp. dry red wine

How
Simmer 30 minutes. Makes about 1 cup.

SAUCE FILIPINO

This is the stuff they use to put zip in their surfboards.

What
½ cup raisins
½ cup chopped apple
½ cup pineapple juice
1 tsp. curry powder
1 tsp. dry mustard
¼ cup light molasses
2 tbsp. wine vinegar

½ tsp. salt
¼ tsp. cayenne pepper
¼ tsp. cinnamon
¼ tsp. ground cloves

How
Simmer raisins in pineapple juice until they are plump.
Add vinegar and simmer 5 minutes until raisins are soft.
Add apple and simmer 10 minutes. Mix all other ingredients
together and add. Simmer 15 minutes, or until thick. Blend
if you have a blender, otherwise whip until smooth. Great
with ham and chicken, or barbecued pork.

CHUCK WAGON SAUCE

What
1 8 oz. can tomato sauce
1 cup ketchup
1½ cups cider vinegar
½ cup brown sugar
1 tsp. caraway seed
1 tsp. cumin seed
1 tsp. allspice
¼ tsp. crumbled bay leaf

How
Simmer all ingredients together 40 minutes. Strain. Chuck
wagon franks are cooked right in this sauce.

STEAK SAUCE

Some people insist on a steak sauce with their barbecued
steak, to be applied at the table before eating. This sauce
does the steak less damage than some sauces, which is all that
can be said for any sauce.

What
1 cup tomato catsup
¼ cup Worcestershire
2 tsp. paprika
1½ tbsp. dry mustard
2½ cups melted butter
½ cup lemon juice

How
Heat together the butter, Worcestershire, paprika, and mustard. Remove from heat and stir in lemon juice. Serves about 40 regular guests, or 4,000 gourmets, who will not use it!

BARBECUE SAUCE

Especially for barbecued ribs.

What
1 cup butter
1 cup finely minced onions
½ cup vinegar
½ cup brown sugar
1 tsp. grated garlic
1 tbsp. horseradish
2 tbsp. Worcestershire sauce
1 tbsp. dry mustard
1 tbsp. salt
1 tsp. fresh black pepper
1 cup chili sauce
1 cup tomato puree

How
Simmer onions in butter for 10 minutes. Add all other ingredients and simmer 10 minutes longer. Blend or whip

together until smooth. If you are a baster, this one is good. Special on spareribs, good on pork or chicken.

STUFFINGS

Mushroom stuffing—for four to five pounds of meat or poultry.

What
½ cup chopped celery
½ cup chopped onion
¼ cup butter
1 tsp. salt
½ lb. mushrooms, sliced or chopped
4 cups bread crumbs, or cooked rice

How
For seasoning, season for each type of meat or dish as below. For the basic stuffing, saute celery and onion in butter for 3 to 4 minutes, then add mushrooms and simmer 3 minutes more. Pour in bread crumbs and seasonings and mix well.
For Stuffed Fish:
Season with 1 tbsp. lemon juice, ½ tsp. savory, and a finely chopped small tomato.
For Stuffed Lamb:
½ tsp. dried mint and ½ tsp. thyme.
For Stuffed Pork:
Season with ½ tsp. thyme, ½ tsp. sage, ½ finely chopped apple, and moisten with apple juice or apple sauce.
For Stuffed Poultry:
Season with ¾ tsp. savory and ¾ tsp. thyme, ¼ tsp. sage. Moisten with apple sauce, fruit juice, or milk. For duck, moisten with orange juice.
For Stuffed Veal:

Season with ¼ tsp. garlic powder and ½ tsp. savory. Moisten stuffing with milk.

MUSHROOM-APPLE-SAUSAGE STUFFING

What
6 cups breadcrumbs
1 tsp. salt
¼ tsp. pepper
1 tsp. savory
1 tsp. thyme
¼ tsp. sage
½ lb. pork sausage meat
½ lb. mushrooms, chopped
1 cup chopped celery
½ cup chopped onion
½ cup applesauce

How
Mix first six ingredients together, well. Fry out sausage meat until brown, and most of the fat has melted out. Break up finely, and add onion and celery and cook 4 minutes. Drain off all fat, and return 1 tbsp., and simmer mushrooms 3 minutes. Mix in breadcrumb mixture and blend well. Add more applesauce if necessary to get the desired texture for stuffing. When cooking stuffed spareribs on the spit, put foil caps at each end to hold in stuffing.

TURNSPIT DUCK

In my opinion, there are many better ways to cook a duck than on a barbecue. However, if you are addicted to outdoor cooking, this method produces an acceptable duck.

What
1 duck, 4 to 5 lb. dressed
2 tart apples
2 cups orange juice
¼ cup sweet vermouth
1 tbsp. grated orange peel
1 tbsp. lemon juice
Salt and pepper

How
Wipe duck inside and out with damp cloth. Rub inside and out with salt and pepper. Put a whole apple to close neck cavity and halve the other apple and put in body cavity. Fasten neck skin to breast with skewer. Put spit lengthwise through bird and bring up driving forks. Tie wings and legs to spit with oil-soaked string. Cook about 1½ hours basting with the balance of ingredients. Serves 4.

BARBECUED SPARERIBS OAHU

What
3 lbs. pork spareribs
½ cup soy sauce
1 tsp. ground ginger
½ tsp. garlic powder
¼ cup brown sugar
½ cup pineapple juice
Dash Tabasco
3 tbsp. lemon juice
2 tbsp. cider vinegar

How
Mix all ingredients, except ribs. Bring to a boil and let stand 2 hours. Brush both sides of ribs with this marinade and bake ½ hour in a preheated 350 degree oven. When ready to

barbecue, put ribs meat side down on grill and brush with marinade. Turn after 5 minutes and brush with marinade. Continue this process until brown and crisp. Serves 6.

If you want to be Mr. Barbecue Excitement, make a cole slaw to go with your barbecued meats.

COLE SLAW

What
1 firm head cabbage
1 large onion
1 large carrot
1 tart apple
¼ cup chopped green pepper

How
Hollow out cabbage to make a bowl. Shred center, and also shred onion, carrot, and apple. Mix with green pepper. Now, for the dressing.
Blend:
½ cup sour cream
2 tbsp. brown sugar
2 tbsp. cider vinegar
1 tsp. salt
1 tsp. Worcestershire sauce
½ tsp. garlic powder

How
Toss the shredded vegetable with the dressing and pile into the cabbage bowl.

8

Neptune Has a Net

Over the years, seafood, and more especially shellfish, has gotten a reputation as a prop to virility. Be that as it may, the products of the great briny can be a gourmet's delight, or a gustatory horror, depending on the skill of the chef. Fish cookery is an art. Most people have a tendency to overcook fish. The flesh is delicate, and requires cooking only until it will flake easily.

Many fish dishes specify cooking in court bouillon. When this term is used it means a bouillon as follows.

Combine 1 cup water with 1 sliced onion, 1 sliced carrot, 1 bay leaf, 1 sprig parsley, 1 tbsp. vinegar or lemon juice, and a half dozen peppercorns. Boil together for 10 minutes, and allow to cool to room temperature. It is then ready for use in poaching fish. This is done by wrapping fish in a piece of cheesecloth, and laying it in a pan with court bouillon. Cover loosely, and poach gently until fish is tender. When I poach fish, I use enough white wine to really wake the fish up. An inattentive or sleepy fish is not really working at pleasing you.

Other fish dishes call for Mornay Sauce. To make it, start with 1 cup medium white sauce (see Sauce section). Add 2 tsp. grated Parmesan cheese, 2 tbsp. grated Swiss cheese, and ¼ cup dry white wine. Mornay is better made a few hours ahead of using.

139

FILLET OF SOLE, PARMESAN

What
2 lb. sole fillets
1 tbsp. butter
1 cup soft bread crumbs
2 tbsp. minced parsley
½ cup grated Parmesan cheese
Pinch of thyme
2 tbsp. butter
¼ tsp. paprika

How
Rub a piece of aluminum foil with soft butter. Put fillets on foil. Mix the bread crumbs, thyme, parsley, cheese, salt, and pepper. Sprinkle on the fillets. Dribble melted butter over the fish and wrap loosely in foil. Bake at 350 degrees for about 15 to 20 minutes. Sprinkle with paprika and serve.

Now we come to the subject of that epicurean poem, clam chowder. If you love clam chowder, put on your sou'wester, pick up your clam rake, and repeat after me, "There are two kinds of clam chowder, edible and Manhattan. Anyone who would marry the strongly flavored tomato with the delicately flavored clam must either love tomatoes, or have a big hate for clams." In my book, that's a "no, no," and puts you in the plebeian class, if you sin thus.

CLAM CHOWDER SUPREME

If you are fortunate enough to be in an area where fresh clams are available, by all means use them, you lucky host. I use the canned baby clams when fresh clams are not available, and the results are excellent.

What

1 can baby clams, 10 oz.
6 slices bacon, diced
1 tbsp. chopped parsley
1 clove garlic, finely minced
1 cup chicken stock or bouillon
2 tbsp. butter
¼ cup diced onion
¼ cup diced celery
½ tsp. thyme
1 cup diced potato, about ⅜ inch
1 cup milk
1 cup light cream
¼ tsp. paprika
2 tbsp. dry sherry
Salt and fresh black pepper to taste

How

Saute onion, garlic, and bacon in 1 tbsp. butter until onion is golden. Do not burn the butter. Add the juice from the clams, chicken stock, parsley, pepper, thyme, and celery. Simmer 6 minutes. Add the potatoes and cook 7 minutes. Add clams, milk, and cream, and bring up just under the boil but do NOT boil. Add the sherry, 1 tbsp. butter, and paprika. Serve over toast croutons.

Note

So if some nut says he still wants Manhattan chowder, and he's a valued client, say "Okay."

To make it, leave out the milk and cream, and add 1 cup chicken stock, 1 cup canned tomatoes, and ½ tsp. basil flakes. He can eat alone, with only the gnashing teeth of adjacent gourmets.

SHRIMP OMELET AU GRATIN

This is a versatile dish, in that you may use shrimp, cooked

ham, diced cooked pork, or diced chicken, or combinations
to suit your taste.

What
1 package (8 oz.) frozen shrimp
3 tbsp. butter
3 tbsp. flour
2 cups milk
3 eggs
¼ tsp. pepper
¼ tsp. salt
½ tsp. dried basil
2 tbsp. cream
4 tbsp. grated Parmesan cheese
½ cup fine dry breadcrumbs

How
Melt the butter in the saucepan and stir in the flour, until
smooth. Add the milk, salt, pepper, and basil, and stir-cook
until smooth and thick. Stir in the thawed shrimp. Now,
butter a shallow baking dish. Beat the eggs lightly, then
beat in the cream and a good pinch of salt. Heat the baking
dish, and pour the hot egg mixture into it. Bake at 400
degrees until brown and puffy (about 10 minutes). Pour the
shrimp mixture in on top. Mix the crumbs and Parmesan
cheese and spread over the top. Put under the broiler until
brown and bubbly. Serves 4.

SHRIMP JAMBALAYA

What
2 4½ oz. cans shrimp
½ cup diced cooked ham
2 tbsp. melted shortening
½ cup chopped onion

1 cup chopped green pepper
2 cloves garlic, minced fine
1½ cups canned tomatoes
1½ cups shrimp juice and water
1 cup uncooked rice
¼ tsp. salt
1 bay leaf
½ tsp. thyme flakes
¼ cup chopped parsley
Pinch of cayenne pepper

How
Drain shrimp and save liquid. Saute ham in shortening for 3 minutes. Add onion, green pepper, and garlic; saute until tender. Add tomatoes, rice, liquid, and seasonings, except parsley; cover and cook 25 to 30 minutes until rice is tender. Stir frequently. Add parsley and shrimp, and reheat. Serves 6.

GULF COAST SHRIMP BOIL

What
2 lb. raw shrimp, peeled and deveined
3 bay leaves
1 tbsp. whole allspice
1 tsp. crushed red peppers
2 tsp. whole black peppers
2 tsp. whole cloves
2 quarts water
2 medium onions, sliced
6 cloves garlic, bruised
2 lemons, sliced
¼ cup salt

How
Tie spices in cheesecloth bag. Put in the water and bring to

a slow boil. Add onion, garlic, lemon, and salt, and return to a boil. Add shrimp and simmer, covered, for 5 minutes for large shrimp, 3 minutes for small. Remove from heat and let stand, covered, in the spiced water for 3 more minutes. Drain and chill. Serve garnished with whole spices and lemon slices.

SHRIMP CREOLE

When not engaged in producing large families, the happy Creoles engaged in shrimp fishing. I have not established the relationship between shrimp and large families, nor which one caused which effect. The fact remains that the shrimp-fed Creoles were prolific, healthy, and happy as anyone could be, while meeting the dual appetites of gourmandizing and procreation.

What
1 lb. raw, peeled, and deveined shrimp
⅓ cup shortening
¼ cup flour
1 cup hot water
½ cup chopped green onions and tops
4 cloves garlic, minced fine
½ cup chopped parsley (2 tbsp. dry flakes)
¼ cup chopped green pepper (1 tbsp. dry flakes)
1 tsp. salt
2 bay leaves
½ tsp. thyme flakes
Dash of cayenne
1 can (8 oz.) tomato sauce
1 thick slice of lemon
2 cups hot cooked rice

How

Cut large shrimp in half. Melt shortening, blend in flour, and brown, stirring constantly. Add remaining ingredients, except rice. Cover and simmer slowly 20 minutes. Remove bay leaves. Serve over hot rice to 6.

Note

I take a few liberties with this traditional recipe. I use about six slices of side bacon, brown it in half the quantity of shortening, using the bacon fat as the balance. I feel that if the Creoles had been able to take time off from their main diversion to cure some of the wild hogs into bacon, they might have come up with this improvement before I did.

SHRIMP DE JONGHE

What

3 4½ oz. cans large shrimp
1 cup dry bread crumbs
½ cup melted butter or margarine
¼ cup green onions, with tops, chopped
2 cloves garlic, minced fine
2 tsp. chopped parsley
1 tsp. chervil
1 tsp. wine vinegar
½ tsp. thyme flakes
¼ tsp. nutmeg
½ cup sherry, dry or medium

How

Drain shrimp. Cover with ice water and let stand 10 minutes. Combine crumbs with balance of ingredients, and mix well. Place alternate layers of the drained shrimp and the crumb mixture in a well-greased 1-quart casserole. Top with ½ cup dry bread crumbs mixed with 3 tbsp. melted butter. Bake at 350 degrees until brown, about 1 hour. Serves 6.

SHRIMP NEWBURG

What
1 1 lb. package of precooked and frozen shrimp
¼ cup butter
2½ tbsp. flour
¾ tsp. salt
Dash of Tabasco
Dash of nutmeg
1 pint coffee cream
2 egg yolks, beaten
2 tbsp. dry sherry
Toast points

How
Thaw shrimp. Cut large ones in half. Melt butter and blend in flour and seasonings. Add cream gradually, cooking and stirring until thick and smooth. Stir a little of the hot sauce into the egg yolks, then return to pan, stirring and cooking until thick and smooth, about 3 minutes. Add shrimp and heat. Remove from heat and slowly stir in sherry. Serve immediately on buttered toast points, or fill patty shells.

BUTTERED TROUT

What
2 frozen rainbow trout
2 tbsp. butter
1 tbsp. lemon juice
1 tbsp. chive flakes

How

Defrost trout completely. Place on rack in roasting pan, adding about ½ inch of water. Water must not touch fish. Cover and steam until tender, about 20 minutes. Slide fish off rack onto platter. Lemon juice is combined with chives and melted butter and poured over fish.

FROGS LEGS PROVENÇALE

What

4 tbsp. butter
6 pair frozen frog's legs
1 egg, beaten
½ cup fine crumbs, cracker or bread
2 tbsp. tomato paste
½ tsp. garlic powder
1 tbsp. lemon juice
2 tbsp. white wine
½ cup tomato juice
¼ tsp. black pepper
½ tsp. salt
1 tbsp. flour

How

Thaw frog's legs completely. Dip in beaten egg, then in crumbs, and fry in butter until lightly browned all over. Remove from pan. Mix flour, garlic powder, and lemon juice well. Put balance of ingredients into pan and stir-cook until thickened. Add frog's legs and heat. Serves 2–3.

CURRIED SHRIMP

What

2 pkg. (12 oz. ea.) frozen peeled shrimp

1½ tsp. curry powder
1 tbsp. lemon juice
1 tbsp. parsley flakes
1 can (10 oz.) condensed cream of chicken soup

How
Cook shrimp 5 minutes in boiling water. Drain. Heat soup with lemon juice, curry powder, and parsley. Add shrimp and reheat. Serve with instant rice, and chutney. Serves 6.

SHRIMP WITH RICE SNOW

What
1 cup cooked rice
3 tbsp. butter, melted
2 egg yolks, beaten lightly
½ cup whole milk
3 tbsp. butter
3 tbsp. flour
⅛ tsp. salt
½ cup grated Parmesan cheese
½ cup grated cheddar cheese
1 cup milk
2 cups cooked shrimp
2 tbsp. sherry
Paprika

How
Mix cooked rice with melted butter, ½ cup milk, and beaten egg yolks. Pour into buttered ring mold and set in pan of boiling water. Bake at 350 degrees until set (about 20 minutes). In top of double boiler melt 3 tbsp. butter and stir in flour and salt. Add cheeses and 1 cup milk. Stir-cook until smooth and thick. Add shrimp and heat. Unmold rice and serve shrimp mixture in center. Sprinkle with paprika. Serves 8.

SHRIMP CEYLON

What
1 lb. shrimp, shelled and deveined
¼ cup orange marmalade
2 tbsp. lemon juice
¼ tsp. powdered ginger
1 tsp. salt
1 tbsp. curry powder
½ cup water
½ cup cubed apple
1 small onion, cut up
2 tbsp. flour
½ cup cream
¼ cup seedless raisins
¼ cup blanched almonds

How
Put all ingredients except shrimp, cream, raisins, and almonds in blender. Blend on high speed 15 seconds. Put in saucepan and stir-cook 15 minutes. Add shrimp, raisins, and almonds. Stir-cook 10 minutes. Stir in cream. Heat and serve over hot rice. Serves 4.

KING CRAB DEVILS

What
4 slices bread
1 chopped medium onion
¾ tsp. salt
¾ tsp. dry mustard
3 eggs
2 parsley clusters
1 can (6½–7 oz.) king crab, flaked

How

Blender crumb the bread and put into bowl. Blend balance of ingredients except crab on high speed, 10 seconds. Add crab and blend on low 3 seconds. Pour over bread crumbs. Shape into flat cakes, roll in flour, and brown on both sides in bacon fat. Serve with tartar sauce.

SOLE NEPTUNE

What

4 raw fillets of sole
1 cup fish stock or clam juice
½ cup dry white wine
1 cup heavy cream
8 sticks of cucumber, seeded
3 tbsp. butter
¼ tsp. thyme
Salt and pepper
½ tbsp. flour

How

Season fillets with salt, pepper, and thyme. Melt 1 tbsp. butter in saucepan, then add stock and wine. Fold fillets in half and put in pan. Poach 6 minutes at simmer. Remove and keep warm. Boil stock until reduced to ¾ cup. Add cucumber sticks and simmer 5 minutes. Remove and fry in butter on all sides. Mix flour into cream and stir into poaching liquid. Stir-cook until thickened. Arrange cucumbers around fillets and pour on sauce. Reheat under broiler or in hot oven. Serves 4.

SEA CHICKEN PIE

What

2 tbsp. butter
2 tbsp. flour

1½ cups milk
2 diced carrots
2 diced potatoes
1 chopped onion
1 cup peas
1 7 oz. can flaked tuna
½ tsp. salt
¼ tsp. white pepper

How
Make a white sauce with the butter, flour, and milk. Boil potatoes, carrots, and onions in salted water. Drain and mix with peas and white sauce. Put in greased casserole. Top with buttered crumbs, or instant mashed potato. Brown in 400 degree oven. Serves 4.

HALIBUT FLEURETTE

What
6 halibut steaks
2 tbsp. butter
½ cup water
¼ tsp. paprika
½ cup dry white wine
Salt and pepper

How
Put steaks in shallow baking dish, dot with butter and pour the water and wine over the top. Sprinkle with salt and pepper. Cover with foil, leaving steam vents in foil, and bake in a 475 degree oven, 15 minutes. Serve with:

SAUCE FLEURETTE

Strain 1 cup stock off the baked fish. Mix 2 tbsp. butter

and 2 tbsp. flour in a pan. Slowly stir in the fish stock, with 2 tbsp. white wine, pinch of nutmeg, ½ cup milk. When thickened and smooth, season with salt and pepper. Add 2 tbsp. chopped parsley, 1 tsp. chopped chives, then 1 tbsp. butter and 1 tbsp. lemon juice. Serve over the halibut steaks, or any other baked, white-fleshed fish.

BAKED HALIBUT CREOLE

What
4 halibut steaks
4 slices bacon
1 thinly sliced onion
¼ tsp. salt
¼ tsp. pepper
¼ tsp. curry powder
1 tsp. sugar
⅓ cup bread crumbs
¼ cup sliced black olives
3 tbsp. dry white wine
1 cup drained, cooked tomatoes
2 tbsp. melted butter

How
Cut bacon into 1-inch pieces and spread half of them in a shallow baking dish. Put half the onion slices on top of bacon. Lay in the halibut steaks. Sprinkle with seasonings. Put balance of bacon and onions on top. Butter the bread crumbs, mix in the olives, and spread on top. Bake uncovered at 375 degrees for ½ hour. Serves 4.

COD PROVENÇALE

What
1 lb. fresh or frozen cod
4 tbsp. vegetable oil

2 small onions, chopped
1 garlic clove minced
½ cup flour
1 tbsp. chopped parsley
4 tomatoes, quartered and seeded
3 tbsp. pitted black olives
Salt and pepper

How

Cut fish into small squares. Mix flour, salt, and pepper in a paper bag, and shake the fish pieces in the flour until well coated. Heat oil in a heavy skillet, and cook onions and garlic until soft and yellow. Do not burn. Remove onions and garlic to a baking dish. Brown the fish pieces in the pan, and place on top of the onions. Cook the tomatoes and olives gently and add to the dish. Keep warm in slow oven until ready to serve.

FILLETS FLORENTINE

What

Use fillets of any white fish, cod, haddock, halibut.
2 lb. fillets, fresh or frozen
1½ lb. broccoli (2 pkg. frozen)
2 tbsp. grated Parmesan cheese
1 cup Mornay sauce

How

Cook fish in court bouillon. Cook broccoli as usual, and drain. Lay in buttered baking dish, and lay fish on top. Pour Mornay on top, sprinkle with the Parmesan, and bake fifteen minutes at 400 degrees. Serves 4.

STUFFED HADDOCK

Use about a 3 lb. haddock, cleaned and with head and tail

off. Wipe thoroughly inside and out with damp cloth. Salt inside and out, slit open full length, and lay out flat. Stuff with rice-tomato stuffing, and close with skewers. Turn closed side down and gash across the back, about four gashes. Insert strips of fat pork or bacon in the gashes. Bake about 45 minutes in a 450 degree oven. Serves 6–8.

STUFFING

What
1 cup cooked rice
1 small onion, minced fine
2 cups drained cooked tomatoes
¾ tsp. salt
⅛ tsp. pepper
½ tsp. curry powder
1 tbsp. sugar

How
Mix well and stuff the fish. Leftover stuffing can be placed around the fish and baked with it.

FILLETS SPENCER

1 lb. fillets of haddock, cut in four pieces. Wash and dry. Dip in milk and roll in cracker crumbs. Place in a buttered baking dish, and pour 5 tbsp. melted butter over the top. Bake in 550 degree oven about 10 minutes. Serve with egg sauce. Serves 4.

SOLE FOUQUET

Put 4 fillets of Dover sole in a baking dish. Add 2 cups water, 1 sliced onion, 1 bay leaf, and ¼ tsp. thyme. Sprinkle with salt and boil 7 minutes. Strain off stock and save. Saute ½ cup sliced mushrooms in 4 tbsp. of butter. Blend in 4 tbsp. of flour. Stir in 2 cups fish stock, and stir-cook smooth and thick. Add 1 finely chopped peeled tomato (¼ cup canned), 2 tbsp. dry white wine, and 1tbsp. Parmesan cheese. Pour sauce over fish, sprinkle with paprika, and brown under broiler. Serves 4.

FISH BALLS

Wash 1 lb. salt codfish in cold water. Break or cut up in small pieces. Boil with 3 cups cubed potatoes. Drain well and mash smoothly. Add 1 tsp. butter, 2 eggs, beaten, ¼ tsp. pepper. Beat all together until well mixed. Drop by spoonsful into deep fat, at 375 degrees.

COD SOUFFLE

Saute in 2 tbsp. butter, ½ finely chopped green pepper, 1 small onion finely chopped. When onion is transparent, add 1 cup cooked flaked codfish, 2 cups mashed potatoes, and 2 well-beaten egg yolks. Beat egg whites stiff and fold in. Put in buttered casserole and bake 20 minutes at 400 degrees. Serves 4.

FISH TIMBALES

Mix ¼ cup fine breadcrumbs with ⅔ cup milk and 2 tbsp. melted butter. Stir-cook until well blended. Add 1 cup chopped cooked fish, 1 tsp. chopped parsley, and 2 lightly beaten eggs. Add salt and pepper to taste. Put in custard cups, set in pan of hot water, and bake at 375 degrees until firm to touch. Serve with medium white sauce and green peas, to 4.

LOBSTER SAUCE

This sauce is a must on boiled lobster, whether served hot over piles of lobster meat, or placed over the meat in lobster shells when baking or broiling lobster.

To make it, blend ½ cup melted butter with 1¼ cups flour, 1 tsp. prepared mustard, ¼ cup wine vinegar, ¼ tsp. Worcestershire sauce, juice of a quarter lemon, and ½ cup grated Parmesan cheese. Mix thoroughly, and stir in 6 cups hot milk. Cook-stir until well thickened. Saute ½ cup sliced mushrooms in 1 tbsp. butter, and add 1 cup dry white wine and 1 cup soft breadcrumbs. Mix into sauce, and remove from heat.

BAKED STUFFED LOBSTER

Split a 1½ lb. boiled lobster. Remove meat and cut into bite-sized pieces. Clean shells, and put into baking pan, allowing tails to curl a little. Return meat to shells, and cover with the following mixture.

In a saucepan blend 2 tbsp. butter with 4 tbsp. flour, ½ tsp. salt, ¼ tsp. prepared mustard, ½ tsp. paprika, and 2 cups milk. Stir-cook until smooth, and add ½ cup grated cheddar cheese, and stir until well melted and blended. Top with buttered crumbs, after pouring the sauce over the meat. Sprinkle with Parmesan cheese and paprika. Brown in hot oven or under broiler.

BROILED STUFFED LOBSTER

Made as baked stuffed lobster, or if broiled from raw state, prepare as follows.

Use a 1 lb. live lobster. Hold big claws and split from mouth to end of tail with a sharp pointed knife. Remove stomach and intestinal sac, and small sac back of head. Crack the big claws and lay lobster open, flat. Clean out body cavity, saving tomali. Brush meat with melted butter, and stuff lobster with the following stuffing.

Lobster Stuffing

Blend the juice of $\frac{1}{4}$ lemon, the lobster tomali, and 6 finely crushed soda crackers. Add 3 tbsp. melted butter, and $\frac{1}{2}$ tbsp. dry white wine. Stuff cavity and cover with an inverted pan while lobster is broiling. When meat shrinks from shell, remove cover (about 20 minutes at 500 degrees), and broil until crumbs brown. Serve lobster with a sauce made of half melted butter and half dry sherry. You may vary the sherry according to your individual taste, or use another wine if you prefer.

LOBSTER IMPERIAL

Clean the meat from 4 1 lb. lobsters, and cut into bite-sized pieces. Clean shells. Mix with the following sauce, and stuff shells. Brown in hot oven or under broiler.

Sauce

Blend 2 cups medium white sauce with 2 cups mayonnaise, $\frac{1}{2}$ cup finely chopped onion, 2 tsp. lemon juice, 1 tsp. prepared mustard, $\frac{1}{2}$ tsp. Worsectershire sauce, $\frac{1}{4}$ tsp. salt, and a pinch of pepper. Saute $\frac{1}{2}$ cup sliced mushrooms in butter, and add to sauce. Mix with the lobster meat.

LOBSTER NEWBURG

Newburg sauce is a calorie catastrophe, which would have resulted in some very fat lobsters had they been stuffed with it while alive. Start with the meat from a 2 lb. lobster, cut into bite-sized pieces. Now, in the top of a double boiler, mix $\frac{1}{4}$ cup butter, $\frac{1}{2}$ tsp. paprika, $\frac{1}{2}$ cup dry sherry, and when well mixed add lobster meat. Cook 2 minutes over boiling water, and sprinkle with 2 tbsp. flour, stirring lightly. Beat 2 egg yolks into 2 cups coffee cream, and add to lobster. Fold in and cook, stirring, until smooth and thick. Serve with toast, or in patty shells.

LOBSTER L'ARMORICAINE

What
6 frozen lobster tails
6 tbsp. butter or margarine
3 tbsp. instant minced onion
1 cup white wine
2 cups beef broth or bouillon
¼ cup brandy
1 cup drained canned tomatoes
¼ tsp. thyme
2 tbsp. flour mixed with 1 tbsp. butter
2 tbsp. tomato paste
Salt and pepper

How
Thaw and split lobster tails. Saute, meat side down, in butter 8 minutes. Turn and cook 5 minutes. Add onions, saute 2 minutes. Add brandy, and ignite. (Stand away when lighting). Add balance of ingredients except tomatoes and flour-butter mixture. Cover and simmer 20 minutes. Stir in butter-flour mixture and stir-cook until thickened. Add tomatoes and heat. Season to taste.

LOBSTER THERMIDOR

Split and remove the meat from two, 2 lb. boiled lobsters. Clean shells. Prepare as for lobster Newburg, and add 1 cup

sliced mushrooms, sauteed in butter. Stuff shells and put
1 whole button mushroom on top of each half lobster.
Sprinkle with mild grated cheddar cheese, and brown under
broiler. Serves 4.

PLEASANTVILLE LOBSTER

1½ cups cut-up lobster meat.
Heat 1 cup milk, and add ½ cup soft bread crumbs, 1 beaten
egg, ¼ tsp. dry mustard mixed with 1 tsp. lemon juice, ¼
tsp. onion juice, 1 tbsp. melted butter, ¼ tsp. thyme, ½ tsp.
salt, pinch of pepper. Mix in lobster and 1 tbsp. dry sherry,
and put mixture into ramekins or casserole. Bake at 400 degrees until brown, about 10 to 12 minutes. Serves 6.

CRABMEAT PIE

What
2 cups cooked crabmeat
3 beaten eggs
⅓ cup melted butter
½ tsp. dry mustard
½ tsp. Worcestershire sauce
1 tsp. salt
¼ tsp. black pepper
1½ cups milk
2 tbsp. chopped green pepper
½ cup cracker crumbs
1 cup buttered bread crumbs
1 tbsp. Parmesan cheese

How
Mix all ingredients except last two, very thoroughly. Place
in buttered baking dish. Bake 35 min. at 350° F. Top with

buttered crumbs and sprinkle with Parmesan. Serves 4 or snacks for more.

CRAB DE LUXE

Saute 1 small onion and 1 small green pepper, both finely chopped, in 3 tbsp. butter. Blend in 2 tbsp. flour, then add 1 cup hot milk, salt, pepper, and paprika, and cook until thickened. Add 1 cup crabmeat, and heat. Serve on toast or in patty shells.

CRAB SOUFFLE

Prepare 1 cup thin white sauce. Remove from heat and beat in 1 egg yolk, well beaten. Season to taste with salt, pepper, and paprika. Fold in the stiffly beaten egg white. Add the crabmeat, and stir in. Turn into buttered baking dish. Place dish in pan of hot water and bake 20 to 25 minutes, at 400 degrees in oven.

Note

This souffle can be made with salmon, shrimp, lobster, or leftover fish.

OYSTERS GERVASE

What
1 qt. oysters
4 tbsp. butter
6 green onions, chopped, with tops
¼ cup bacon, crumbled fine
1 tsp. parsley flakes
¼ tsp. garlic powder
¼ tsp. thyme

1 tsp. Worcestershire sauce
Chicken bouillon
2 cups medium cream sauce
Salt and pepper to taste

How
Saute onions in butter 3 minutes. Drain oysters and reserve liquor. In a dry skillet, brown oysters until lightly crusted on both sides. Add to onions in pan. Make cream sauce, using oyster liquor and if extra liquid is needed, use chicken bouillon. Add to pan with balance of ingredients and stir-cook slowly 5 minutes. Serve in patty shells or on toast points. Serves 4.

OYSTER FRICASSEE

Simmer 1 quart of fresh oysters in their own liquor until edges curl. Remove with skimmer. Strain liquor through double cheesecloth. Add enough milk to make 2 quarts.

Melt 4 tbsp. butter and add 4 tbsp. flour. Add the oyster liquor and 1 tsp. chopped parsley. Beat lightly 2 eggs. Pour some of the sauce into the eggs, and mix well. Return to sauce, and cook until thickened. Add $\frac{1}{2}$ tsp. salt and 1 tsp. paprika. Pour in the oysters and, if you like, 1 tbsp. white wine. Stir and cook 2 minutes. Serve to 8 on toast, mashed potatoes, or in shells.

OYSTERS AND MUSHROOMS

Drain 1 cup of oysters and reserve juice. Cook in hot frying pan until edges curl. Put them in a hot dish. Saute 1 cup chopped mushrooms in butter, and transfer to dish with oysters. Add to the pan enough butter to make 3 tbsp. Blend in 3 tbsp. flour. Stir in 1 cup hot milk and 1 cup oyster liquid. Cook until thick and smooth, then add 1 tsp. onion juice, ½ tsp. lemon juice, and ½ tsp. salt. Beat an egg, and add the sauce to it, then return to the saucepan, with the oysters. Cook 1 minute, stirring, and serve on toast or in patty shells.

PIGS IN BLANKETS

Season 1 dozen oysters with salt and pepper. Wrap a half slice of bacon around each oyster, and fasten with a toothpick. In a skillet, put some bacon fat, and roll the little pigs around until the bacon is crisp. Serve on toast quarters.

FRIED SHELLFISH

Do not precook any shellfish before frying. Dip lobster into boiling water to kill quickly. Remove shells, and intestinal tracts. Rinse scallops well. Pinch stomach contents out of clams. Flour each shellfish individually, and dip in a wash made by beating an egg into ½ cup water. Mix cornmeal with fine cracker crumbs and seasonings. Roll the fish in, until coated. Fry at 375 degrees.

I do not intend to add instructions on cleaning and filleting fish. I assume that any host-chef will sidestep messy work that is so readily done for him!

9

Inside the Fowl Line

ROASTING TIMETABLE

Type	Weight	Oven temp. Degrees F.	Minutes per pound
Chicken	3 to 6 lb.	350	25 to 30
Duck	5 to 7 lb.	350	25 to 35
Turkey	6 to 12 lb.	325	18 to 20
	13 to 18 lb.	300	20 to 25
	19 to 25 lb.	300	16 to 18
Goose	8 lb.	450 and 300	24 to 25

Stuffing is a must, and stuffing makes the bird, provided you have done everything else according to directions. Stuffing is somewhat elastic as to recipe, provided you have the basic stuffing correct. You can add chopped chestnuts, chopped cooked giblets, clams, oysters, or cooked sausage meat to basic stuffing. Use of your favorite wines will change the flavor, and provide a welcome difference to the traditional flavors.

BASIC STUFFING

What
3½ cups stale bread crumbs
1 tbsp. poultry seasoning

163

1 tbsp. butter
1½ tsp. salt
¾ cup finely chopped celery
¼ tsp. pepper
¼ cup finely chopped onion

How
Pour ¾ cup boiling water over the crumbs and butter. Mix and let stand 10 minutes. Add balance of ingredients. Pack lightly into cavity, as dressing swells in roasting.

FRIED CHICKEN

Cut one 2½ lb. broiler into serving pieces. Season flour with salt and pepper, and shake pieces in a bag with the flour, after dipping them in cold milk. Fry in 2 tbsp. fat mixed with 6 tbsp. butter. Fat should be deep enough to reach well up on the sides of the chicken pieces. Keep pan covered, and when chicken is well browned on one side, turn and cover again, to brown other side. Cook slowly until tender, making sure the pieces are not touching, as they will not brown where they touch.
Check that you have at least 2 tbsp. fat left for making:

CREAM GRAVY

To the 2 tbsp. fat, add 2 tbsp. flour, and blend. Blend in enough water to make a thin paste. Season and scrape in the crust from the roasting pan for flavor. Add 1 cup of milk and cook till thick. Serve on the side, with the chicken.

COQ AU VIN

The French are famous for their capers with chicks stewed with wine. I do not propose to enter into a discussion of

French morals. I do, however, recommend one of the more printable and edible results of their chicken research, called simply coq au vin. The quantities given serve 4 to 6, depending on the appetites of the guests and the generosity of the host.

What

3½ lb. chicken, cut up for serving.
3 tbsp. butter
3 tbsp. oil (olive preferred)
¼ lb. salt pork or bacon, diced
¼ cup flour, seasoned with ¼ tsp. salt, ⅛ tsp. pepper and ¼ tsp. thyme
10 small onions (canned may be used)
10 medium whole mushrooms
1 clove garlic, crushed
¼ tsp. parsley flakes (1 sprig)
1 bay leaf
½ cup dry red wine
¼ cup warm brandy

How

Dredge chicken pieces in seasoned flour, and brown in the oil and butter. Do not burn the butter. Transfer chicken pieces and juices to large casserole. Add onions, mushrooms, garlic, bay leaf, and salt and pepper to taste. Pour brandy over chicken and flame. When flame goes out, add wine. Cover, and bake at 350 degrees until chicken is tender, about 1 hour. If using canned mushrooms and/or onions, add only in the last ten minutes of cooking. Spoon the sauce over the chicken when serving.

CHICKEN SUPREME

4 tbsp. melted butter

4 tbsp. flour
1 tsp. salt
¼ tsp. white pepper
8 large mushrooms
4 thick slices of baked Virginia ham
4 breasts of small broilers, already broiled

How
Stir flour into melted butter, and add seasonings. Stir in and
stir-cook 2 cups rich chicken stock. When smooth and thick,
serve over dish. Saute mushrooms in butter until nicely done.
Put one broiler breast atop each slice of ham, then add 2
mushrooms and pour the sauce over the top.

PARIS BAKED CHICKEN

Saute halves of two 2 lb. broilers in butter, with 16 medium-
sized mushrooms and 16 small white onions. When chicken
is lightly browned, cover and bake at 350 degrees for 45
minutes. Remove chicken from pan, then add 1¼ cups red
wine. Simmer a few minutes, then blend in 1 tbsp. flour,
mixed well with 2 tbsp. cold water. Stir in 1 cup chicken
stock, and cook until thickened. Season chicken, and return
to pan and reheat. Serves 4.

BROILED CHICKEN

What
4 halves of 1½ lb. broilers
2 tbsp. melted butter, mixed with 2 tbsp. white wine,
½ tsp. thyme, ¼ tsp. salt, and ¼ tsp. pepper

How
Wash and dry chicken, and place skin side down on broiler

rack. Brush with wine and butter, and broil 10 minutes, 3 inches below heat. Turn, baste, and broil 10 minutes more, until skin is crisp and brown. Serve brushed with the wine and butter sauce, or Hollandaise, if you prefer.

SOUTHERN BELLE CHICKEN CUTLETS

What

2 large broiler breasts
4 tbsp. butter
1 egg yolk beaten with 1 tbsp. oil
½ cup cracker crumbs
½ cup toasted almonds
6 tbsp. flour
½ tsp. salt
½ tsp. paprika
¼ tsp. pepper
1½ cups chicken stock
1 tbsp. parsley flakes
1 tsp. lemon juice
2 tbsp. dry sherry

How

Skin and bone out chicken breasts. Pound flat, about ¼ inch. Mix flour, salt, pepper, paprika. Roll cutlets in flour, brush with egg yolk, and roll in crumbs. Brown in 2 tbsp. of the butter, on both sides, about 8 minutes. Remove from pan. Remove pan from heat and add 2 tbsp. butter and 2 tbsp. flour. Mix smoothly. Add parsley and chicken stock, and mix well. Stir-cook over low heat until thick and creamy. Crush nuts finely or blend in blender. Add nuts, sherry, and lemon juice to sauce, and mix well. Add chicken and reheat. Serves 4. This dish may be held in a covered baking dish until ready to serve. Oven temperature should not be over 200 degrees.

CHICKEN LIVERS AU VIN

What
1 lb. chicken livers
½ cup whole wheat flour
1 green pepper, halved and sliced
1 small onion, sliced thinly
8 medium mushrooms
1 tbsp. lemon juice
Dash of cayenne pepper
1½ oz. Burgundy or rosé wine

How
Season flour with salt and pepper, and coat chicken livers thoroughly. Fry in butter or margarine, until lightly browned. Add onion and green pepper, and saute 5 more minutes. Cut mushrooms in 2 and sprinkle with lemon juice. Saute, tossing with livers for 3 minutes. Add wine and sprinkle on cayenne pepper. Cover and simmer 5 minutes. Sprinkle with salt and pepper lightly. Serve to 4 on toast points, or with toast fingers or English muffins.

SCALLOPED CHICKEN AND NOODLES

What
6 lb. boiling fowl, cut up
1½ qt. water
1 bay leaf
6 peppercorns
½ tsp. salt
4 tbsp. butter
4 tbsp. flour
¼ tsp. salt
¼ tsp. pepper

2 tbsp. white wine
2 cups buttered bread crumbs
1 6 oz. package noodles

How
Put water, salt, bay leaf and peppercorns in large saucepan, with cut-up chicken. Cover and cook until meat comes off bones easily, about 1 hour. Remove chicken pieces, strain stock, and save. In a skillet, mix butter and flour, salt and pepper. Stir in 2 cups stock, and cook until thick and smooth. Add wine. Cook noodles as directed, and drain. Remove skin and bones from chicken, and cut into bite-size pieces. Layer noodles and chicken in casserole. Pour sauce over, top with bread crumbs. Brown lightly at 400 degrees. Serves 6.

CHICKEN CHASSEUR

What
1 3 lb. broiler, cut in serving pieces
1 cup dry Sauterne
Salt and pepper
½ tsp. ginger
¼ lb. fat smoked bacon, diced fine
1 tbsp. parsley flakes
2 cloves garlic, minced
1 cup button mushrooms

How
Put chicken and wine in skillet. Cook fast for 10 minutes, covered. Add garlic, parsley, and diced bacon. Season with salt, pepper, and ginger. Brown chicken pieces and bacon. Add mushrooms, cover, and lower heat. Cook 10 minutes. Serve with garlic bread to 4 friends.

BAKED ROCK CORNISH HEN MADEIRA

A goody from Trinidad.

What
4 Rock Cornish hens
½ cup water
2 tbsp. butter
Juice of 2 oranges
Juice of ½ lemon
Grated peel of 1 orange
Grated peel of ½ lemon
2 tsp. dry mustard
½ tsp. ginger
½ tsp. salt
¼ tsp. pepper
1 cup currant or grape jelly
½ cup Madeira wine

How
Wipe hens inside and out with damp cloth. Season with salt and pepper. Bake uncovered in 375 degree preheated oven, until lightly browned, basting often with butter and water. Meanwhile, boil grated peel in the orange and lemon juice for 10 minutes. Add balance of ingredients and simmer 10 minutes more. Serve sauce over birds to 4 good friends.

DUCK MARSALE FLAMBÉE
(Sicilian Style Duck)

What
3½ (about) lbs. duck, cut in serving pieces
2 tbsp. butter
2 tbsp. olive oil
¼ cup chopped fat bacon

⅛ tsp. thyme
1 bay leaf
1 clove garlic, minced
½ cup Marsala (or sherry)
½ cup wine vinegar
Salt and pepper
1 dozen small white onions
1 tsp. tomato paste mixed in ½ cup water
1½ cups stuffed olives
1 tsp. grated lemon rind
2 tbsp. grated orange rind
¼ tsp. cayenne pepper
3 slices orange, halved
2 oz. cognac
Lemon juice

How

Cook onions in water with 2 tbsp. lemon juice for 8 to 10 minutes. Brown duck with oil, butter, and fat bacon. Add bay leaf, thyme, garlic during browning. When well browned, pour off all but 2 tbsp. fat from pan. Pour wine and vinegar evenly over the pieces, and season with salt, pepper, and cayenne. Cook on high heat until wine and vinegar have evaporated. Add tomato paste mixture. Cover and cook slowly about 40 minutes. Uncover and add olives, onions, orange, and lemon rind. Mix in and cook 10 minutes. Put duck pieces on hot platter with onions and olives around the outside. Warm brandy, pour over, and flame.

The Sicilians serve this with bread rubbed with garlic and fried in olive oil.

ROAST TURKEY

Make stuffing, according to basic stuffing recipe, figuring 1 quart stuffing for an 8 lb. bird. Stuff neck where craw was

removed, and sew up. Stuff body and sew up opening. Turn
wings and legs back against body and tie securely. Brush
with butter or oil, and season with salt and pepper. Brown
at 400 degrees for 20 minutes, lying on breast, then turn and
repeat on the back. Add 1 pint of chicken stock to the pan,
cover, and bake covered at 300 degrees according to time-
table. Turkey is done when leg moves easily at the joint, or
190 degrees on meat thermometer.

Note
To females inside the fowl line: when your host is a taxi-
dermist be careful of his work-to-rule technique. A taxider-
mist first stuffs the bird, then mounts it!

ROAST GOOSE

The meat of goose is exceptionally tasty when properly
cooked. Most people try to roast a goose as they would any
other bird, and this results in a greasy and unpalatable dish.
With a goose, the idea is to extract most of the plentiful
oil before serving. To do this, start with a 450 degree oven.
Put the goose in, uncovered, lying on its breast on a rack.
Roast 25 minutes. Turn over and roast another 25 minutes.
Pour off the oil and cool the bird enough to handle.

Meanwhile you have prepared and partially skillet cooked
your favorite dressing. Season the goose inside and out, stuff,
and truss. Finish, covered, in a 300 degree oven, putting
2 tbsp. bacon fat and a pint of good stock in the pan. Roast
according to the chart, deducting the time already cooked
uncovered from the total time; in other words, 50 minutes
from the total, gives the remaining time to finish.

10
The Fleur-de-lis Is a Lily

No book on the gentle art of cooking would be complete without a section on French cookery. France has long been touted as the fountainhead of gourmets and gourmands. While I freely admit that the French nation is credited with rating the production and consumption of food as third amongst their most popular diversions, eating is still highly esteemed as a pleasant stopover to recharge the batteries for the top-rated sports. They did have a few eccentrics like Escoffier and Brillat-Savarin who rated food above all other vocations and avocations, but they were considered second-class citizens because of devotion to items that were only third in national interest. However, their efforts were newsworthy if only because reports on their progress in this field were more printable than were reports on the other two top-rated preoccupations. The Frenchmen have never fully understood why they achieved all the fame for cookery, but this is a matter of communication, rather than of primary interest. Having disposed of derivation and motivation, and order of importance, we can now proceed.

POTAGE PARMENTIER

A diversionary term for potato soup.

173

What
1 lb. potatoes, peeled and cut up
2 leeks, opened, cleaned, and cut up
2 onions, peeled and sliced
1 carrot, peeled and diced
1 stalk celery, with leaves, cut up
1 tbsp. chopped parsley
1 tsp. salt
¼ tsp. fresh ground black pepper
½ cup whipping cream
¼ cup butter
1 tbsp. chopped chives
2 tbsp. dry white wine, optional

How
Put all the vegetables and seasonings in 2½ quarts water.
Cover and cook for 2½ hours. (Season with ½ tsp. thyme,
if extra flavor is desired.) Drain vegetables, reserving juice.
Sieve, or blend vegetables in blender. Return to pot with
liquid, butter, and cream. Reheat and check for seasoning.
Add the wine, if desired, and serve.

BOURRIDE AIOLI

Bourride is famous for its flavor of sauce Aioli. Aioli is wild
with garlic, and it is believed *Aioli* was a yell generated
when a stranger got downwind of a bourride eater.

Sauce Aioli

What
6 cloves garlic
1¾ cups mayonnaise

1 tbsp. lemon juice

How

In your blender, blend garlic, lemon juice, and ¼ cup mayonnaise. Remove from blender and mix in balance of mayonnaise. Now, take off your mask and start the

Bourride

What
4 cups water
¼ cup white wine
¼ tsp. wine vinegar
1 onion, sliced
1 tbsp. parsley flakes
1 bay leaf
¼ tsp. dill flakes
½ tsp. salt
¼ tsp. pepper
3 lbs. of white fish, in fillets
3 egg yolks

How

Cook all ingredients except fish and egg for 10 minutes. Add fish, wrapped in cheesecloth and poach 10 minutes. Remove to a hot platter. Strain broth and simmer down to 1½ cups. Now, put broth in top of double boiler over hot simmering water. Beat egg yolks, and heat in ½ cup of broth, adding slowly as you beat. Return to double boiler and cook-stir until thickened. Stir in 2 cups Aioli sauce until thick and creamy. Put a thick slice of bread in each soup plate and top with a serving of fish. Pour on plenty of sauce. (It is said that a Bourride eater can knock out a Breathalyzer with one well-directed breath). Serves 4 to 6.

GARBURE BASQUE (Ham, Bean, and Vegetable Soup)

What
1 lb. dried navy beans
6 cups water
1 ham butt, 3 to 4 lb.
6 sliced onions
8 cloves garlic, minced fine
1 crushed chili pepper
1 green pepper, cut in strips
1 lb. lima beans
4 turnips, sliced
1 cabbage, sliced fine
3 carrots, sliced
1 pkg. frozen peas
12 pork sausages
2 tbsp. dry red wine

How
Cover dried beans with water and boil 2 minutes. Let stand
3 hours, covered. Add the ham and start cooking. Add
onions, garlic, green pepper, hot pepper, lima beans, carrots,
and turnips, and simmer 3 to 4 hours. Then add cabbage
and peas, and cook until vegetables are a thick puree. Taste
and season. Add wine. Remove ham, and keep hot. Slice
when ready to serve. Serve with crusty bread to 8 or 10.
Make sure your date eats with you, or get ready for a kissless
evening.

COQUILLES ST. JACQUES (Scallops in Shells)

No doubt you will look at the length of this recipe and
conclude it's a drag. However, this dish is a terrific experience in taste when made properly. It is not clear whether

this dish was invented by St. Jacques as one of his saintly tasks, or whether he was sainted for the invention of the dish, which seems more reasonable in view of its excellence.

What
1½ lb. scallops
6 green onions, with tops
1 bouquet garni (celery, leaves, parsley, thyme, bay leaf)
1½ cups dry white wine
¼ lb. mushrooms
⅓ cup water
Juice of 1 lemon
Salt and pepper
3 tbsp. flour
4 egg yolks
7 tbsp. butter
1 cup whipping cream
Grated Parmesan cheese
Bread crumbs

How
Wash scallops and dry on absorbent paper. Place in saucepan with 2 tbsp. butter and chopped green onions. Add bouquet garni and barely cover with wine. Season with salt and pepper, lightly. Bring quickly to a boil, then simmer 5 minutes, very slowly. Drain and save the broth for the sauce. Cut scallops into small pieces. Chop mushrooms fine, and saute in 2 tbsp. butter. Add the ⅓ cup water, lemon juice, and ¼ tsp. salt, and a pinch of pepper. Simmer gently 4 minutes. Melt 3 tbsp. butter in saucepan, and blend in 3 tbsp. flour. Add the broth saved from the scallops and mushrooms and stir-cook until thick and smooth. Cook slowly 3 more minutes and add scallops. Beat egg yolks and mix with cream. Add the mixture to the sauce, stir-cooking just under the boil. Add mushrooms and correct for seasoning. Put into individual ramekins or scallop shells, sprinkle with

Parmesan and buttered crumbs, and glaze under broiler. Serves 6 gourmets to a state of euphoria. Takes some time and trouble, but a short-cut to fame.

BOUILLABAISSE

The exact recipe for bouillabaisse has always been a mystery, often even to the French chefs who are reputed to have invented it. With true Gallic savoir faire, they change ingredients according to the change of seasons and availability of ingredients, or even how they feel about life at the moment creativity hits them. They also have a tendency to leave lobster, oysters, mussels, or clams in their shells in the melange when they serve it. This is fine if you are wearing a rain cape and gum boots while eating. At the risk of being dubbed a culinary traitor, I shell the shellfish and mollusks and leave the shells out of the concoction. The result is just as flavorful, if less spectacular. For serving 3 to 6.

What
2 lb. fillet of any white fish
2 cups crab, lobster meat, shrimp, or a combination
1 cup oysters, clams, or combination
1½ cups cooked or canned tomatoes
1 tsp. garlic powder
2 tbsp. green pepper flakes
2 leeks, white part only
2 tbsp. melted butter
2 tbsp. olive oil
1 tbsp. parsley flakes
½ tsp. each, thyme, basil, and black pepper
½ cup dry white wine
1 bay leaf
2 cups fish stock, including clam juice

1 big pinch of saffron
1 long loaf crusty French bread

How

Cut fish into 2-inch squares, and saute gently in butter on both sides, 4 minutes total. Remove from heat. Heat olive oil in large saucepan or kettle. Saute sliced leeks and all seasonings until leeks are just golden. Add fish, fish stock, and tomatoes, and simmer 5 minutes. Add the crab and/or lobster and shrimp. As soon as pot returns to a boil, add the wine, and do not boil again. Drop in clams and/or oysters and simmer 5 minutes. Sprinkle on saffron and it's ready to serve. During this time you have been frying slices of the French bread golden, in butter. Stand the slices in a tureen, around the sides. Seat your guests, and pour in the bouillabaisse. If one should sneer that it doesn't look like the one he had in Marseille, toss in any loose shells you have around into his soup dish. Anything to please a guest!

QUICHE DE LANGOUSTE

Sounds more mysterious and exotic than lobster pie, which it is.

What

Meat from 2 1½ lb. lobsters (or the same amount of canned)
Pastry for 9-inch pie shell
2 tbsp. chopped onions
¼ cup cognac or white wine
Salt and pepper
¼ cup butter
1 cup cream
4 eggs
Dash of nutmeg
Lobster coral and tomalley, if you have it.

How
Line a 9-inch pie plate with the pastry. Form a sheet of
foil into the pie, and fill with dry beans or peas to weight
the crust into form while baking. Bake according to directions. Remove foil and weights. Then saute onion in butter
until golden, add lobster and heat through. Add cognac or
wine, season to taste. Put it in the pie shell. Mix coral and
tomalley with 1 tbsp. cream in pan, cook 1 minute, and
pour over lobster. Beat eggs and remaining cream together,
and season. Pour over lobster, dust with a little nutmeg
and bake about 35 minutes at 375 degrees. Serves 6 for a
snack, or 3 for a pièce de résistance.

DAUBE DE PROVENÇALE

This is a beef dish made in a *daubière,* which is a deep
earthenware pot made in Provence. Any heavy pot or Dutch
oven will do as well. Make a day ahead and skim before
reheating.

What
⅔ cup olive oil
5 to 6 lbs. chuck, tied
1 cup red wine
1 tbsp. salt
1 tsp. black pepper
1 tsp. oregano
1 tsp. rosemary
1 bay leaf
2 cloves
1 carrot, cut up
1 pig's foot
½ lb. salt pork
6 peeled carrots
6 garlic cloves, peeled

1 bay leaf
1 tsp. rosemary
½ tsp. thyme
24 black pitted olives
8 large tomatoes, or 1 large can of canned tomatoes

How

Put olive oil, wine, salt, pepper, 1 tsp. oregano, 1 tsp. rose-mary, 1 bay leaf, 2 cloves, and carrot in a pot and bring to a boil. When cool, put in the meats and let stand 24 hours. Weight down under surface of marinade during that time, and turn a couple of times. Remove meat from marinade and put in cooking pot. Strain the marinade and pour in pot. Add balance of ingredients, except tomatoes and olives. Simmer, covered, or place in 300 degree oven for 2½ hours. Add tomatoes and olives and simmer 45 minutes more. Remove meat and let stand to drain a few minutes, before serving. Slice and serve on a platter with some of the marinade as sauce.

BLANQUETTE DE VEAU

What

1 shoulder of veal in 1-inch cubes
1 clove garlic
1 onion stuck with three cloves
2 carrots
½ cup dry white wine
¼ tsp. thyme
½ lb. mushrooms
1 tbsp. lemon juice
1 tsp. salt
¼ tsp. pepper
15 small onions
¼ cup butter

¼ cup flour
2 egg yolks
½ cup heavy cream

How
Put veal, onion and cloves, carrots, thyme, and salt in a
pot and cover with water. Simmer, covered, 1½ hrs. Remove
the veal and cook the broth down to 1½ cups. Blanch
mushroom caps in broth and remove. Cook onions in water
with 1 tsp. lemon juice until tender and almost dry. Add
to broth. Melt butter and mix in flour. Add broth and stir-
cook until thick and smooth. Beat egg yolks and cream
together, and stir-cook in the sauce until smooth and thick.
Stir in lemon juice, add the veal, and heat. Serves 8.

FILET DE BOEUF BOUQUETIÈRE

What
1 5 to 6 lb. beef filet (you can hock the family jewels!)
6 strips bacon
½ tsp. thyme
½ tsp. rosemary
½ cup Madeira wine
½ tsp. lemon juice

How
Trim the fat off the filet. Rub with melted butter, and the
herbs. Roast at 450 degrees 40 minutes for rare, 50 minutes
for medium. (Any guest who requests well done should be
fed hamburger with ketchup!) After 20 minutes roasting,
brush with melted butter, and top with bacon. Finish
roasting. Serve with a Madeira sauce, made as follows.
    Make a gravy of the pan juices, then add the wine and
lemon juice.
    The *bouquetière* in this dish is the vegetables with which

you surround the meat when serving. You can let yourself go with a mixture of whatever vegetables are in season. Green and yellow are colorful, of course. For potatoes, small new potatoes or potato balls boiled, then browned in fat are good.

LE GIGOT QUI PLEURE
(Weeping Leg of Lamb)

It took a little time to find out what all the weeping was about. Developed it was from the original way of making this dish, where the lamb was placed on a rack by the chief Inquisitor (chef?), so that it could weep its juices into the pan of vegetables below. Bet you're glad you found this out in time to prevent your weeping with the lamb. As the French say, "It is of a sadness, n'est çe pas?"

Start with a leg of lamb, 6 lb. or more. Stud meat with slivered garlic cloves, making incisions with a pointed knife. Rub with salt, pepper, and rosemary, then with melted butter. Roast on rack at 350 degrees for 1 hour. Slice 3½ lbs. of potatoes, thin. Put in layers in a baking dish, dotting each layer with butter, and sprinkling with salt, pepper, garlic powder, rosemary, and thyme. With baster, remove about 2 tbsp. of fat from under the roast, and sprinkle on the potatoes. Bake in the oven with the lamb, until done and meat thermometer shows 175 degrees in center of lamb. Slice lamb and put slices on top of the potatoes. Pour over the juices released in slicing. Serves 6 to 8.

STEAK AU POIVRE (Pepper Steak)

Press cracked black peppercorns into four minute steaks. You can buy bottled cracked peppercorns if you have mislaid your hammer. Use a rolling pin or the heel of your hand to press the pepper in. Grease lightly a heavy frying pan, and when pan is really hot, sear steaks on both sides. Finish cooking, turning often until done to your taste. Put a pat of butter atop each steak, and rinse pan with red wine, and pour over steak.

BOEUF BOURGUIGNONNE

What

6 slices bacon, cut in 1-inch pieces
3 lb. beef chuck, cut in 1-inch cubes
2 cans condensed beef broth
1 large carrot, sliced
2 tbsp. instant minced onion (or flakes)
3 tbsp. flour
1 tbsp. tomato paste
1 tsp. garlic powder
1 bay leaf
½ tsp. thyme
1 lb. mushrooms
1 lb. small white onions
1 tsp. salt
¼ tsp. pepper
2 cups red Burgundy
2 tbsp. butter, mixed with 2 tbsp. cooking oil
¼ cup flour, creamed with 2 tbsp. butter

How

Cook bacon crisp in Dutch oven. Remove. Mix flour and salt and dredge meat well in flour, until well coated. Brown all around in the fat. Remove. Put in balance of flour, and stir into fat until smooth. Put in all the broth except ½ cup. Add wine, tomato paste, and seasonings. Return bacon and beef to pan and stir-cook 5 minutes. Cover and simmer 3 hours. Brown onions in oil and butter, and remove. Then brown mushrooms lightly. Return onions and the reserved ½ cup of broth to pan and simmer, covered, ten minutes.

When beef is done, form the flour, creamed with the butter, into small balls and add to liquid. Stir over low heat until thickened. Add mushrooms and onions and reheat. Serves 8 to 10.

COQ AU RIESLING
(Chicken with Riesling Wine)

This is an Alsatian dish and uses the delicious white wine of the region. However, I have used a California Riesling with equally good results.

What

2 chickens, 3 to 4 lb. each, quartered, or 6 broiler breasts
Flour, salt, and pepper
¼ cup butter
2 tbsp. vegetable oil
Dash nutmeg
1 tsp. thyme
1 leek, well washed
1 sprig parsley
1 onion stuck with 2 cloves
⅓ cup cognac
1½ cups Riesling
2 slices salt pork
12 mushroom caps
18 small white onions, peeled
sugar to glaze
3 egg yolks
¾ cup heavy cream
2 tbsp. chopped parsley
¼ cup butter

How

Dredge the chicken pieces in flour, seasoned with salt and pepper. Heat the oil and butter in a heavy skillet and place the chicken in, skin side down. Cook dark meat first, as it takes longer than white meat. Brown well and turn and brown other side. When chicken is well browned, add nutmeg, thyme, leek, parsley, and onion. Pour cognac over and ignite. When flame dies down, add wine and bring to boil. Reduce heat and simmer, and cook gently 20 to 25 minutes until chicken is tender. While chicken is cooking, cut the salt pork into small pieces and saute in butter until golden. Transfer to pan with chicken. Saute the mushroom caps in the pork fat. Saute onions in ¼ cup butter. Sprinkle with a little sugar to glaze and season with salt. Cover the pan and steam gently, until tender. Keep warm. When chicken is done, remove to hot platter. Garnish with the onions and mushrooms. Reduce the sauce to 1½ cups. Beat the egg yolks with cream, and stir in a little of the sauce. Return to sauce, and stir-cook until smooth and creamy. Do not boil. Serve sauce separately, garnished with chopped parsley. Serve with buttered noodles and Riesling wine, to 6 guests, who have probably been belting the wine while you slaved.

COTELETTES À LA KIEV
(Breast of Chicken)

What
2 chicken breasts, boned and beaten thin
4 tbsp. green butter (see Sauces)
1 cup flour
1 egg, lightly beaten
1 cup vegetable oil
1 cup fine bread crumbs
Salt, pepper
¼ tsp. thyme

How
Sprinkle salt, pepper, and thyme on each chicken piece and rub in. Put 1 tbsp. cold green butter on each piece and fold

in sides. Then fold ends over and fasten with toothpicks. Dip into flour, then into egg, then coat with bread crumbs. Deep fry in oil (should be 375 degrees) for 5 minutes. Drain and remove picks. Serves 4, or 2 who love Chicken Kiev.

The French are known for being a creative people (after all, look at their birth rate!), but they are hidebound in tradition. If you like water with your meals, or coffee with your dessert, forget it, for the French will have no truck with your foreign foibles. Pass up the aperitifs, and drink a dry or medium wine before dinner. Their aperitifs, whether bitter or sweet, stun your taste buds and spoil your enjoyment of the unique flavor of:

CANETON STRASBOURG
(Duck with Brandied Cherry Sauce)

What

1 5 lb. duckling, ready-to-cook
1 clove garlic, peeled and split
1 cup beef gravy
$\frac{1}{2}$ tsp. thyme
$\frac{1}{4}$ tsp. black pepper
1 cup Beaujolais
$1\frac{1}{2}$ tbsp. black currant jelly
$1\frac{1}{2}$ tbsp. grated orange peel
2 tbsp. brandy
2 cups stoned black cherries

How

Rub duckling inside and out with garlic. Mix salt, pepper, and thyme, and rub on duck, inside and out. Place duck on its back on rack in roasting pan, and roast uncovered for $2\frac{1}{4}$ hours. Turn over the last 40 minutes of cooking. Remove to warm platter. Pour off fat from roasting pan, and add rest of ingredients, except cherries. Bring to a boil on top of range, and stir-cook 5 minutes. Drain cherries and add to sauce. Heat slowly 3 minutes. Return duck to pan and cover with sauce. Reheat in oven 10 minutes, and serve with shoestring potatoes, or small potato pancakes. Serves 4 or 5, depending on what happened to the rest of the Beaujolais!

POULET SAUTÉ À LA MARENGO
(Sauteed Chicken)

What
3 lb. cut up frying chicken
2 rock lobster tails
2 tbsp. tomato paste
½ tsp. chervil
2 tbsp. parsley flakes
4 tbsp. butter
4 eggs
1 cup canned mushroom gravy
½ cup white wine
1 cup garlic flavored croutons
Salt and pepper

How
Brown chicken in butter in large skillet. Season with salt and pepper. Add rock lobster, tomato paste, chervil, gravy, half the parsley, and wine. Cover and cook 25 minutes. Add croutons, heat, and turn onto hot serving platter. Top with 4 fried eggs and sprinkle with parsley. Serves 4 to 5. I am not sure what the fried eggs are added for. Maybe the French do, as this is how they insist Chicken Marengo should be.

SUPRÊMES DE VOLAILLE
(Chicken Breast Supreme)

What
Meat from 3 chicken breasts, pounded thin
2 tsp. dried grated lemon rind
2 tbsp. bottled lemon juice
1 cup cream
6 pats butter
¼ lb. butter
2 tbsp. sherry
Salt and pepper
2 tbsp. grated Parmesan cheese
¼ tsp. savory

How
Season chicken breasts and saute 4 minutes on each side in butter. Remove to shallow baking dish. Put in balance of ingredients except Parmesan and butter pats in skillet and cook-stir until slightly thickened. Pour over chicken, put a pat of butter on each piece, and sprinkle with the cheese. Brown lightly under broiler and serve. Serves 4 or 5.

SUPRÊMES MILANESE
(Chicken Breast Milan Style)

What
2 chicken breasts, boned and pounded thin
¼ lb. butter
¼ tsp. rosemary
4 slices lemon
1 cup flour
½ cup fine bread crumbs
1 egg

1 tbsp. milk
½ tsp. salt
¼ tsp. pepper
½ cup grated Parmesan cheese

How

Put flour and seasonings in paper bag. Beat egg with milk. Mix cheese and bread crumbs. Put chicken pieces into bag and shake until coated with flour. Dip into egg wash, and roll in crumb-cheese mixture. Saute brown in hot butter (foaming hot) in skillet, 4 minutes on each side. Serve, decorating each piece with a lemon slice.

POULET À L'ESTRAGON
(Tarragon Chicken)

What

3 chicken breasts, boned, skinned and halved
1 can (6 or 8 oz.) chicken pâté
1 can condensed chicken broth
1 can chicken gravy
1 tsp. tarragon flakes
6 sprigs parsley

How

Put chicken in saucepan with ⅔ tsp. tarragon and the chicken broth. Cover and cook until tender—about 20 minutes. Remove and cut a pocket in each piece and stuff with 1 tbsp. of chicken pâté. Heat gravy in another pan with balance of tarragon. Add chicken pieces and reheat just until hot. Serves 6.

TRUITE AMANDINE
(Trout with Almonds)

What

4 to 6 fresh trout, ¾ to 1 lb.

Milk
Seasoned flour
1/4 lb. butter
1 tbsp. cooking oil
6 tbsp. slivered, blanched almonds
Juice of half a lemon
4 tbsp. finely chopped parsley (or flakes)

How

Season inside of trout, and dip them in milk, then in flour.
Saute in half the butter and half the oil, until golden brown
on both sides. Remove from pan, and drain remaining fat.
Put balance of oil and butter in pan, and brown the almonds, shaking continuously until golden. Add lemon juice
and parsley, and heat two minutes at a slow bubble. Pour
over trout, which has been kept hot, on a heated platter.
Serves 4 to 6.

SCALLOPS AU GRATIN

What

1 dozen scallops
1/2 pt. dry white wine
2 tbsp. finely chopped green onions (shallots)
4 tbsp. heavy cream
1 tbsp. butter
1 tbsp. flour
1 egg yolk
5 or 6 medium mushrooms, sliced
1/2 tbsp. lemon juice
Salt and pepper

How

Melt butter in pan. Add scallops, wine, shallots, lemon juice,
and sliced mushrooms. Simmer 5 to 7 minutes, covered. Mix

flour with cream, and then egg yolk. Stir smooth. Add a little hot sauce to mixture and whisk in. Return to pan and cook 5 minutes, stirring. Serve in patty shells.

COOKING THE ARTICHOKE

An artichoke is related to the thistle. It is the only vegetable you have more of when you finish eating than when you started. If you are addicted to weeds of the more-or-less edible variety, here is how you prepare one (or more). Make sure they are green and fresh looking. With a pair of kitchen shears cut off all the thorns, and pull off the bottom row of leaves. Cut off enough of the top to make the plant about 3 inches high. Cut off stems. Dip in water with a tablespoon of lemon juice in it, to prevent vegetable turning brown. Shake dry.

ARTICHOKES ITALIANO

What
4 artichokes
3 cloves garlic, crushed
⅓ cup olive oil
¼ cup water
½ tsp. salt
¼ tsp. pepper
1 tsp. mint flakes

How
Prepare artichokes as directed above. Cut in quarters and scrape out fuzzy choke. Put them in a saucepan with oil, water, garlic, and mint. Cover and steam slowly until tender. Serve on a heated platter, with liquid from the pan poured over the artichokes. Serves 4 who like artichokes, or 16 who can take 'em or leave 'em.

STUFFED ARTICHOKES PALERMO

What
4 artichokes (globe)
1 lb. sweet Italian sausage meat
1 cup sliced mushrooms
3 tbsp. grated Parmesan cheese
1 tbsp. chopped parsley flakes
1 egg
½ tsp. salt
¼ tsp. pepper
½ cup tomato sauce
1 cup bread crumbs
3 tbsp. butter
½ cup water
1 tbsp. lemon juice

How
Put one inch of boiling water in a roast pan or large casserole. Add lemon juice. Stand the artichokes in the pan and cover. Cook 20 minutes. Drain upside down and cool. Saute sausage meat in butter until nicely browned, and remove to cool. Toss the bread crumbs in remaining butter and fat in pan until well coated. Crumble sausage meat and mix well with egg, Parmesan, mushrooms, and salt and pepper to taste. Mix in parsley. Spread the leaves of the artichoke gently, pull out the conical center, and scrape out the fuzzy choke. Put the artichokes in a large casserole. Stuff artichoke centers with the dressing, pushing down between the leaves as well. Top with the crumbs. Mix tomato sauce with water and pour into casserole. Bake at 375 degrees uncovered about 30 minutes. Baste now and then. Serves 4.

POTATOES DUCHESSE

By appointment to the Duchess of Lard.

What
2 lb. potatoes, peeled and quartered
¼ lb. fresh butter
½ tsp. salt
¼ tsp. pepper
1 egg yolk

How
Boil potatoes in water with the salt. Let dry after draining.
Mash well. Add butter and pepper and mix well in top of
double boiler. Add the egg yolk and mix in, cooking a few
minutes over the hot water. Hold hot until serving.

POMMES DE TERRE EN CRÊME
(Potatoes in Cream)

Peel and slice thin, six large raw potatoes. Slice thin ¼ lb.
mushrooms. Mash a clove of garlic in melted butter, then
butter a baking dish with the butter. Chop one small onion
fine, and mix with 2 tbsp. chopped parsley. Put a layer of
potato slices in the baking dish, then a layer of mushrooms,
and repeat until used up. Sprinkle each layer with Parmesan cheese. Pour over top 1 pint heavy cream, and dot
with ¼ lb. butter, cut in pieces. Bake at 375 degrees. When
almost done, about 40 minutes, sprinkle with Parmesan and
brown lightly. Not very slimming, but very satisfying.

JAMBON PERSILLES (Parsley Ham)

This stuff is real groovy for a picnic. Start with 3 cups of
any clear broth, or make it with bouillon cubes. Dice enough
cooked ham, ½ inch, to make 3 cups. Soften 1½ tbsp. unflavored gelatin in 1 cup of cool broth. Heat 2 cups broth
and add gelatin mixture. Mix diced ham with 1 cup chopped
parsley, and press firmly into bowl. Pour cooled gelatin over

ham, so it just covers when settled. Chill with a weighted plate on top of the ham. Serve with a mixture of hot mustard and finely chopped gherkins.

OIGNONS A LA MONEGASQUE
(Monaco Onions)

This means onions Monegasque style. I know of a prominent tomato, who resides in Monaco, but she runs more to princes than to onions!

Start with three dozen small white peeled onions, and 1½ cups medium dry white wine. Put them in a pan with 1 tbsp. wine vinegar and 3 slices of lemon, ¼ inch thick. Cover and simmer until onions are almost tender but still firm in center. Stir in 2 tbsp. tomato paste and ½ cup each Sultana and white raisins. Add 1 tsp. salt and ¼ tsp. fresh ground pepper. Cook about 5 minutes to plump raisins and spread the flavor. Remove onions, and reduce sauce until almost a glaze. Pour over the onions and chill. Serve as an hors d'oeuvre, or with cold meat. Serves 8 to 10.

SAUCISSE ET POMMES DE TERRE EN SALADE (Sausage and Potato Salad)

Use large sausages, kielbasa or cotechino. The first is Polish and the second Italian. Put whichever sausage you use into a pan with 1 cup finely cut green onions and enough medium dry red wine to cover. Simmer gently and after 35 to 40 minutes, slice and serve with some of the sauce from the pan.

SALADE AUX POMMES DE TERRE, CHAUDE (Hot Potato Salad)

What
2 lb. small new potatoes, or potato balls

⅓ cup salad oil
2 tbsp. wine vinegar
¼ cup finely chopped onion
¼ cup chopped parsley

How
Boil potatoes in salted water until done but not soft. Put oil and vinegar into a pan, and add the potatoes. Heat together, season, and when hot, add onion and parsley. Toss well together and serve hot. Some of the red wine broth with chopped green onion makes a nice addition to the flavor. Some of the mustard sauce as for Jambon Persilles goes well with the sausage.

11

Stews Are International

A stew is not necessarily the host who sampled too much of the cooking brandy. *Stew* is a loose term used to describe anything from a watery concoction full of floating islands of guck, to an epicurean delight just short of Heaven. Whether it is a trapper making a beaver-tail stew as a by-product of a beaver skin, a hungry Eskimo stewing his mukluks, or a continental chef exercising his talents to produce an irresistible blend of inspired ingredients, stews are perennial and international. Continental chefs produce complex masterpieces of loving care, while Penn-Dutch farmers make a husky stew in which the spoon will stand proudly erect.

CHUCK WAGON STEW

What
1 lb. stewing beef, cubed ¾ inch
3 carrots, cut in ¾ inch chunks
2 medium onions, quartered
3 medium potatoes, diced ¾ inches
4 stalks celery, cut ¾ inch long
1 cup shredded cabbage
2 tbsp. bacon or beef fat

1 tsp. salt
¼ tsp. black pepper
1 bay leaf
¼ tsp. paprika
4 tbsp. flour

How
Shake the beef cubes in a bag with the flour, salt, and pepper until well coated. Brown cubes of beef well in the fat. Add 1 can consomme and 1 can water, with bay leaf and paprika. Simmer 1 hour until meat is tender. Add celery, onions, and carrots, and simmer 20 minutes. Add potatoes and cabbage and simmer 15 minutes more. Add water if necessary. Mix the flour from the bag with ½ cup water, and add to stew. Simmer 5 minutes and correct for seasoning. Serves 4 to 6.

ENGLISH BEEF STEW

What
2 lb. flank steak
2 tbsp. salad oil
4 carrots
4 onions
4 medium potatoes
1½ cups boiling water
¾ cup Worcestershire sauce
½ tsp. salt
¼ tsp. pepper
8 whole cloves
Flour

How
Cut beef in ¾ inch cubes. Roll in flour and brown all around in fat. Transfer to stew pot, with fat and browned flour. Add all other ingredients except cloves and flour. Tie cloves in

cheesecloth and add to stew. Simmer 1½ hours covered. Remove cloves. Stir 2 tbsp. flour into ½ cup water and add to stew. Cook and stir now and then about ten minutes. Serves 4.

GIBLET STEW CHASSEUR

What

1 quart chicken giblets
½ cup butter
½ cup minced onions
¼ cup flour
½ cup minced green peppers
1 pint tomato puree
1 pint chicken stock or bouillon
½ cup diced potatoes
½ cup diced carrots
½ tbsp. salt
½ tsp. pepper
2 tbsp. dry sherry (optional)

How

Cut up gizzards and saute with onions in the butter for about 15 minutes, on low heat. Cut hearts in two, and saute 10 minutes more with gizzards. Add livers and green peppers and stir and cook 5 minutes. Add stock and puree, stir-cook smooth. Add seasonings, potatoes, and carrots, and cook 20 minutes. Mix flour smoothly with a little cold water and add to stew. Stir-cook 5 minutes. Serves 4 or 5 hunters.

STEWED CHICKEN WITH RICE

What

1 5 lb. chicken, cut up
1 tsp. salt

¼ tsp. pepper
⅔ cup flour
⅓ cup butter
½ tsp. oregano
¼ tsp. thyme
¼ tsp. sage

How
Season chicken pieces with salt and pepper and roll in flour.
Fry in butter until brown all over. Cover with water and add
seasonings. Simmer 1 hour, covered. Serve with cooked,
herbed rice.

BEEF STEW WITH DUMPLINGS

What
2 lb. beef round, cubed ¾ inch
½ cup lard
1 tsp. salt
¼ tsp. pepper
½ cup flour
1½ quarts beef stock
½ cup diced carrots
1 cup diced potatoes
½ cup chopped onion
2 cups canned tomatoes

How
Season meat with salt and pepper. Roll in flour and brown
in lard. Cover with stock and simmer 1 hour until meat is
tender. Add vegetables and simmer until tender, 20 to 30
minutes, depending on size of dicing.

Dumplings

What
1 cup flour
2 tsp. baking powder

½ tsp. salt
½ tbsp. butter
½ cup milk

How
Stir flour, salt, and baking powder well together. Rub the butter well into the flour, add milk, and mix. Drop by large spoonfuls onto boiling stew. Cover and cook 20 minutes, no peeking, please. Dumplings can be temperamental!

BEEF DAUBE

This is a sort of European pot roast with overtones of stew, or is it undertones. Groovy hosts please note that pot roast is not made with marijuana!

What
1 5 lb. round of beef
6 slices bacon
1½ tsp. salt
1 tsp. pepper
½ cup flour
1 gallon beef stock, or water
1 bay leaf
¼ tsp. thyme
1 tbsp. minced parsley
1 clove garlic, slivered
½ cup chopped onions
½ cup chopped turnip
½ cup chopped carrot
2 tbsp. red wine

How
Lard beef with bacon cut in 1-inch strips. Rub flour, salt, and pepper well into meat. Put in large pot with ½ cup of oil, and brown on all sides. Cover with the stock and add sea-

sonings. Cover and cook about 2 hours. Add turnips, carrots, and onions and cook 30 minutes longer. Serve hot or cold, adding wine after you take the dish off heat.

CHICKEN PAPRIKA

This dish is Austrian and is to be eaten with dark beer and an Austrian accent.

What
2 2½ lb. chickens, cut up
1½ cups chicken broth
3 coarsely chopped onions
½ cup butter
1 tbsp. paprika
1 tsp. salt
2 tbsp. flour
1 tbsp. parsley
1 cup dairy sour cream

How
Cook chicken necks and giblets in water to cover, for 1 hour. Melt butter in a heavy skillet and brown chicken lightly all around. Add onions and cook until golden, then sprinkle with paprika. Add the salt and a half cup of the chicken broth. Cook slowly 15 minutes, uncovered, turning chicken once. Add another cup of chicken broth, mixed with 2 tbsp. flour. Cook 15 minutes uncovered, and 15 minutes covered. Remove chicken pieces to hot platter, then stir sour cream into the gravy, and heat until it begins to bubble. Pour over the chicken and sprinkle with parsley. Serve with hot rice—ach du lieber!

CHICKEN VIENNESE

What
4 lb. roasting fowl, cut up

1 lemon, quartered
1 tsp. salt
5 tbsp. butter
1 lb. tiny white onions, peeled
½ lb. mushrooms, sliced
2 cups dry white wine
¼ tsp. dried tarragon
1 cup heavy cream

How
Rub chicken pieces with cut lemon. Let stand 15 minutes.
Melt butter in heavy skillet, and cook chicken over low heat
until browned all over. Sprinkle with salt, and add onions
and mushrooms. Pour in the wine, add the tarragon, and
cook covered for 45 minutes, over low heat. Stir in cream
slowly. Serve with egg foam dumplings, to 6.

EGG FOAM DUMPLINGS

What
3 egg whites
3 egg yolks
¼ tsp. salt
3 tbsp. flour

How
Beat egg whites with salt until stiff. Beat yolks with flour
until smooth. Fold yolk mixture into whites. Drop the mixture by tablespoonfuls into boiling stock or gravy, and cook
covered 5 minutes.

LAMB IN DILL SAUCE

Dining with a Swedish accent.

What
2 quarts water

2 tsp. salt
3 dill stalks, or 1½ tsp. flaked dill
2 tbsp. butter
3 lb. lamb neck, in 2-inch chunks
2 tbsp. flour
1½ tbsp. vinegar
2 tsp. sugar
¼ tsp. white pepper
1 egg yolk
12 medium potatoes
2 tbsp. dry white wine

How
Put water, salt and dill stalks in heavy kettle. Add lamb
when water is boiling. When liquid boils again, turn heat low
and cover. Cook 1½ hours. Add potatoes and cook another
¾ hour. Drain stock off lamb. Remove lamb and potatoes
from kettle. Add butter to kettle and melt; add flour and
stir in. Add 2 cups of stock, and stir in. Add balance of
ingredients except egg yolk and wine. Cook until thickened.
Add a little of the sauce to the beaten egg yolk, and blend
well. Add wine. Return to the kettle and cook 3 minutes
more. Add lamb and potatoes and heat slowly. Serve the
sauce over the lamb and potatoes, to 6. Serve with green salad.
The aquavit and Ludafisk set are high on this dish. Brings 'em
right out of orbit!

COLLOPS, SCOTCH VARIETY

It is said that the smell of this dish brings the Scots storming
out of the heather with their appetites at the ready.

What
1 medium onion, chopped
1 lb. ground beef

½ lb. ground lean mutton
1 tsp. salt
½ tsp. pepper
2 tbsp. oatmeal
1½ cups strong stock and 1 cup water, or 2 cups water and
  2 bouillon cubes
2 tbsp. shortening
2 tbsp. brandy

How
Cook onion in shortening until light yellow. Add beef,
mutton, salt, pepper, and 1 tsp. savory, and brown lightly.
Add stock and cover. Simmer 1 hour. Add the oatmeal, and
stir in. Cook 10 minutes. Remove from heat, add brandy,
and serve. Usually served over mashed potatoes, to 6.

YUGOSLAV STEW

For some reason lost in the annals of time, this was called
"Priest's lunch."

What
3 lb. beef brisket, cubed
8 small onions
4 potatoes, peeled and diced
3 stalks celery, diced
3 tomatoes, cut in quarters
¼ cup chopped parsley
2 cloves garlic, minced
1 tsp. salt
2 tbsp. paprika
2 bay leaves
6 peppercorns
2 cans beef bouillon and 2 cans water

How
Combine all ingredients in a heavy kettle. Cover and cook over low heat for 2 hours. Serve from kettle with crusty bread to any 6 priests you may have as guests. Even the laity likes it in Yugoslavia!

PORTUGAISE FISH STEW

What
½ cup cooked rice
1 cup olive or salad oil
3 medium onions, chopped
½ cup canned tomato sauce
2½ lb. white fish
1 clove garlic, minced
1 tbsp. chopped parsley
1½ tsp. salt
¼ tsp. pepper
1 cup dry white wine

How
Put oil in large skillet. Add onions and cook until yellow. Add filleted fish, rice, tomato sauce, garlic, parsley, salt, pepper, and wine. Cover and cook 10 minutes. Uncover and cook slowly 10 more minutes. Serves 6.

CHERRIED DUCKLING

I hate to accuse the Frenchmen of being hooked on cherries, but what with cherries jubilee and cherried duckling, I am at least suspicious.

What
1 5 lb. duckling, quartered
1 tsp. salt

3 cups dark pitted cherries
2 tbsp. butter
½ cup Madeira wine
2 tsp. flour
2 tbsp. water

How
Sprinkle duckling with salt. Brown in butter in heavy kettle.
Drain cherries, and save juice. Add ½ cup juice and the
wine, and cook, covered, over medium heat for about 20
minutes until duckling is tender. Remove duckling to warm
platter and skim off excess fat. Mix the flour and water
smooth, and stir into juice in kettle. Cook until slightly
thick. Add cherries and heat. Serve sauce over duckling to
4 smiling French guests.

WHITE VEAL STEW

Here's a gourmet-tempter—cradled in Normandy, eaten anywhere.

What
2 lb. boneless breast of veal, cut in 2-inch cubes
1 large onion stuck with 1 clove
4 cups cold water
2 tsp. salt (try 1 first, and add?)
Large carrot, cut in half
1 tbsp. chopped parsley
½ tsp. French savory
½ tsp. marjoram
12 small peeled onions
½ lb. mushrooms, sliced
¼ cup butter
3 tbsp. flour
Juice of half a lemon
2 egg yolks

½ cup light cream
½ cup dry white wine

How
Put veal, salt, and water in a large saucepan, and bring to a boil. Skim after boiling 5 minutes. Add the onion, carrot, marjoram, parsley, and savory; cover and simmer 1 hour. Meanwhile, cook the small onions in boiling salted water until tender. Slice mushrooms and saute in 2 tbsp. of butter. Turn heat low and blend in the flour, after removing mushrooms. Add remaining butter and blend in. Add veal stock, adding water if necessary to make 1½ cups. Add lemon juice and half the wine. Cook until slightly thickened. Beat egg yolks with cream and add to stock. Heat for 10 minutes, just under boiling, stirring. Combine veal, onions, and mushrooms. Sprinkle with balance of wine, then pour sauce over all. Hold hot in oven, and serve to 6 guests whom you wish to impress with your expertise in foreign cookery. G-O-O-D.

CHICKEN IN WINE

This palate zinger is a sort of chicken-wine stew from Southern France, where the grapes hang low and the people are high—or they should be, from the amount of wine they drink and cook with. Start this one with a bottle of medium red wine, so you can taste as you go, now and then. Uncork the wine and taste to see if it is dry enough—m-m-m, it is? Now, just once more to make sure—okay, are you ready?

What
2 3 lb. chickens, cut up
24 small white onions
½ lb. salt pork, in fine strips
½ lb. fresh mushrooms, sliced

¼ tsp. each, pepper and paprika
1 tsp. salt
⅛ tsp. nutmeg
¼ cup flour
2 cups dry red wine
½ tsp. sugar
2 cloves minced garlic
2 celery tops
⅛ tsp. thyme
⅛ tsp. rosemary
6 sprigs parsley
1 large bay leaf

How
Combine salt, pepper, paprika, nutmeg, and flour in a paper bag. Shake to blend, and shake chicken pieces in the bag, a few at a time, until well coated. Cook salt pork strips in skillet until brown, and discard. Cook chicken pieces until brown on all sides, in the pork fat. Add onions and brown lightly. Saute mushrooms lightly, then pour off fat. Add remaining ingredients except flour and cook, covered, until chicken is tender, about 1 hour. Remove chicken, celery, parsley, and bay leaf from pan. Blend flour with enough water to be smooth, and stir into stock in pan. Stir-cook until thick, then return chicken to pan and reheat. Serves 6.

STUFFED CABBAGE STEW

This one is courtesy of Czechoslovakia, and I am assured it has been carefully Czeched for goodness!

What
1½ lb. ground lean pork
¾ lb. lean ground beef
Large head of green cabbage

⅔ cup raw rice
1 slice bacon, minced, raw
1½ lb. sauerkraut
1 20 oz. can tomatoes
1 crushed bay leaf
½ cup water
1½ tsp. salt
1 medium onion, chopped fine
1 cup sour cream (optional)

How
Remove a dozen of the large outside leaves of the cabbage, and blanch 4 minutes in boiling water. Drain well. In a bowl, combine pork, beef, onion, 1 tsp. salt, pepper, minced bacon, and rice. Mix well and divide into 12 equal balls. Place 1 ball in each cabbage leaf and roll up loosely, tucking ends under securely. Chop remaining cabbage coarsely. Put a layer of drained sauerkraut in the bottom of a large kettle, using half of it. Arrange half of the chopped cabbage on top of the kraut. Pour in half of tomatoes. Arrange 6 of the stuffed cabbage rolls on top of cabbage in kettle. Repeat. Sprinkle bay leaf and ½ tsp. salt over top. Add ½ cup of water. Cover and cook slowly 2 to 2½ hours. If desired, stir sour cream in gently before serving. Serves 6.

ARROZ CON POLLO

Spanish foolery—*arroz* is rice and *pollo* is chicken. Devious, isn't it? Or maybe you knew it all the time? This makes the title just a throwaway line. Eats nicely, though.

What
1 3 lb. chicken, cut in pieces
½ cup olive (or salad) oil
2 medium onions, chopped
1 clove garlic, minced

3 cups chicken broth
2 medium tomatoes
¼ tsp. pepper
1 tsp. oregano
2 tsp. salt
¾ cup fresh or frozen peas
4 pimentos, cut in strips
2 tbsp. chopped parsley
1 cup raw rice
2 tbsp. dry red wine

How
Make broth with 2 cups water and then add the chicken giblets and cook 30 minutes. Brown chicken pieces in oil, making sure oil is about ¼ inch deep in the skillet; cook slowly to brown on all sides. Remove from pan and fry onions and garlic until tender. Put chicken back in pan. Add wine and water to chicken broth to make 3 cups, and add to pan with tomatoes, salt, pepper, and oregano. Cover and simmer 20 minutes. Add peas, pimento strips, 1 tbsp. parsley (1 tbsp. parsley to be saved for garnish), and the rice. Cover tightly and cook 30 minutes until rice is soft and liquid is absorbed. Serves 4.

PENN-DUTCH CHICKEN STEW

What
1 5 lb. boiling fowl, cut up
2 small onions, peeled
1 stalk celery with top
1 carrot
1½ tsp. salt
½ tsp. pepper
2 tbsp. flour
¾ cup cold water

How

Put chicken, vegetables, and seasonings in deep kettle. Add water to cover. Bring to a boil, skim after 5 minutes. Cover and cook slowly 2 hours. Remove vegetables and discard. Stir in flour and water, and cook smooth.

FLUFFY DUMPLINGS

What

1½ cups sifted all-purpose flour
2 tsp. baking powder
½ tsp. salt
1 egg, beaten
½ cup milk

How

Sift flour, baking powder, and salt together. In another bowl, beat egg until it's light, then beat in milk. Mix quickly into dry ingredients. Batter should be heavy and rather dry, but completely moistened. Drop by tablespoonfuls on top of stew. Cover and cook for 15 minutes, without peeking. Peeking makes heavy dumplings! Serves 6.

OXTAIL STEW

What

3 lb. oxtails, cut 2 inches long
8 medium onions, peeled
½ lb. sliced mushrooms
½ chopped green pepper
6 medium potatoes, halved
2 tsp. salt
¼ tsp. pepper
1 tbsp. parsley flakes

8 peppercorns
4 tbsp. flour
¼ cup water
3 tbsp. shortening

How

Put 3 tbsp. flour, 1 tsp. salt, and the pepper into a bag, and coat the oxtails well, shaking in the bag. Brown in the shortening in a deep kettle. Chop 2 onions and add. Cook until soft. Add parsley, peppercorns, and 1½ cups hot water, then cover and cook slowly 2 hours. Add remaining onions and the potatoes, 1 tsp. salt and more water, if necessary. Cook 45 minutes. Add mushrooms. Mix 1 tbsp. flour and ¼ cup water, and add. Stir in and cook until thickened. Sprinkle chopped green pepper in just before serving. Usually served with green salad, crusty rolls, and red wine, to 6 lusty bone-chawers. Oxtail is for diners who like sticky-good meat with great flavor.

SOUTHERN SHORT RIB STEW

Besides being found where you're thinking, Southern short ribs are found on the Southern menus!

What

3 lbs. short ribs, cut serving size
1 20 oz. can tomatoes
¼ cup chopped onion
1 cup coarsely chopped celery
1 cup diced carrots
1 cup water
1 tsp. salt
½ tsp. dry mustard
½ cup dry red wine
1 tsp. Worcestershire sauce

⅛ tsp. Tabasco
3 tbsp. flour
3 tbsp. shortening

How
Trim excess fat from ribs and coat with flour. Cook ribs in shortening until well browned on all sides. Add tomatoes, salt, and water. Cover and cook over low heat until tender, about 1½ hours. Add chopped onions, celery and carrots, dry mustard mixed with Worcestershire, and Tabasco. Cook slowly, uncovered, for 30 minutes. Add a little water if necessary. There should be a thin gravy when finished. Serves 4. Usually served with steamed rice, hot cornbread, and pickle relish.

OYSTER STEW

Here comes that alleged aphrodisiac stew, for true believers!

What
1 quart oysters
¼ cup butter
½ cup minced celery
2 quarts milk
1 tbsp. minced parsley
1 tsp. salt

How
Drain oysters, saving liquor. Pick out any pieces of shell. Strain liquor. Place oysters in pan with butter and celery, and simmer 5 minutes. Scald milk and oyster liquor together. Add oysters and seasonings. Reheat and serve.

Oyster crackers, tossed in melted butter, and heated, go well with this, as a change from the mundane.

12

Hot Dishes from Erin

I searched all over for some famous old Irish recipes like shamrocks marinated in Irish Mist, or pig's trotters in Dublin Stout. I finally had to settle for colleens with Irish coffee, which wasn't too bad at all, now that I have reflected on it. The combined lift was great.

No collection of Irish dishes would be complete without several preparations of that grand old Irish staple, called a *pratie* in the Irish fields and homes, and the potato in less enlightened parts of the world. Together with usquebaugh (pot-still whiskey) the pratie has fueled some fine brannigans and energized the sires of many fine colleens. For the colleens, a deep bow to Eire, and for the whiskey, a fast side-step. (I tried it!) Some of those distillers-in-the-bog use forked lightning and brimstone as ingredients of their alleged potables. So, with these cautionary comments to guide you through the friendship rites, I leave you to enjoyment of the scenery (colleens), the quaint pubs, and the down-to-earth cooking of Ireland.

DAPPLED LAMB FRICASSEE WITH PIMENTO DUMPLINGS

I had this delightful dish in a small hotel within sight of the great Guinness Breweries. They used a Guinness product for flavoring, namely GYE (Guinness Yeast Extract). I have substituted Kitchen Bouquet or Liquid Oxo with equally good results.

What
1 large onion, chopped
1 clove garlic, minced or 1 tsp. garlic powder
2 tbsp. vegetable oil
2 lb. lean lamb shoulder, cubed 1 inch
3 tbsp. flour
1 16 oz. can tomatoes
1 cup water
2 tsp. salt
1 tsp. ground cumin
¼ tsp. ground coriander
¼ tsp. pepper
2 large carrots, halved and cut 1 inch long
2 stalks celery, sliced
1 package frozen green peas

How
Saute onion and garlic in the oil until soft. Add lamb cubes, dredged in flour, and brown slowly all around. Stir in tomatoes, water, salt, pepper, cumin, and coriander. Simmer, covered, 1¾ hours. Stir in carrots and celery, and simmer 15 minutes. Now mix:

Pimento Dumplings
Combine 2 cups biscuit mix, ⅔ cup milk, and ¼ cup finely chopped pimento. Stir lightly until evenly mixed. Now, add the frozen peas and 1 tsp. Kitchen Bouquet to the fricassee. When boiling, drop the dumpling batter in tablespoons on top. Do not cover. Cook 10 minutes, then cover. Cook until dumplings are puffed and dry on top (about 10 minutes). This serves 8 Irish gourmets, but the chef generously

allowed me to eat it also, even though I did not have the
stamp of the shamrock.

GALWAY PUB OYSTERS

This gourmet's poem comes from a little pub quite close to
Galway Bay. Their oysters are wonderful. Suitably armed
with a bottle of liquid friendship, I induced the chef to let
me watch the preparation of this dish.

What
6 potatoes, peeled and sliced thin
1 onion, sliced thin
½ tsp. salt
⅛ tsp. pepper
½ tsp. thyme
2 tbsp. chopped parsley
6 slices bacon
1 dozen oysters
½ pint oyster liquor
½ pint cream
3 tbsp. melted butter
1½ tbsp. flour

How
Butter a good sized flat baking dish, about 8 x 10 inches,
about 2 inches deep. Layer the potato slices and onion slices
in the bottom. Sprinkle on half the parsley, salt and pepper,
and all of the thyme. Lay the bacon slices on top, pour on
half the oyster liquor, and bake 40 minutes at 375 degrees
until bacon and potatoes are both browned lightly. Mix
the flour and the rest of the seasoning with the cream and
oyster liquor. Pour over the bacon and potatoes, and bake
until sauce starts to bubble vigorously. Drop in the oysters

and bake 5 minutes, just until the edges start to curl. Serve at once.

My memory of this dish will always be as green as the rest of Ireland!

IRISH CONSOMME

Enough for Conan the Conqueror!

This is a slow-simmered stimulant, best made a day ahead.

What
3 lb. beef shank and 1 pig hock, or pig's foot
3 quarts water
1 leek
3 large onions, unpeeled
2 large carrots
4 stalks celery
6 whole cloves
2 bay leaves
½ tsp. thyme flakes
8 peppercorns
2 tsp. salt
1 bunch parsley, tied well
4 tbsp. Irish whiskey

How
Bring meat to a boil, with cold water. Skim when scum rises. Add all the seasonings except whiskey. Add the vegetables slowly so pot does not stop boiling. Split and wash the leek and split the onions before adding. Cover and simmer 7 hours. Skim again, if necessary. Strain through sieve, using 2 layers of linen. Pour into jars or milk bottles. Chill. To serve, remove the fat and heat, then add the whiskey. This is a fine soup or gravy stock. Up the Irish!

POT ROAST PORK TENDERLOIN

This is a lusty and tasty (and expensive) pot roast.

What
2 pork tenderloins
1 cup fresh bread crumbs
Grated peel of half lemon
2 bacon slices, diced
1 onion, minced fine
1 lemon, halved
2 tbsp. butter
1 tsp. sage
½ tsp. salt
¼ tsp. pepper
1 egg
1 tbsp. butter
Flour
2 cups consomme
2 tbsp. stout

How
Split each tenderloin open along its length, cutting only far enough so you can lay it open. Rub all over with the cut sides of the lemon. Melt 2 tbsp. butter and add the onion; cook until soft. Remove pan from heat and add bread crumbs, sage, salt, pepper, and grated peel. Mix well and break an egg over the top, and mix well again. Put the stuffing on one side of each opened tenderloin, and turn up the tip. Put the second tenderloin on top, and turn tip under, inside the two. Sew or tie together. Roll in flour. Fry the diced bacon and add 1 tbsp. butter. Brown the pot roast in the fat, all around. Cover and bake at 350 degrees for an hour and twenty minutes. Remove to hot platter. Add 1 tbsp. flour to the drippings in the pan. Stir-cook until browned. Add the consomme and stout, and stir until the gravy is

smooth and slightly thickened. Serves 4 to 6, according to size of fillets.

IRISH POTATO STUFFING

What
8 medium potatoes
4 tbsp. melted butter
1 cup chopped onions
½ cup chopped celery
1 cup bread crumbs
½ tsp. sage
½ tsp. celery salt
½ tsp. savory
1 tsp. salt
¼ tsp. pepper
2 eggs, beaten

How
Pare potatoes, and boil under tender. Drain and mash. Add remaining ingredients and mix well. Stuff any kind of fowl. Any Irish guest will stuff himself!

BERKS COUNTY DUMPLINGS

What
6 medium potatoes
10 slices bread
1 grated onion
1 tsp. minced parsley
2 eggs, beaten
½ tsp. salt
¼ tsp. pepper

How

Peel and grate potatoes. Soak bread in cold water, then squeeze out as much water as possible. Mix together bread and seasonings, then add grated potatoes and eggs. Mix well. Form into walnut-sized balls and drop into boiling, salted water. Cover closely and cook 15 minutes without peeking.

DAIRY FARM POTATOES

What

2 lb. potatoes
½ tsp. salt
¼ tsp. pepper
⅛ tsp. nutmeg
⅛ lb. butter
½ cup milk
¾ to 1 cup of heavy cream

How

Peel and quarter potatoes, and boil until tender. Drain well and mash over hot water in a double boiler. Add salt, pepper, nutmeg, and butter and mix well, then stir in the milk and stir for 5 minutes over the boiling water. Put the mixture in a covered tureen, and pour the cream over. Cream should be just under boil, when poured in. Hold hot in slow oven, if not serving at once.

COUNTRY BAKED POTATOES

Use large potatoes, 1 per serving. Parboil 15 minutes, then bake (with skins) in 350 degree oven 45 minutes. Cook sausage meat and mash with cream, breaking up fine. Slice top off potatoes, and scoop out inside, leaving a wall to hold the sausage and cream mixture. Mash the potato scooped out, with grated cheddar cheese, and pile on top of potatoes. Brown lightly under broiler or in 450 degree oven.

IRISH DUMPLINGS

What
2 tbsp. fat
1 tbsp. minced onion
½ cup well-drained grated raw potato
5 cups boiled potato, riced and cooled
1 tsp. salt
¾ cup flour
2 eggs, lightly beaten

How
Fry onion in fat until golden. Add grated potato and cook until mixture forms a sort of paste. Let cool, and mix in other ingredients. Drop in walnut-sized balls into boiling, salted water. Cook until dumplings rise to the top, and are cooked through, about 15 minutes. Lift out in strainer, or drain.

SCALLOPED POTATOES

2 lb. raw potatoes
1 cup thinly sliced onion
½ tsp. salt
¼ tsp. pepper
½ cup cracker crumbs
1 pint milk
¼ cup butter
2 tbsp. sherry

How

Peel and slice potatoes thinly. Place a layer in individual greased casseroles, or 1 large casserole. Sprinkle with seasonings and crumbs. Dot with butter, and continue procedure until all the potatoes are used. Add milk and sherry. Cover and bake 1 hour at 350 degrees.

POTATOES ANNA

What

2 lbs. raw potatoes
¾ tsp. salt
¼ tsp. pepper
¼ cup butter

How

Peel and slice potatoes, thinly. Lay them pie fashion (in circles, overlapping) around a deep, buttered, pie pan. On each layer of potatoes sprinkle seasonings and dot with butter. Cover pan and bake 30 minutes at 375 degrees. Cut into pie-shaped pieces and serve.

DUCHESS POTATOES

2½ lb. potatoes
½ cup milk
¼ cup thin cream
2 tbsp. butter
1 tsp. salt
¼ tsp. white pepper
1 egg, separated

How

Pare potatoes and boil soft. Let steam 5 minutes after draining. Mash, then whip in seasonings and beaten egg yolk, and whip smooth. Form into balls, or any form that suits your fancy. Brush with egg white, and brown in 375 degree oven or under broiler.

POTATOES DELMONICO

What

4 cups chopped, cooked potatoes
1½ cups thin cream
2 tbsp. butter
½ tsp. salt
1 tsp. onion juice
¼ tsp. white pepper

How

Place potatoes in greased baking pan. Combine remaining ingredients and pour over potatoes. Bake 20 minutes at 350 degrees.

PRATIE SOUP

4 potatoes, peeled
¼ tsp. salt
⅛ tsp. pepper
1 leek
1 quart Irish consomme
½ pint water

How

Boil everything together until potatoes and leek are soft.

Remove them and mash, or rice into the stock. Beat well into the stock. This is a heart-warming dish when eaten hot, and is also eaten cold with sour cream and chives. May your shamrocks never turn blue!

PUFFED CAULIFLOWER

This is not only good in Ireland, but a tasty dish any place. Its richness must have contributed materially to the girth of some of the country colleens I saw.

What
1 cauliflower
2   tbsp. butter
2 tbsp. all-purpose flour
½ cup cream
1½ cups milk
1 tsp. salt
½ cup medium strong cheddar cheese
½ tsp. pepper
½ tsp. dry mustard
2 eggs, separated

How
Separate the cauliflower into flowerets, and boil 15 minutes, until barely tender. Drain well. Melt the butter and stir in the flour. Add milk and stir-cook until smooth. Add cream and heat. Add all of the cheese but 2 tbsp., and the dry mustard, and mix thoroughly. Beat egg yolks lightly, then add a little of the sauce and stir in. Return to sauce and stir in well. Beat the egg whites, stiff. Fold gently into the sauce. Put the cauliflower into a baking dish and cover with the sauce. Sprinkle with the reserved cheese and bake at 350 degrees for 25 to 30 minutes. Serves 5 or 6.

IRISH COFFEE

"A long life, and may your bones rest in Erin," say the Irish.
This coffee may delay the process. Make strong, fresh coffee.
Serve in large cups or tall, heat-proof glasses. For each serving
use 1½ tsp. fine sugar, 1 jigger Irish Whiskey, 1 to 2 tbsp.
whipped cream. Heat glass in hot water, and dry the outside
only. Add sugar, and a little coffee to melt it. Add the whiskey
and swirl a little. Fill glass to 1 inch below brim. Float on
the whipped cream. Do not shake or mix. Enables you to
jump a large bog on the third drink. Kindly do not stand up
while the room is in motion!

SNOWCAP AMBER

This is a light and delightful dessert. It is good with ice
cream, or even whipped cream, at which point you stop
thinking of calories and say, "Begorrah, who cares?"

What
6 to 8 peeled, cored, and sliced apples
¼ cup butter
¼ cup brown sugar
½ cup white sugar
3 egg whites
⅓ cup, plus 1 tsp. white sugar
2 tsp. water
1 tsp. vanilla, or 1 tbsp. Irish whiskey

How
Melt the butter in the frying pan, then the ½ cup white
sugar and the ¼ cup brown sugar, and stir until melted.
Add the apples and stir until well coated. Cook uncovered
over medium heat for 10 minutes, turning. Cover and simmer
over low heat for 20 minutes. Remove from heat and mash

apples with a fork, add the vanilla or whiskey, and stir well. Pour into 8-inch pie plates. Preheat oven to 350 degrees. Beat the egg whites and the 2 tsp. water together until stiffening. Add 1/3 cup sugar, a teaspoon at a time, beating between each addition. Spread over the apples, and sprinkle with 1 tsp. sugar. Bake for 30 to 35 minutes. Serves 6.

Also good cold, but do not refrigerate.

13

Gourmet Stunts
with Hamburger

So, you've decided to serve some variation of ground meat dish when entertaining friends. Some second-class citizen may elevate his, or her, nose, and say "hamburger," in a critical tone. Look incredulous. Elevate your own nose three degrees higher than did your critic, and answer sternly, "Ground steak is hardly hamburger. Ground steak is more flexible in the hands of a master chef than is solid steak." The gimmick is to never admit that you have even heard of hamburger. You can intimate that you select special cuts of meat for grinding, to insure the very best in flavor. This sidesteps the necessity of your admitting that you couldn't get into your bank vault to get out a Chateaubriand, or maybe couldn't float a loan to buy one. There are certain truths in your claim, also, provided you have the requisite skill to produce flavorful meat patties. In combination, two or more of ground meats such as beef, veal, pork, lamb, bacon, or sausage, can produce taste tempters par excellence. If you are clued up enough to use monosodium glutamate (M.S.G. or Accent), and the proper flavorizers such as wines and spices, you can prove your point about the superiority of ground meats in cooking.

If you are serving meat patties buffet style, putting them

on toast rounds, buns, or zwieback makes them easier to handle.

To keep meat patties juicy and rich, mix and shape lightly, and do not overcook. Beef is better when a little pink is seen inside. Pork patties, of course, must be cooked through.

To offer continuous combinations of flavor, it helps if you stock powdered mushrooms, dry onion soup mix, celery, onion, and garlic powder. These, in combination with recommended herbs and spices from the spice chart can make you a sought-after host. Whether or not this is good rests with you, and the ends in view.

SWEET AND SOUR MEATBALLS

What

1 8 oz. can cranberry sauce
1 8 oz. can tomato sauce
1 lb. ground beef
½ lb. ground pork
2 tbsp. dry onion soup mix
2 tbsp. salad oil
⅓ cup water
3 tbsp. lemon juice
1 tbsp. brown sugar
½ tsp. salt
⅛ tsp. each, pepper, garlic powder, oregano, thyme, and chili powder.

How

Mix meats well with seasonings, and shape into balls the size of a walnut. Roll in flour and brown in oil. Remove and add balance of ingredients to pan. Bring to a boil, turn down to simmer, and add the meatballs. Simmer 35 minutes, covered the last 20 minutes. Stir now and then to prevent sticking. Serve with or over rice. Exotique!

PANHANDLE CORN PIE

What
1 lb. hamburger
1 tsp. chili powder
1 14 oz. can corn niblets
1 large onion, chopped
1 tsp. salt
½ tsp. pepper
1 8 oz. can tomato sauce
3 cups mashed potatoes
2 tbsp. flour

How
Brown meat and onions in fat. Break up fine, and remove from pan. Retain 2 tbsp. fat in pan. Add flour and mix well. Add balance of ingredients except potato, and simmer 15 minutes. Turn into loaf pan, and top with mashed potatoes. Bake at 375 degrees until potatoes brown on top.

CHILI CON CARNE

Because of a diversity of opinion and locale, chili can be anything from liquid fire to a heart-warming meal. This recipe is for one that will not set fire to your socks, yet will prevent the ice in your highball from chilling you unduly!

What
2 lb. coarsely ground beef
½ cup minced onions
⅓ cup lard
1 pint tomato puree
½ tsp. minced garlic
3 tbsp. chili powder
1 tsp. sugar

1½ tsp. salt
1 #2 can spiced chili beans (or red kidney beans)

How
Fry beef, onions, and garlic in lard until cooked. Dissolve chili powder in 2 tbsp. water, and add with sugar and salt. Cook slowly until meat is very tender, with tomato puree. Stir in beans and heat well. Serve with rice timbales or spaghetti. Keeps well in refrigerator.

MEXICAN HASH

What
1 lb. ground meat
½ cup minced onion
½ cup minced green pepper
1 cup corn niblets
1 pint bread crumbs
½ pint tomato sauce
1 tsp. salt
½ tsp. cayenne pepper

How
Fry hamburger and onions until done. Remove and mix well with all other ingredients. Put in greased loaf pan and bake 50 minutes at 325 degrees. Serves about 10.

SALISBURY SURPRISE

Women love these filled goodies.

What
1½ lb. ground beef
1 tsp. salt

⅛ tsp. pepper
½ cup finely chopped onion
¾ cup undiluted evaporated milk
¾ cup rolled oats

How
Mix beef, seasoning, onion, milk, and rolled oats. Shape
into 12 flat patties. Place a portion of whatever type of filling
you fancy, in the center of half the patties. Cover with the
other patties, and pinch edges together. Brown well on both
sides under broiler. You can let yourself go on seasonings if
you wish. A choice of oregano, rosemary, garlic powder, or
sage may be used, as your taste or discretion dictates.

POWDER RIVER STEAK

Chopped steak de luxe—yummy in the winter—or anytime.

What
1 lb. ground beef
½ tsp. salt
½ tsp. chili powder
⅛ tsp. pepper
Pinch of garlic powder
¼ tsp. parsley
1 dash Tabasco
1 egg, beaten
¼ cup chopped onion (fine)
¼ tsp. oregano
1 14 oz. can of kidney or red chili beans
8 round slices of cheese
8 rounds of toast

How
Mix meat, seasonings, and eggs thoroughly. Shape into 8
patties. Brown in 1 tbsp. fat in fry pan, with onions. Remove

and keep warm. Add beans and dash with *Tabasco* (careful!). Heat to simmer. Place patties on toast rounds in baking pan. Spoon the beans over top, and top each pattie with a cheese slice. Toast under broiler until cheese melts. Watch any growing children who may be around, or you will get none for yourself. Snax for 8, food for 4.

PARMASTEAKS

What

1 lb. bround beef (better with half beef and half pork)
⅓ cup dry bread crumbs
3 tbsp. finely chopped onion
⅓ cup creamy French dressing
½ tsp. savory
¼ lb. grated Parmesan cheese
1 egg, beaten
½ tsp. salt
¼ tsp. pepper
6 slices French bread, sliced ¾ inch thick

How

Combine all ingredients except bread, mixing lightly but thoroughly. Shape in 6 patties the size of the bread, and broil on both sides until brown. Mix Parmesan cheese with 3 tbsp. softened butter, and spread both sides of the bread. Broil on both sides until slightly browned. Serve the patties on the toast.

BIFTEK AND MUSHROOMS

What

1½ lb. ground beef, or beef and pork
¼ tsp. garlic powder
⅛ tsp. pepper

¾ tsp. salt
¾ cup evaporated milk
¾ cup soft bread crumbs
1 can mushrooms
2 tbsp. finely chopped onion
¼ tsp. thyme
⅛ tsp. pepper
2 tbsp. butter

How
Mix all ingredients except butter and mushrooms. Form into
12 thin patties, and fry on both sides in a small amount of
butter. Remove and keep hot. Slice all but six of the mushrooms. Add balance of butter to pan, brown mushrooms
and slices lightly. Remove whole mushrooms and set aside.
Sprinkle flour into the pan (about 1 tbsp.) and cook, stirring. Place the chopped mushrooms on 6 of the patties. Top
with the other 6 patties, and place 1 mushroom on top of
each.

SALISBURY STROGANOFF

Surprised? Well, I was, the first time I tasted this. Regard-
less of the fact that you are using ground beef, this has a
taste that will really put you over the top as a chef extraor-
dinaire.

1½ lb. ground round or chuck
4 tbsp. tomato soup
¾ tsp. salt
¼ tsp. garlic powder
3 tbsp. finely minced onion
1 tsp. Worcestershire sauce
¼ tsp. savory
1 tsp. chopped chives
¼ cup sour cream

1 tbsp. tomato paste
1 tbsp. dry red wine
¼ tsp. fresh black pepper
1 tbsp. bacon fat

How

Mix together meat, garlic powder, bacon fat, Worcestershire, savory, salt, and pepper. Shape into small patties and fry lightly, until brown on both sides. Add onions to pan after removing patties, and brown lightly. Add sour cream, tomato soup, tomato paste, and wine to pan, and mix. Return patties to pan, and simmer until heated. This would make not only Stroganoff happy, but maybe Stravinsky and Stokowsky!

BOULETTES RIGAUD

What

1½ lb. ground lamb, or lamb and pork
1 tsp. salt
1 cup soft bread crumbs
¼ tsp. black pepper
2 tbsp. minced onions (fine)
1 tbsp. Worcestershire sauce
1 tbsp. dry red wine
12 slices side bacon
1 tsp. marjoram

How

Combine all ingredients except bacon. Shape into small thick patties. Wrap bacon around patties and secure with toothpick. Brown slowly in frying pan, and serve with bacon gravy.

BACON GRAVY

This is wonderful with all chopped meat patties. Warm

2 tbsp. bacon fat in pan. Add 2 tbsp. flour. Let sit five minutes to expand. Stir in 1 cup stock or bouillon, and return to heat. Cook and stir until thick, adding more stock or water until of desired consistency. Season with salt and pepper, and ¼ tsp. savory, if you like it. Any other seasoning spice, selected from the chart for its relationship to the meat you are cooking, is good.

KILLARNEY STEAKS

Called Killarney steaks because of the potato used with the meat.

What
1 lb. ground beef
2 cups coarsely grated potato
3 tbsp. fiinely chopped onion
1 tsp. salt
⅛ tsp. pepper
¼ tsp. marjoram
¼ tsp. M.S.G.
1 egg, slightly beaten
2 tbsp. butter
2 tbsp. flour
2 cups milk

How
Combine meat, potato, onion, seasonings, and egg, with 2 tbsp. of the milk. Shape into patties and fry brown on lightly greased griddle or pan. Remove to hot platter. Add butter to pan, remove from heat and stir in flour. Add milk, stirring in well, and cook until smooth and thickened, stirring steadily. Season to taste, pour over patties, and serve.

BEEF CRESCENTS WITH CURRY SAUCE

What
½ lb. ground beef
¼ tsp. salt
¼ tsp. curry powder
Pinch black pepper
1 tbsp. mayonnaise
1 tbsp. pickle relish
8 thin slices cooked ham
1 8 oz. can refrigerated crescent rolls

Curry Sauce

What
1 cup dairy sour cream
1 tbsp. butter
½ tsp. curry powder
¼ tsp. onion powder
Salt and pepper to taste

How
Combine beef, salt, curry, and pepper, and shape into fingers about 3 inches long. Fry until browned all around. Unroll crescent rolls, and separate into 8 triangles. Brush meat fingers with mayonnaise, roll in ham, place on base of triangle, dot with pickle relish and roll up. Bake on ungreased cookie sheet at 375 degrees for 10 to 15 minutes. Heat the ingredients of curry sauce together, but do not boil. Serve over rolls.

MEXICAN MEAT PIE

What
½ lb. diced beef (or ground)
½ lb. diced pork (or ground)

½ tsp. salt
¼ tsp. pepper
2 tbsp. cooking oil
3 tbsp. minced onion
¼ cup minced green pepper
1 tbsp. parsley
1 tsp. chili powder
1 cup buttered crumbs
¾ cup tomato puree, or undiluted tomato soup

How

Mix meat, and season with salt and pepper. Sprinkle with
1 tbsp. flour, and mix in. Cook onions, green pepper, and
parsley until soft. Combine all ingredients except crumbs,
and put in loaf pan. Cover with the crumbs and bake at 350
degrees for 45 minutes.

FRICATELLIS

What
1 lb. ground pork
½ tsp. salt
¼ tsp. pepper
¼ cup bread crumbs
1 tbsp. white wine
1 egg, beaten
¼ tsp. sage

How

Combine all ingredients. Form into thin patties and pan
fry until browned and well done. Excellent with scalloped
potatoes. Serves 4.

MEAT PIE

What
1 lb. lean ground beef

2 hard-boiled eggs
1 tsp. salt
½ cup cooked green peas
½ cup diced cooked carrots
1 pint brown gravy
1 recipe pie paste
2 tbsp. dry red wine

How
Fry beef until tender. Dice eggs and mix with meat, seasonings, peas, and carrots. Place in individual casseroles, pour on gravy to cover, top with pie paste, and cook for 20 minutes in 400 degree oven.

SALISBURY STEAK

What
¾ lb. ground beef
½ lb. ground pork
1 finely minced onion
1 tbsp. minced parsley
¼ tsp. celery salt
2 egg yolks

How
Simmer onions and parsley in butter until soft. Combine with balance of ingredients. Form into round steaks, place on greased baking sheet, and bake 20 minutes at 350 degrees.

MOCK FILET MIGNON

What
1 lb. ground rump or round
1 tbsp. beef suet
½ tsp. salt

½ tsp. sugar
¼ tsp. paprika
¼ tsp. pepper
4 slices bacon

How
Mix together all ingredients except bacon. Form into round, flat cakes 1 inch thick. Wrap with bacon slices, and secure with toothpicks. Broil or pan broil on both sides until brown.

SALBURGERS

What
1 lb. ground lean beef
2 tbsp. ground suet
½ cup bread crumbs
1 beaten egg
¼ cup finely minced onion
1 tsp. salt
¼ tsp. black pepper
½ tsp. grated garlic

How
Combine all ingredients and mix well. Mold into salburgers the right size for the buns you are using. Pan broil on both sides. Serve on hot toasted buns.

BEEF LOAF

What
1½ cups ground beef chuck
1 minced onion
2 tbsp. bacon fat
1 tsp. salt
1 tsp. sage

½ cup milk
2 tsp. Worcestershire sauce
1 cup soft bread crumbs

How
Saute onion in fat. Combine with balance of ingredients, and mix well. Pack into a greased loaf pan, and bake at 325 degrees for 1½ hours.

PINWHEEL MEAT ROLL

What
¾ lb. ground lean beef
¼ lb. ground lean pork
½ cup minced onion
2 tbsp. fat or oil
2 tsp. salt
1 egg, beaten
1½ cup chopped cooked carrots
2 tbsp. milk
6 tbsp. dry bread crumbs
¼ tsp. sage

How
Brown onion in fat, add carrots and ½ tsp. salt and mix well. Combine egg, crumbs, milk, sage, remaining salt, and onion and mix well. Place mixture between two sheets of waxed paper and roll ¼ inch thick. Remove top sheet of paper, and spread the mixture on the meat. Roll up jelly roll fashion. Bake at 350 degrees for 1 hour. Serves 4.

NEAPOLITAN MEAT LOAF

Since this loaf uses poultry stuffing, it is assumed the Neapolitans love stuffing. Makes a pretty tasty loaf, though.

What
1 lb. lean ground beef
½ lb. lean ground pork
1 onion, chopped fine
1 tsp. salt
⅛ tsp. black pepper
2 tbsp. dry red wine

How
Mix all this together and set aside. Now prepare:

Stuffing

What
3½ cups stale bread crumbs
1 cup tomato soup
1 tbsp. butter
1 tbsp. poultry seasoning
1½ tsp. salt
¼ tsp. black pepper
1 finely chopped onion
¾ cup finely diced celery

How
Pour the hot water (¾ cup) over the butter and crumbs.
Let stand a few minutes. Add the seasonings, then mix in
well the rest of the ingredients. Thorough mixing is a must.
Now, in a greased loaf pan, put a layer of meat, about ½
inch thick, then a layer of stuffing, and repeat until all is
used. Bake in preheated oven, at 350 degrees for 1 hour.
Serve hot or cold to 6.

14

All Those Leftovers

Whole books have been written on the using up of leftovers. Use of leftovers is a matter of character. If you have one of those ancestral memories attendant on the long use of clichés like "Waste not, want not," you have a problem, in that it gives you an acute pain in some sensitive area to throw anything into the garbage. You *must* reform.

I have stayed at boarding houses where I suspected that their only purpose in cooking was to produce leftovers for the week ahead. On the other hand, they may have had a bundles-for-boarding-house club and pickup service in the neighborhood.

I have been desperately trying to conjure up a recipe that uses a piece of stale cake, some limp lettuce, two tablespoons of dried-out yoghurt, 1 chicken wing, and a quarter of an avocado, to produce a taste-tempting dish. This effort was strictly from Endsville. After this failure I advise against using your refrigerator as dead storage between table and Disposall.

This attitude does not exclude the possibility of using some substantial leftovers that have a real future, like leftover roasts, corned beef, or spaghetti meat sauce.

In the fullest use of leftovers, a meat grinder is a valuable tool, as is a blender. You can change, hide, and blend ingredients into an entirely new and more palatable form.

PÂTÉ CHINOIS

Means Chinese paste in French—silly, eh?
This traditional dish is a kind of shepherd's pie. It's a fine way to use leftover roasts, or parts of several kinds of roasts. Start by grinding 1 lb. of the meat.

What
3 tbsp. brown jelly gravy,
    or
3 tbsp. cream
1 tbsp. bacon fat
1 onion, minced fine
1 can creamed corn
⅛ tsp. pepper
4 to 6 servings instant mashed potato
¼ tsp. thyme
Salt to taste

How
Fry onion in fat until soft. Mix well into meat with gravy and seasonings. Level in a casserole, and place corn on top. Prepare potatoes according to package directions, and spread on top. Bake at 350 degrees, until corn bubbles up around potatoes, about 25 to 30 minutes.

BAR HARBOR SALAD

What
1 cup leftover fish, flaked
4 firm   tomatoes
2 tbsp. capers
½ cup minced celery
2 tsp. prepared horseradish
½ cup chili sauce
1 bunch watercress

How

Quarter tomatoes without cutting through bottoms. Scoop out insides. Combine fish flakes, capers, celery, horseradish, and chili sauce. Fill tomatoes with this mixture. Serve on watercress. Garnish with sweet pickles and small pickled onions.

FLAKED FISH WITH MUSHROOMS

What

⅔ cup sliced mushrooms
2 tbsp. butter or margarine
4 tbsp. flour
½ tsp. salt
Pinch of pepper
2 cups milk
2 cups flaked fish
1 tbsp. chopped parsley
Toast slices

How

Saute mushrooms in butter 3 minutes. Blend in flour, salt, and pepper. Gradually add milk over very low heat, stirring until thick. Add fish and parsley, and reheat. Serve on toast.

MANHATTAN FISH CHOWDER

What

1 onion
2 tbsp. fat or oil
1 potato, peeled and diced
1 cup diced celery
1¼ cups cooked or canned tomatoes
¼ tsp. salt
¼ tsp. pepper

1½ cups whole kernel corn, cooked
1 cup flaked fish
Grated Parmesan cheese

How
Mince onion, and saute in fat. Add tomato, potato, celery, salt, and pepper. Simmer, covered, 15 minutes. Add corn and fish and heat. Serve over toast or toasted hard roll, split.

BAKED CURRY OF BEEF

What
1½ cups medium white sauce
1½ tsp. curry powder
2 cups chopped cooked beef
1½ cups cooked or canned peas
1½ cups cooked or canned carrots
3 tbsp. minced onion
2 hard-boiled eggs, sliced
¼ tsp. salt
¼ tsp. white pepper
2 cups cooked rice
Chutney

How
Combine white sauce and curry powder, well. Add beef, peas, carrots, and onion. Season, and mix. Pour into baking dish and top with the rice. Bake 20 minutes at 400 degrees. Garnish with chutney and egg slices. Serves 4.

CHOP STEWY

What
2 cups cubed lamb, cooked

2 tbsp. fat (bacon fat is best)
3½ cups water
1 tsp. salt
1 tsp. Worcestershire
1 cup finely diced celery
2 onions, chopped
1 cup canned peas
4 servings noodles

How
Brown lamb in fat. Add water, salt and Worcestershire, onions and seasonings. Cover and cook 20 minutes. Add drained peas, and heat. Drain off liquid. For 2 cups liquid, add 1½ tbsp. flour, stirred smooth with ¼ cup of water. In a separate saucepan, cook the sauce slowly, stirring all the time, until thick. Add sauce to meat mixture and heat, stirring. Serve over hot, cooked noodles. Noodles are better if they are buttered and held hot in the oven a few minutes before serving.

CORNED BEEF SLAW

What
2 cups cooked corned beef, cubed
1½ cups grated carrots
2 cups shredded cabbage
¼ cup chopped sweet pickle
¼ cup French dressing (shaken with pinch of garlic powder)
⅓ cup salad dressing or mayonnaise
Lettuce

How
Combine corned beef, carrot, cabbage, pickle, and 3 tbsp. mayonnaise. Serve on lettuce leaves, and garnish with remaining mayonnaise. Serves 4.

CREAMED HAM CAROLINA

What
1 can condensed mushroom soup
1/4 cup milk
1 cup cooked ham, cubed
2 hard-boiled eggs
3 tbsp. dry sherry
1/8 tsp. savory
1/8 tsp. pepper

How
Heat soup in top of double boiler over hot water. Add milk and stir. Add ham and eggs, sliced, with seasonings. Heat and add sherry, after removing from heat. Serve over hot cornbread or buttered toast.

HAM AND CHUTNEY SANDWICHES

Combine 1 cup cubed ham with 2 tbsp. chopped chutney. Spread on Vienna rolls, spread with mayonnaise. Lamb, roast beef, or other leftover meat, singly or in combination, can be used.

KING COLE PIE

What
2 cups cold beef, cubed
1 can cream of celery soup
1 can cheese-and-bacon soup
1½ cups biscuit mix
2 tbsp. butter, mixed with 2 tbsp. sherry

How
Combine beef with soups. Put in baking dish. Prepare bis-

cuit dough according to package directions. Roll out into
½ inch strips, ½ inch thick. Cover pie with woven pattern
of strips. Brush with melted butter-sherry mixture. Bake at
450 degrees for 25 minutes, in preheated oven.

QUICK SPAGHETTI CASSEROLE

What

4 cups cooked spaghetti
1 can condensed tomato soup
2 cups of any leftover meat, or a mixture of meats, or franks
1½ cups soft bread crumbs
2 tbsp. melted butter
1 tsp. oregano flakes

How

Melt soup in casserole while oven is warming up. Stir in
spaghetti and meat. Butter the crumbs with the melted
butter, and top the spaghetti mix with them. Sprinkle on the
oregano flakes evenly, and if you wish, sprinkle on a few
tsp. of dry wine. Bake in oven at 325 degrees for 20 to 25
minutes.

VEAL AND HAM MOUSSE

This is not the kind of mousse you can hunt in the woods.
While veal and ham is specified, any mixture of chopped
cooked meats will make the dish.

What

1 cup chopped cooked ham
1 cup chopped cooked veal
¼ cup chopped celery
2 tbsp. pickle relish
1 envelope (1 tbsp.) unflavored gelatin

2 tbsp. cold water
⅛ tsp. paprika
2 tbsp. minced parsley
¾ cup whipping cream
French dressing
Stuffed olives

How
Soften gelatin in cold water. Dissolve over hot water. Combine veal, ham, paprika, celery, and parsley. Whip cream, and fold in gelatin. Fold into meat mixture. Rinse individual or large mold in cold water. Pack gently with mousse. Chill until firm and unmold onto lettuce. Shake pickle relish with French dressing, and serve on the side. Serves 4 or 5.

CHICKEN CASSOLETTES

This uses up leftover chicken, giblets, etc. Melt 2 tbsp. butter and brown ½-inch bread cubes in the butter. Make 2 cups of cubes. To 1 can of macaroni and cheese, add 1 cup cooked chicken cubes. Mix in baking dish, and top with buttered bread crumbs. Pour over the top 1 can creamed corn. Bake in 350 degree oven 20 minutes.

CHICKEN SALAD

Use any leftover light and dark meat from chicken, including chopped giblets, if any.

What
2 cups chicken, cubed
1 cup finely diced celery
1 tbsp. grated onion
¼ tsp. salt

Pinch of pepper
Pinch of thyme
½ cup mayonnaise or salad dressing

How
Mix all the above together thoroughly. Serve on lettuce
leaves or in lettuce cups. If desired, garnish with asparagus
tips or pimento strips. Serves 4.

TURKEY HASH

You can use turkey, chicken, or duck in this dish.

What
2 cups cubed cooked turkey (small cubes, or chopped)
3 tbsp. minced onion
3 cups chopped cooked potatoes
½ cup milk
2 tbsp. minced parsley
2 tbsp. bacon fat (or oil if preferred)
¼ tsp. savory

How
Combine all ingredients except fat. Make patties and roll
in flour or fine crumbs. Brown slowly in fat. Serves 4. Serve
with tossed salad or cooked vegetable salad.

CURRIED CHICKEN CASSEROLE
(Or Beef, Or Lamb)

What
2 cups medium white sauce
1 tsp. curry powder
3 cups chopped cooked chicken

½ cup sliced mushrooms
3 cups cooked rice

How
Put all ingredients into a casserole and mix thoroughly.
Sprinkle 1 tsp. paprika over the top. Bake at 350 degrees
20 to 25 minutes. Serves 4.

TURKEY MUSHROOM SOUP

For this one you hammer the carcass of a roast turkey apart,
or otherwise reduce it to pot dimensions. If you crack a few
bones in your frenzy, so much the better, as bone marrow is
very flavorful. When you get it in the pot, add 6 cups water,
1 carrot. Split one celery stalk, top and all, and one small
onion, halved. Add ¼ tsp. salt, pinch of pepper, pinch of
thyme. Simmer 2 hours. Add ¼ cup raw rice, cover again
and simmer 20 minutes, until rice is tender (could take
30 minutes, rice can be stubborn in stock). Add 2 cans
cream of mushroom soup, and 2 cans water or milk. Garnish
with sliced Brazil nuts, or as they do in the South, chopped
peanuts. Serves 4 to 6.

15

Quickies and Make-aheads

Those cats who "just drop in to take pot-luck" hardly deserve to be fed à la gourmet. The term *pot luck,* I believe, derived from people who dropped in on a short-tempered host without warning, and the pot he absently-mindedly threw in their direction missed them. In my book, they should not always be so lucky. However, if you are going to be chicken, and not toss the uninvited guests out, here are a few things you can whomp up in a hurry. I know you are always torn between inventing a ptomaine special to teach them a lesson, and showing them that you can rise to the occasion with something palatable. They should hold their breath. Here is a sudden sort of soup you can make in ten minutes, and it's a pretty good stick-to-the-ribs dish.

OFF-THE-CUFF POTAGE PARMENTIER

What
5 slices bacon
½ cup fine-chopped celery
3 cups milk
1 tsp. salt
1½ cups boiling water
½ tsp. pepper

1 large onion, minced fine
¼ tsp. savory
1½ to 2 cups instant potato flakes

How
Fry bacon and drain on absorbent paper. To fat in pan, add onions and celery, and stir-cook until lightly browned. Add crumbled bacon, water, milk, and seasonings. Simmer 5 to 7 minutes, and whip in the potato flakes. Simmer 3 minutes and serve. 2 tbsp. dry white wine makes this good-good.

SAUSAGE WITH APPLE-WINE GRAVY

Most everyone has sausage, wine, and canned applesauce around. For this dish, you fry ½ lb. sausage until nicely browned. Remove from pan, and stir in fat and flour, equal quantities. Return pan to heat, and stir in ½ cup water, then 4 tbsp. applesauce, ¼ tsp. each salt and pepper, and stir-cook adding water as needed to make a smooth gravy. Add 2 tbsp. sherry. Return sausage to pan and heat 3 minutes. Keep sausage hot in gravy until serving.

APPETIZER SPARERIBS

What
2½ lb. fresh spare ribs, cut 2 inches long
2 slices onion
¾ cup sugar
2 tbsp. cornstarch
½ tsp. curry powder
⅛ tsp. ground cloves
¾ cup water
⅓ cup cider vinegar
2 tbsp. soy sauce
1 clove garlic, crushed

How

Cut ribs into single ribs, and cover with water, with 1 tsp. salt. Cover and boil for 45 minutes until meat is just tender. Drain, and chill. Mix sugar, cornstarch, curry, and cloves in a saucepan. Add balance of ingredients and stir-cook until sauce thickens. Bring oven to 350 degrees. Put ribs in pan on rack, using a large enough pan to baste all ribs. Brush with sauce, turning and brushing until a nice glaze results. Hold in a 250 degree oven until serving. These ribs may be made ahead and kept several days in the refrigerator, if you put them in a bowl and pour the sauce over them. Reheat long enough to renew the glaze.

MAKE-AHEAD SPARERIBS

What

3 to 4 lbs. spare ribs
1 onion, sliced thin
1 lemon, sliced thin
1 cup ketchup
⅓ cup Worcestershire sauce
1 tsp. chili powder
2 cups water
Dash of tabasco

How

The day before you want these ribs, arrange them, fat side down, in strips, in shallow roasting pan. Place slices of lemon and onion on top, and roast, uncovered in a 450 degree oven for 30 to 40 minutes. Combine the balance of the ingredients in a small saucepan and bring to a boil. Baste ribs with the sauce. Reduce heat to 350 degrees, and bake one hour, basting frequently. For serving, reheat in foil, in a 300 degree oven or on a hibachi or barbecue. Serves 4, or sometimes only 2 guests—depending on what kind of guests you have.

VEAL AND HAM LOAF

Serve hot or cold.

What
2 lb. lean veal shoulder
1 lb. minced raw ham
1 cup finely crushed soda crackers
1 can tomato soup (as is)
6 tbsp. fine-chopped onion
½ tsp. oregano
1 tsp. Worcestershire sauce
¼ tsp. pepper
1½ tsp. salt
1 tsp. paprika

How
Combine all ingredients except the water. Spoon the mixture into a greased loaf pan, and press down well into corners. Pour over the loaf ½ cup boiling water, and bake at 350 degrees for 1½ hours. If serving cold, chill with a weight on the meat to make a firm loaf. Serves 6 to 8, or makes very good sandwiches.

SUDDEN SEAFOOD CASSEROLE

This can be made with canned seafood, shrimp, lobster, crab, tuna, or any leftover fish you may have. You can also use several different soups as a base, such as cream of mushroom, celery, or asparagus.

1 cup cooked rice, and 1 cup cooked seafood, or up to 3 cups per undiluted can of soup, with 3 cups rice. Put rice in the bottom of a casserole, and spread evenly. Spread drained seafood on top. Cover with 1 can cream soup, and sprinkle with 3 tbsp. sherry. Combine ½ cup breadcrumbs

with ⅓ cup melted butter. Spread evenly on top of soup. Bake uncovered at 375 degrees for 35 minutes. Garnish with watercress or strips of pimento. This is an elastic dish and you can build it up for any number of (gr-r-r) uninvited guests.

RANCH WAGON BAKED BEANS

What

3 20 oz. cans baked kidney beans, deep browned beans, or any kind that suits your fancy
1 large onion, chopped
1 garlic clove, minced
3 tbsp. salad oil
½ cup diced celery
1 8 oz. can tomato sauce
1 tbsp. cider vinegar
1 tbsp. chili powder
3 tbsp. ketchup

How

Brown the onion and garlic lightly in salad oil. Add the celery and stir-cook 3 minutes. Remove from the heat and add the tomato sauce, vinegar, chili powder, and ketchup. Add the beans and mix well. Simmer over low heat for 1 hour, or until most of the liquid is evaporated. Serve hot on toast, or with toast, or garlic bread. Serves 6 to 8 wagoneers.

CORNED BEEF CASSEROLE

What

1 10 oz. can cream of celery soup
1 cup cooked green beans
1¾ cups hot water

1 12 oz. can corned beef, chopped
1⅓ cups precooked rice
½ cup canned French fried onion rings

How
Mix soup with hot water and add green beans. Pour half of
the soup mixture into a 1½ quart casserole. Spread corned
beef over soup, evenly. Sprinkle in a layer of rice. Pour in
remaining soup mixture. Cover and bake 10 minutes. Stir
mixture gently, level off, and cover with onion rings. Return
to oven and bake 25 minutes longer, uncovered.

CHEESE FISH BAKE

What
1 lb. fillets of any white fish
110 oz. can cheddar cheese soup
1 tbsp. instant minced onion
1 tsp. dried parsley
¼ tsp. marjoram

How
Preheat oven to 400 degrees. Place fish in greased baking
dish. Pour soup over top. Sprinkle evenly with onion, parsley,
and marjoram. Bake 30 minutes. Serves 3 to 4.

SEA ISLAND BEEF STEW

What
2 cups cooked rice
2 tbsp. melted butter
1 1½ lb. can beef stew
1 8 oz. can small onions
½ tsp. curry powder
Pinch each of cinnamon, clove, ginger

How

Mix butter and rice, spread in bottom of baking dish. Stir stew, onions, and spices together, spread over rice. Bake 35 minutes at 350 degrees. This may be topped with buttered crumbs, or slivered toasted almonds. Serves 4.

PIEDMONT LASAGNA

What

1/2 lb. lasagna noodles
1 cup cottage cheese
1/4 cup dairy sour cream
1 lb. lean ground beef
2 tbsp. vegetable oil
1/2 tsp. salt
2 10 oz. cans spaghetti sauce with mushrooms
1/4 cup grated Parmesan cheese
1/4 tsp. white pepper
1/2 lb. mozzarella cheese
2 tbsp. vegetable oil

How

Cook noodles according to package directions. Drain and toss with 2 tbsp. oil, until well coated. Combine cottage cheese with sour cream. Brown beef in remaining 2 tbsp. oil. Stir in spaghetti sauce, salt, and pepper. In a 9 x 9 x 2 inch baking dish spread 1/3 of the noodles. Pour in 1/3 of the meat sauce. Spoon 1/2 the cottage cheese mixture over the meat sauce. Sprinkle with 1/2 the Parmesan cheese. Cut eight thin slices of mozzarella. Cube remaining cheese and sprinkle 1/2 the cubes into baking dish. Repeat the noodle, meat sauce, and cheese layers. Top with noodles, sauce, and cheese remaining. Lay the mozzarella slices over the top, and bake 40 to 45 minutes in 350 degree oven. Serves 8 or 9.

SNOW-CAPPED FRANKS

What

8 large frankfurters
1 4½ oz. pkg. of instant mashed potato with sour cream sauce mix

How

Split franks lengthwise, almost through. Prepare potato according to package directions. Lay franks open in flat baking dish and pile potatoes on each as stuffing. Spread top with sour cream sauce. Bake in 450 degree oven until lightly browned, about 12 minutes. Serves 4.

TUNA RAREBIT

What

1½ cups tuna fish
½ tsp. salt
¼ lb. grated cheddar cheese
1 tbsp. Worcestershire sauce
2 tbsp. dry sherry (optional)
1 tbsp. butter
1 tbsp. flour
½ tsp. dry mustard
1 cup milk
1 egg

How

Melt butter, stir in flour until well mixed, then blend in mustard. Gradually add milk, stirring over low heat until thickened. Beat egg with grated cheese, and stir slowly into sauce. Cook-stir until thick and creamy. Add salt, Worcestershire, and tuna, and heat. Remove from heat and stir in sherry. Serves 4.

TUNA SCALLOP

What

1 6 oz. pkg. noodles
2 cups tuna fish
1 cup grated mild cheddar
3 tbsp. butter
2 tbsp. flour
1¼ cups milk
Pinch of salt and pepper
2 tbsp. dry white wine

How

Cook noodles according to package directions. Drain and toss with 1 tbsp. butter until coated. Melt 2 tbsp. butter and add 2 tbsp. flour. Blend well and stir in milk slowly, and stir-cook until smooth and thick. Put a layer of noodles in baking pan, then a layer of tuna, sprinkle with cheese, and repeat until you run out of stuff. Bake 20 minutes at 400 degrees.

SALMON À LA KING CROQUETTES

What

2 cups salmon
2 eggs
½ cup chopped cooked mushrooms
2 tbsp. water
2 tbsp. butter
2 tbsp. flour
¾ cup milk
¼ cup dry breadcrumbs

How

Melt butter, stir in flour, and add milk. Stir-cook until thick. Combine salmon, sauce, and mushrooms and chill

well. Form into small patties and dip into egg beaten with
water. Dip in crumbs and fry in hot fat.

CLAMBURGERS

What
2 cups minced clams or whole baby clams
2 eggs
⅔ cup dry bread crumbs
2 tbsp. lemon juice
1 tbsp. onion juice
2 tbsp. minced parsley
½ tsp. salt
Pinch of pepper
4 large round soft buns, buttered

How
Beat eggs, add drained clams, crumbs, lemon juice, onion
juice, and seasonings. Shape into 4 flat round cakes, and
saute in oil or bacon fat, browning both sides on medium
heat. Split buns, toast under grill, and butter them. Serve
the clam cakes on the buns.

CRAB AND CHEESE FONDUE

What
1 cup crabmeat
1 cup fine-diced celery
3 tbsp. mayonnaise
1 tbsp. prepared mustard
¼ tsp. salt
8 thin bread slices
2 eggs
1 cup milk

8 slices of cheese
1 tbsp. Worcestershire sauce
2 tbsp. dry sherry

How
Combine crab meat, celery, mayonnaise, mustard, and salt.
Spread on bread to make four sandwiches. Cut sandwiches
in two. Alternate layer of sandwiches and layer of cheese
in a greased baking dish. Beat eggs, add milk, Worcestershire,
and sherry. Pour over sandwiches. Cover baking dish and
bake at 325 degrees for 45 minutes. Serves 4.

CORNED BEEF HASH

2 cups chopped corned beef, mixed with 3 cups chopped,
cooked potato, 8 tbsp. minced onion and ½ cup milk. Season
with salt and pepper, and squeeze into patties. Dust with
flour, an brown on both sides in fat or oil. Serves 4.

CORNED BEEF PATTIES

What
2 cups chopped corned beef
½ cup fine chopped onion
1 cup cooked rice
2 eggs
1 tbsp. Worcestershire sauce
½ tsp. salt
¼ tsp. pepper
4 tbsp. tomato juice

How
Combine beef, rice, and onion. Beat eggs with tomato sauce,
or juice, Worcestershire, salt, and pepper. Add to beef mix.
Fry in patties, in bacon fat or oil. Serves 4.

SHEPHERD'S PIE

What
1 lb. ground chuck of beef
1 lb. ground lean pork
1/4 cup fine chopped onion
2 eggs, beaten
2 1/2 cups crushed crackers
1/4 tsp. pepper
1/2 tsp. salt
1/2 tsp. sage
1/2 cup evaporated milk
1/2 cup minced onion (green)

How
Combine beef, pork, onions, cracker crumbs, beaten eggs, and seasonings. Add milk and mix all together, well. Put in greased loaf pan and bake 1 hour, at 350 degrees. Top with 6 to 8 servings of mashed potato (instant will do) and bake another half hour until potatoes are browned. Serves 6 to 8.

HAM CUTLETS

What
2 cups ground cooked ham
1 tbsp. chopped parsley
1 tbsp. ketchup
1 egg
1 tbsp. butter
2 tbsp. water
1 tbsp. flour
3/4 cup milk
Dry crumbs

How
Combine ham, parsley, and ketchup. Beat egg with water.

Melt butter and stir in flour. Add milk and stir-cook until thick. Add to ham mixture and chill thoroughly. Shape in small cutlets. Roll in crumbs, then in beaten egg, then in crumbs. Fry in deep fat or oil at 375 until done. Serves 4.

SOUTHERN HASH

This is not an election in Mississippi, as you may have feared!

What
1 lb. lean ground veal
2 large onions
3 tbsp. fat or oil
2½ cups cooked tomatoes
1 cup cooked rice
1 tsp. chili powder
1 tsp. salt
¼ tsp. pepper

How
Slice onions and brown in fat. Add veal and brown well. Add balance of ingredients and simmer covered until rice is tender. Serves 4.

16

Hawaii Calling

Of course you could go down to Hawaii for your food, where a bunch of splay-footed descendants of Duke Kahanamoku come roaring in out of the surf on surfboards and stomp your wallet flat.

While you sit on your fat lanai, the natives will serve you marinated fish with pineapple chunks in hollowed-out coconut shells, or marinated fish with shredded coconut in hollowed-out pineapple shells. This profitable caper enables the natives to eat off bone china at home. Of course at times they offer a palliative sauce made of bananas mashed into coconut milk and fermented. When laced with 100 proof rum this is really something else.

At one time shrimp formed the base of many native dishes. However, since shrimp became so popular in American dishes, the natives can no longer afford shrimp as a meal at home. Instead, they eat cheaper things like pheasant sprinkled with gold dust, and garnished with emeralds, all as a result of selling native shrimp dishes to the tourists.

They also have a sticky mess called poi, that is eaten with the fingers. The most that can be said for poi is that it tastes a little like used glue, and is unlikely to replace steak and potatoes as an American staple. I also doubt that a plantain leaf will ever supplant our Delft china as a serving dish.

At dinners in the Polynesian Islands, native girls in grass

skirts decorate the good things with colorful leaves and grasses. It is said that the fringes of grass do nothing to prevent easy access to the more delectable dishes.

There is, however, no gainsaying the fact that a judicious marriage of the fruits and juices of Polynesia with some of our North American viands can be most fortunate. So, get your favorite lei and your grass skirt and pitch your own private luau. Keep those wahine happy.

Note
In the Hawaiian hotels, they also serve dishes from all over Polynesia, Indonesia, and China, reflecting the nationalities of their chefs.

DIAMOND HEAD STEAKS

If you can visualize a grass-skirted gourmet shivering with delight, you have some idea of the result you can get with this inexpensive dish. The flavor is frabjous. The descriptive phrase is luau-wow!

What
1 lb. ground lean beef or lean pork
2 tbsp. chopped onion
1 tbsp. soy sauce
½ tsp. salt
½ tsp. ground ginger
½ tsp. sugar
⅛ tsp. garlic powder
1 tsp. wine vinegar
1 can sliced pineapple

How
Drain pineapple and save juice. Make a teriyaki sauce by combining soy sauce, ginger, sugar, garlic powder, and salt

with the wine vinegar. Mix 2 tsp. of this sauce with the meat
and onion. Add 2 tbsp. of pineapple juice and mix well.
Shape into 4 thick patties. Brown well in frying pan or under
broiler. Dip pineapple slices in the remaining teriyaki sauce
and grill for a few minutes. Serve patties between pineapple
slices, with sweet potatoes, to 4.

FILLET OF SOLE OAHU

What
1 lb. fillet of sole
1 egg
¼ cup cornmeal
1 firm   large banana

How
Beat egg lightly with 1 tbsp. milk. Season cornmeal with
salt and pepper. Dip fillets into egg, then roll in cornmeal.
Put in a pan in a 400 degree preheated oven, and bake 10
minutes. Slice banana in 4 slices, lengthwise. Brush with
pineapple juice and sprinkle with parsley. Lay a slice on each
fillet, and bake 10 minutes more. Heaven can wait.

Alternate
If you grill the fillets, grill lightly 5 minutes, 3 inches under
broiler. Then add banana slices, top with buttered crumbs,
sprinkle with lemon juice, and brown lightly.

SHRIMPS PARADISE

What
3 cans (4½ oz. each) large shrimp
1 large pineapple
2 large oranges

1 avocado
1 tbsp. lemon juice

How

Drain shrimp. Cover with ice water and let stand 10 minutes. Drain. Cut pineapple in half lengthwise. Core and remove meat leaving sufficient shell for serving in. Peel and section oranges. Peel and slice avocado, and sprinkle slices with lemon juice to preserve color. Fill shells with orange, pineapple meat, and avocado slices. Arrange chilled shrimp on top. Serve with Paradise Salad Dressing.

PARADISE SALAD DRESSING

What

2 tbsp. lemon juice
2 tbsp. dry white wine
1 tbsp. honey
½ tsp. salt
½ tsp. paprika
½ cup salad oil

How

Combine all ingredients and chill. Shake well before serving.

PATIO SHRIMP PLATE

What

3 cans (4½ oz. each) large shrimp
Lettuce
1 large cucumber, sliced

How

Drain shrimp. Let stand 10 minutes in ice water, and drain.

Arrange on crisp lettuce, with cucumber slices. Serve topped with patio shrimp sauce.

PATIO SHRIMP SAUCE

What
1 cup sour cream
1 tbsp. horseradish
½ tsp. salt
1 tbsp. grated onion
½ tsp. paprika

How
Combine all ingredients and blend well.

POLYNESIAN LAU-LAU

What
¼ lb. diced salt pork
3½ cups boiled chicken, diced
¼ cup peanut oil
2 lb. Swiss chard, or Chinese cabbage
1 cup chopped green onions
2 tsp. M.S.G.
1 tbsp. candied ginger, chopped fine
2 tsp. sugar
½ tsp. black pepper
¼ cup lemon juice
1 tbsp. cornstarch
1 tbsp. water
3 cups cooked rice

How
Saute pork in oil until lightly browned. Add chicken and stir-fry 3 minutes. Add chopped chard and onions and stir-

fry 5 minutes. Add sugar and seasonings and stir in thoroughly. Remove chicken and vegetables. Combine cornstarch, water, and lemon juice and stir-cook until thickened. Return chicken and vegetables to pan and toss in the sauce. Serve over hot rice. Serves 6.

LAMB CHOPS PELEE

What
2 lamb chops
2 rings of pineapple
¼ tsp. salt
¼ tsp. ginger
2 Maraschino cherries
1½ oz. white rum

How
Rub salt, pepper, and ginger into both sides of chops. Broil until properly done. Broil pineapple rings until lightly browned. Put chops on heated metal platter. Top with pineapple rings and cherries. Warm rum, pour over chops. Ignite and serve flaming to a couple of gourmet firebugs.

GINGER PINEAPPLE HAM

What
4 slices tenderized ham, ½ inch thick
1 can pineapple slices
½ cup bread crumbs
3 tbsp. butter
½ tsp. ground ginger
2 tbsp. flour, or 1 tbsp. cornstarch
½ tsp. chervil
2 tbsp. white wine

How

Saute ham slices in butter until lightly browned. Remove. Stir flour or cornstarch into butter, then add pineapple juice, stir-cooking until thick and clear. Add ginger and chervil and stir in. Remove from heat and stir in wine. Add enough pineapple gravy to the bread crumbs to moisten. Season with salt and pepper. Top pineapple slices with bread crumb mixture, and brown lightly under broiler. At the same time heat the ham in the gravy, without boiling.

POLYNESIAN CHICKEN
(Without Grass Skirt)

What

1 4 lb. roasting chicken
1 medium onion
1 #2½ can (3½ cups) sliced pineapple
4 tbsp. fat or salad oil
⅓ cup flour
1 tsp. salt
Pinch of pepper
2 thin slices ham
4 cups hot cooked rice
1 avocado

How

Saute ham lightly in 3 tbsp. salad oil. Wash chicken and dry, then disjoint. Mince onion and cook until tender in pan, after removing ham. Mix flour and seasoning, then dredge chicken pieces in the flour. Brown in pan with onion. Measure pineapple syrup and add enough water to make 2 cups. Add to chicken, cover, and simmer gently 1½ hrs. Dice ham and toss with rice. Saute pineapple slices in another pan with remaining fat or oil. Peel avocado. Halve lengthwise and remove seed. Slice thinly crosswise. Place rice in center of serving platter, and arrange avocado slices, pine-apple, and chicken around the mound of rice. If desired, gravy may be thickened to desired consistency and served over rice.

SEA ISLAND LOBSTER

What
2 cups lobster chunks
2 tbsp. butter
2 cups unsweetened pineapple juice
2 tbsp. flour
1/4 tsp. salt
1/2 tsp. curry powder

How
Melt butter, and stir in flour. Add pineapple juice slowly, stir-cooking until thickened. Add seasonings and lobster chunks and stir in. Heat to serving temperature. The natives serve this dish on a coolapoola leaf which they say grows in the shape of a bowl and tastes like fermented coconut milk. While you are looking for one of these leaves, I'll serve the dish in a scooped-out pineapple half, or even a soup plate. Judging from some of the recipes, the forest on the fringes of the luau bases must be piled high with coconut shells and scooped-out pineapple shells, from making these exotic dishes.

SEA ISLAND DRESSSING

Oho, you noticed the three esses in the dresssing. My Poly-nesian waiter sounded like a leaky steam valve, and every ess in a word was at least a trio, if not a quartet! That's com-munication, but whether you make this dressing with one ess or three, there's a new taste adventure for you.

What

1 cup unsweetened pineapple juice
1 egg
1 cup vegetable oil
2 tbsp. wine vinegar
2 tbsp. lemon juice
2 tbsp. sugar
¼ tsp. salt
1 tsp. chervil flakes
1 tsp. dry mustard

How

This dressing is easiest to make in a blender. You can use an electric mixer, instead of blender, also. Beat vinegar thoroughly into the egg. Add lemon juice and beat in. Dribble the oil in a few drops at a time. When emulsion starts (emulsion is thickening), add the oil faster and keep beating. Add all the seasonings and beat in, then beat in the pineapple juice. Excellent with shellfish, tossed salad, or fruit salad.

CURRIED PINEAPPLE AND SAUSAGE

What

1 lb. small pork sausages
8 slices canned pineapple
½ tsp. curry powder
1 cup pineapple syrup
1 tsp. cornstarch
2 cups hot cooked rice

How

Fry sausage. Remove, then brown pineapple slices in the sausage fat. Drain on absorbent paper. Mix cornstarch and curry powder, then add pineapple syrup. Remove all but 2 tbsp. of fat from pan. Add syrup and cornstarch mixture.

Stir-cook until thickened. Put rice in center of serving platter. Arrange sausage and pineapple around rice. Pour sauce over.

PORK CHOPS HAWAIIAN

What
8 pork chops
½ tsp. ground cumin
8 slices canned pineapple
½ tsp. salt
½ tsp. pepper
1 tsp. cornstarch

How
Brown chops quickly on both sides. Trim heavy fat off outside and fry out until 2 tbsp. of fat are in pan. Take chops out and season them, then roll in flour and return to pan. Finish cooking them slowly, making sure they are nicely browned. Remove from pan. Stir cornstarch into fat, then stir in enough of the pineapple juice to make a thick sauce. Serve chops with a slice of pineapple on each, and pour sauce over the top.

WAIKIKI BEANS

What
1 20 oz. can deep brown beans
1 large firm banana
½ cup pineapple chunks
1 tsp. lemon juice

How
Quarter banana lengthwise, then into 1-inch lengths. Toss with the lemon juice, and 2 tbsp. pineapple syrup. Stir into

the beans, with the pineapple chunks. Put in baking pan, sprinkle with buttered crumbs, and bake 30 minutes at 325 degrees. Not likely to make Cordon Bleu dish-of-the-month, but pretty tasty fare, nonetheless.

CHICKEN SALAD HAWAIIAN

What
1½ cups diced cooked chicken
1½ cups diced cooked ham
½ cup diced celery
¾ cup diced apple
Mayonnaise enough to moisten the foregoing
1 head lettuce
10 small or 5 large pineapple slices
2 medium tomatoes
10 stuffed olives

How
Combine chicken, celery, ham, and apple. Moisten with mayonnaise. For each serving arrange a mound of the chicken mixture in center of a bed of crisp shredded lettuce. Top each serving with 1 or 2 of the pineapple slices, depending on size. Insert carrot sticks through hole in center of slices. Garnish with tomato wedges and olives.

STUFFED PORK HAM ALOHA

What
1 fresh pork ham, 10–12 lb.
12 bananas
1 quart bread crumbs
1 tbsp. salt
1 tsp. cayenne pepper

1 cup applesauce
1 cup milk

How
Bone ham for stuffing. Dice half the bananas, and mix with crumbs, seasonings, applesauce, and milk. Press into the ham cavity. Sew up opening. Sear in 400 degree oven for 20 minutes. Reduce heat to 300 degrees and cook 3½ hours. About 10 minutes before the ham is done, slice remaining bananas lengthwise, and cover the meat with them. Allow to brown. Carve and serve.

HAWAIIAN SEA CHOWDER

Zingy, zesty stuff.

What
½ lb. salt pork, diced
2 tbsp. oil
1 large onion, chopped
1 lb. any white fish, cubed
1 lb. new potatoes, sliced
2 tbsp. lemon juice
4 tbsp. pineapple juice
4 ripe tomatoes, sliced
½ pint boiling water
½ pint milk
½ tsp. salt
¼ tsp. freshly ground black pepper

How
Saute diced pork until golden, and remove. Saute onions in fat until transparent. Add diced fish, sliced potatoes and tomatoes. Toss and fry five minutes. Add pork, water, and juices, and simmer slowly, covered, ½ hour. Add milk and simmer 5 minutes more.

Note

If you have a few shrimp to add the last 10 minutes of cooking, they add color to the dish, and maybe a little extra glamor. Serves 6 to 8.

CHINESE SWEET-SOUR PORK

Served over fluffy rice, or over chow mein noodles, this is a superb dish.

What

1½ lbs. lean pork shoulder, cut in strips, ¼ x ½ x 2 inches
2 to 2½ cups pineapple chunks
¼ cup brown sugar
2 tbsp. cornstarch
¼ cup wine or cider vinegar
2 tbsp. soy sauce
½ tsp. salt
½ tsp. white pepper
½ cup green pepper strips
¼ cup sliced green onions

How

Brown pork in 1 tbsp. hot peanut oil or other fat. Add soy sauce and ½ cup water and simmer slowly about ½ hour. Add cornstarch and sugar, mixed with ½ cup pineapple syrup. Add vinegar and seasoning. Cook-stir until sauce thickens and is well cooked. Add pineapple chunks, green pepper, and onion. Cook two minutes and serve with extra soy sauce.

CHICKEN LAU LAU

I first ate this dish in Hong Kong, but later found it just

as good at Trader Vic's. They used taro leaves in the East but I have used Swiss chard or Chinese lettuce with equally good results.

What
¼ lb. sliced salt pork
3½ cups large chunks of boiled chicken
¼ cup peanut oil
2 lb. Swiss chard, or Chinese lettuce
1 cup chopped green onions
2 tsp. M.S.G.
2 tsp. sugar
1 tbsp. finely chopped candied ginger
½ tsp. pepper
¼ cup lemon juice
1 tbsp. cornstarch
1 tbsp. cold water
3 cups cooked rice

How
Saute pork slightly. Add chicken and stir-fry in hot oil for 5 minutes. Add greens and cook 5 minutes. Add onions and seasonings and cook for another minute. Combine cornstarch, water, and lemon juice. Push chicken and vegetables to one side. Add cornstarch, and cook until gravy thickens. Correct to taste for seasonings, and thin with a little more lemon juice if desired. Serve over fluffed rice.

SHRIMP CHOW MEIN

What
2 cups cooked or canned shrimp
¼ cup salad oil
1 cup chopped onion
1 can condensed cream of mushroom soup
1 cup chopped celery

1 can bean sprouts
1 cup chopped green pepper
2 tsp. cornstarch
¾ cup cold water
¼ cup soy sauce
⅔ cup broiled sliced mushrooms
⅔ cup water chestnuts
4 cups hot chow mein noodles

How
Stir-fry onion, celery, and green pepper in oil for 2 minutes.
Add soup. Mix cornstarch, soy sauce, and water, and stir
into hot soup mixture. Stir-cook until thickened. Cut shrimp
in half lengthwise, add with mushrooms, water chestnuts,
and bean sprouts. Heat and serve over chow mein noodles,
with extra soy sauce on the side.

PINEAPPLE SHRIMP

What
24 large shrimp
1 tbsp. cornstarch
¼ pint pineapple juice
2 tbsp. soy sauce
1 tbsp. honey
1 tbsp. wine or cider vinegar
¼ tsp. powdered ginger
1 cup pineapple chunks

How
Blend cornstarch with pineapple juice, until thoroughly
mixed, and smooth. Stir-mix with soy sauce, honey, ginger,
and vinegar. Stir-cook until smooth and thickened. If shrimp
are raw, cook in boiling water, salted, for 7 minutes. Cool in
water they were cooked in, shell and clean. Cook lightly in

pan with butter until lightly browned. Add to sauce, and serve to 4, or 6 snackers.

NA PAPAI HOOPIHAPIHA
(Stuffed Crab)

What

½ lb. shredded cooked crabmeat
1 tbsp. butter
2 tbsp. chopped onion
1 tomato, peeled, seeded and chopped
¼ tsp. garlic powder
1 tsp. lime juice
Salt and pepper
2 tbsp. pineapple juice

How

Melt butter and saute onion 1 minute. Add tomato and garlic powder, and saute 2 minutes. Add crab and pineapple juice. Season to taste, put in crab or scallop shells. Sprinkle with lime juice, and serve. Makes 4 snacks.

CHINESE WALNUT CHICKEN

What

2 chicken breasts, raw, boned and cut in thin strips
¼ cup salad oil
1 cup coarsely broken walnuts
1 cup celery slices, sliced thin diagonally
1 cup onion slices
1¼ cups chicken broth
¼ cup soy sauce
1 tbsp. cornstarch
1 tsp. sugar

2 tbsp. sherry
⅔ cup bamboo shoots
⅔ cup water chestnuts
¼ tsp. finely chopped green ginger

How
Brown walnuts in hot oil. Remove to paper for draining.
Sprinkle chicken with salt and stir-cook 5 minutes. Remove.
Cook onion until tender, add celery and ½ cup chicken
broth. Combine sugar, cornstarch, soy sauce, remaining
chicken broth and add to pan. Cook and stir until sauce
thickens. Add ginger, and simmer 2 minutes. Add water
chestnuts and bamboo shoots, then walnuts. Reheat. This is
better if it stands an hour to develop flavor. Reheat or hold
hot over boiling water, at a very slow simmer.

TERIYAKI MARINADE

For beef, pork, chicken, shrimp, lobster. This marinade, both
for marinating and for basting, accounts for the distinctive
flavor of Polynesian and Oriental cooking, on braziers, bar-
becues, and chafing dishes.

What
1 cup soy sauce
1 clove garlic, split
1 tbsp. minced onion
2 tbsp. lemon juice
1 tbsp. sherry
½ tsp. ground ginger
1 tbsp. dark molasses
¼ cup brown sugar (packed)

How
Mix well, or blend in blender, all ingredients. Let stand at
least 24 hours in the refrigerator, to develop full flavor.

CEYLONESE MARINADE

For pork or fowl.

What
½ cup peanut oil
1 tsp. curry powder
½ cup dry white wine
½ cup brown sugar
½ cup soy sauce
⅓ cup minced green onion, with tops
1 tsp. ground ginger
6 coriander seeds or pinch of coriander

How
Blend peanut oil and curry powder. Add remaining ingredients and stir until sugar is dissolved. Let stand an hour to develop flavor. Keep refrigerated when not using.

ORIENTAL DUCK SAUCE

For egg rolls, shrimp, spareribs, pork strips.

What
1 tbsp. dark corn syrup
10 oz. plum, apricot, or peach jam
1 tbsp. white sugar
⅓ cup Indian chutney
1 tbsp. wine vinegar

How
Blend all ingredients in blender. Let stand a few hours to develop flavor.

ORIENTAL SEAFOOD SAUCE

What
1 cup crushed pineapple
1½ tbsp. soy sauce

¼ cup wine vinegar
2 tbsp. white sugar
½ cup chicken broth
1 tbsp. cornstarch
3 green onions, sliced thin
1 small tomato, peeled and diced

How
Put pineapple, soy sauce, and vinegar in saucepan. Mix
sugar and cornstarch, and combine well with chicken broth.
Add to saucepan and stir-cook until it is clear and thickened.
Add onion and tomato. Reduce heat and simmer about
4 minutes. Makes about 2 cups.

HAM STEAK CEYLON

What
4 ham steaks, ½ lb. each
4 sweet potatoes
6 tbsp. flour
6 tbsp. peanut or soya oil
¼ tsp. salt
Pinch of black pepper

Sauce
3 tbsp. peanut oil
1 tbsp. flour
4 tbsp. finely minced onion
½ tsp. dry mustard
½ tsp. tarragon flakes
2 tbsp. brown sugar
8 oz. champagne or pineapple juice

How
Broil ham steaks. Peel sweet potatoes and slice ½ inch thick.

Mix salt, pepper, and flour. Roll potato slices in flour, and fry in oil until lightly browned on both sides. Serves 4.

For the sauce: saute onions in oil until golden. Stir in flour, mustard and tarragon. Stir-cook 3 minutes. Remove from heat and stir in champagne or pineapple juice. Put steaks and potatoes on ovenproof platter. Pour sauce evenly over top and sprinkle with sugar. Heat under broiler.

KALA EMI
(Sparerib Crown Roast)

What

3 lb. meaty pork spareribs, cut in half lengthwise of strip
2 tbsp. soy sauce
1½ tsp. salt
½ tsp. black pepper
3 cups bread cubes
¾ cup chopped prunes
12 water chestnuts, chopped
1 orange, peeled and chopped
1 can pineapple tidbits (9 oz.)
¼ cup syrup from pineapple
½ tsp. tarragon flakes
½ tsp. ground ginger

How

Rub ribs with salt, pepper, and 1 tbsp. soy sauce. Form into circle and skewer ends, making a crown. Cut a circle of heavy aluminum foil, 5 inches larger than the crown. Stand crown on this. Mix balance of ingredients well and stuff the crown. Turn up sides of foil all around and bake at 350 degrees for 1½ hours. Cover with foil the first 45 minutes of baking, then uncover and finish. Have a pretty wahine serve it to 3 or 4!

MAUNA LOA SUPPER

We revised the native recipe a little in the interest of fast and easy preparation. The result is just as tasty as the original slow method of preparation.

What
2½ cups slivered cooked ham
3 tbsp. butter
1 green pepper, cut in strips
2 tbsp. wine vinegar
2 tbsp. brown sugar
½ tsp. dry mustard
½ tsp. salt
Black pepper, fresh
2 tbsp. cornstarch
1 can (15 oz.) pineapple chunks
1⅓ cups pineapple juice and water
1⅓ cups hot water
2 tbsp. chopped green onion tops
1⅓ cups minute rice

How
Fry ham gently in butter, until lightly browned. Stir in green peppers. Mix mustard with a little water, then with pineapple juice and water, vinegar, ½ tsp. salt, and the cornstarch. Add to ham. Stir-cook until thick and transparent. Simmer, covered, 5 minutes. Mix water and sugar with ½ tsp. salt and a pinch of pepper, green onions and minute rice. Make a well in the center of sauce. Pour in rice mixture. Cover and boil slowly 5 minutes. Serves 4 or 5.

17

That Wild, Wild Game

If you are addicted to game, wild or fair, proper handling is necessary to insure gourmet satisfaction. On some game, breast is one of the more delightful parts, and in the hands of the master the results will be all that can be desired. For instance, we offer:

BREAST OF PHEASANT, EN CASSEROLE

What
1 breast of pheasant, skinned
1 slice of ham
¼ cup butter
½ cup chopped mushrooms
¼ cup raw chicken livers, chopped
1 tbsp. finely chopped onion
½ cup beef broth
⅓ cup tomato sauce
Pinch of salt, pepper, thyme

How
Lard breast with strips of ham, rub in seasoning, and brown on all sides in butter. Transfer to buttered casserole. Mix in remaining ingredients. Bake in 350 degree preheated oven

25 minutes. Serve with brown or wild rice cooked in chicken stock, and a tart jelly on the side. Serves 2.

STUFFED WILD DUCK

What
2 mallard ducks, ¾ lb. each
1½ tsp. salt
1 tsp. black pepper
¼ cup white wine
3 tbsp. melted butter
½ cup chopped blanched almonds
4 cups mashed potatoes
2 tbsp. finely minced onions
½ cup finely chopped celery
½ cup rich cream
¼ cup butter
2 beaten egg yolks
1 tsp. salt
½ tsp. black pepper
½ tsp. tarragon flakes
½ cup orange juice
½ cup chicken stock or bouillon

How
Pluck ducks without scalding. Singe and clean. Rub inside and out with wet cloth. Wet another small cloth with the wine and rub inside and out. Saute onions and celery in the ¼ cup butter for 5 minutes. Mix contents of pan with potatoes, nuts, cream, egg yolks, 1 tsp. salt, ¼ tsp. pepper, and the tarragon. Stuff the ducks and sew up openings. Brush with the melted butter, and sprinkle with the pepper and salt. Place uncovered in roasting pan and roast 45 minutes in preheated 350 degree oven. After 15 minutes add orange juice and chicken bouillon. Baste frequently the last 20

minutes of roasting. A wild duck is done when blood does not run out when pierced with a fork. Serves 4.

GINGER-ORANGE DUCK

This recipe removes most, if not all, the wild taste from wild duck.

What
2 mallard ducks
½ tsp. black pepper
4 tsp. salt
2 tsp. ground ginger
2 tsp. thyme
½ cup butter
1½ cups dark honey
⅓ cup orange juice
2 tsp. lemon juice
Thinly sliced peel of 1 orange
2 oranges
½ tsp. dry mustard
2 tsp. arrowroot flour or cornstarch
4 tbsp. brandy
4 tbsp. red wine

How
Place cleaned and plucked ducks in game marinade for 3 to 5 days. Remove from marinade and wipe dry, inside and out. Mix salt, ginger, thyme, and pepper. Rub ¼ of mixture inside each duck. In a saucepan, melt butter and add honey, lemon juice, orange juice and peel, and mustard. Bring just to boil and shut off. Dribble 2 tbsp. inside each duck. Cut oranges into sections, with skin, and stuff into each duck. Pour 3 tbsp. of honey mixture into each duck. Rub balance of ginger and thyme mixture on outside of ducks. Truss and

wrap birds in heavy brown greased paper or aluminum foil. Roast at 325 degrees 2 hours. Unwrap and raise oven to 350 degrees. Roast 35 minutes more, basting often. Mix arrowroot or cornstarch with red wine and stir into pan drippings in a separate saucepan. Stir cook until smooth and thickened slightly. Put ducks on heated serving platter and pour sauce over. Pour in brandy and ignite. Serves 6 to 8.

MALLARD CHAUSSEUR

What
2 mallards, plucked and cleaned
2 cups chopped cabbage
2 cups chopped celery
1 cup chopped onion
1 tsp. dill flakes
½ tsp. thyme
1 egg, beaten lightly
½ cup bacon fat, melted
1 tbsp. Worcestershire sauce
½ cup dry sherry
1 cup bread crumbs
6 strips fat bacon
½ cup Sauterne
Salt and fresh black pepper

How
Wipe birds inside and out with a damp cloth. Rub inside and out with salt and pepper. Mix cabbage, celery, onion, dill, and thyme. Mix in egg, 4 tbsp. bacon fat, Worcestershire, sherry, 1 tsp. salt, and ¼ tsp. black pepper. Now, mix in bread crumbs. Stuff and truss the birds. Put on rack in shallow roasting pan. Bake in preheated 375 degree oven for 10 minutes. Baste with Sauterne and bacon fat, and lower heat to 350 degrees. Roast 20 minutes more, basting twice more. Serves 2 duck lovers or 4 casual diners.

WILD DUCK SOUP

What
4 or 5 duck carcasses, skin, and leftover meat
2 cups ham or beef stock
1½ cups dry white wine
2 tbsp. lemon juice
¼ lb. bacon, diced and fried
1 tsp. salt
½ tsp. fresh black pepper
1 small turnip, cut up
3 carrots, sliced
2 onions, sliced
1 cup chopped celery and leaves
½ tsp. savory
½ tsp. oregano flakes

How
Put all ingredients in large pot. Add water to cover. Bring
to boil and boil 5 minutes. Skim, and turn down to simmer.
Cover and simmer slowly, 2½ hours. Strain off soup. Chill
until fat rises to top and sets. Stock will keep a week, refrigerated. When ready to serve, remove fat and reheat. Serves
6 to 8.

MARINADE FOR GAME

Some people like game, but not the gamey taste. This marinade will heighten flavor and reduce the gamey taste. This
recipe will handle 2 ducks or wild rabbits.

What
2 cups dry red wine
1 cup salad oil
1 cup wine vinegar
2 onions, sliced

3 cloves garlic, sliced
1 tart apple, sliced
2 bay leaves, crumbled
6 peppercorns, cracked
2 tbsp. parsley flakes
1 sliced lemon
½ cup currants

How
Put all ingredients in a crock, and let stand 6 hours. Add game, cover, and keep in cool place or refrigerator 3 to 5 days.

SALMI OF PHEASANT

What
1 Pheasant
2 tbsp. melted bacon fat
6 medium-sized mushrooms
¼ cup white wine
4 tbsp. butter
2 tbsp. flour
¼ tsp. thyme
1 pkg. French cut green beans, frozen
Salt and pepper

How
Brush pheasant with bacon fat and sprinkle inside and out with salt and pepper. Put in baking pan with half the wine and 1 tbsp. butter. Roast at 375 degrees for 35 minutes, basting 4 times during roasting. Wash mushrooms and put in covered saucepan with 1 tbsp. butter, 1 cup water, and balance of wine, simmer covered, 15 minutes. Remove, and remove stems. Save caps, and chop stems finely. Melt balance of butter and stir in flour. Stir in liquid from mushrooms and stir-cook until smooth and thick—add chopped mush-

room stems. Add thyme, salt and pepper to taste. Disjoint pheasant and add pieces to gravy. Reheat before serving. Cook green beans according to package directions. Mound in center of heated platter. Alternate pheasant pieces and mushrooms around the edge. Serves 2 to 3.

ROAST QUAIL

What
8 quail
2 tsp. salt
1 tsp. black pepper
½ cup butter, melted
8 slices bacon
8 slices brown toast
¼ cup dry white wine
½ tsp. sage flakes (¼ tsp. powdered)

How
Pluck, singe, and draw quail. Wipe inside and out with wet cloth. Put ½ tsp. butter inside each. Brush outside with butter. Truss birds with 1 slice bacon around each, fastening with a toothpick if necessary. Put quail in buttered baking dish. Moisten with wine and sprinkle with salt and pepper. Roast at 375 degrees for 25 minutes. Put birds on toast and pour pan drippings over each bird. Serve garnished with water cress and lemon slices. Serves 4 to 6.

PARTRIDGE CASSEROLE

What
2 partridges
½ lb. mushrooms
1 cup milk

¼ cup chopped onion
½ tsp. sage
2 tbsp. butter
2 tbsp. flour
1 bay leaf, crumbled
¼ cup white wine
Salt and pepper

How
Split birds in half, and put in casserole. Add 1 cup hot water,
bay leaf, ¼ tsp. salt, wine, and onion. Chop the mushroom
stems and add. Cover casserole and bake at 325 degrees for
1 hour. Add mushrooms the last 20 minutes of cooking. Pour
off stock from casserole into a saucepan. Mix flour smoothly
into milk, and stir into stock. Stir-cook until smooth and
thickened. Add seasoning to taste, and pour over birds. Reheat and serve. Minted green peas and small parsleyed potatoes are a gracious accompaniment. Serves 4.

ROAST LEG OF VENISON—VOLGA

What
1 leg of venison, 6 to 8 lb.
10 slices of salt pork or fat bacon
2 cloves garlic, split
2 cups sliced onion
1 cup sliced carrot
1½ cups chopped celery
4 bay leaves
1 tsp. salt
½ tsp. black pepper
1 cup flour, whole wheat is best
1½ cups Burgundy or Chianti
3 cups dairy sour cream
1 cup currant jelly

How

Preheat oven to 450 degrees. Put low rack in roast pan. Add vegetables and bay leaves. Wipe roast with wet cloth. Rub with garlic and season all over with salt and pepper. Place on rack in pan and put in oven for ½ hour. Turn and put strips of salt pork or bacon on top. Close oven and reduce heat to 350 degrees. Roast 30 minutes per pound (180 degrees on meat thermometer). Remove roast to hot platter and hold hot until serving. Strain and skim the pan liquid, discarding vegetables. Melt the butter, stir in the ffour, add strained liquid, and bring to simmer, stirring until smooth. Stir in wine, sour cream, and jelly, and simmer slowly until thickened. Pour part over venison and serve balance in gravy boat on the side. Serves up to a dozen, depending on how they like venison.

SADDLE OF VENISON TOBERMORY

What

1 full saddle of venison
2 cloves garlic, slivered
¼ lb. fat salt pork or bacon
Salt and pepper
½ cup Chianti
3 tbsp. flour

How

Using a sharp, fine-pointed knife or the larding needle, insert slivers of garlic all along the fillet. Lard the fillet with thin strips of pork or bacon. Slice balance of pork and cover fillets. Roast in a shallow roasting pan 10 minutes in a 500 degree preheated oven. Baste with stock or drippings. Reduce heat to 350 degrees and roast 1½ to 2 hours, depending on size of saddle. Baste every 10 minutes. Remove meat, hold hot until serving. Mix the flour with 3 tbsp. water and stir and scrape into pan drippings. Add wine and stir-cook until thick. Season to taste. Serve with apple jelly mixed with horseradish.

HASSENPFEFFER

This famous dish is a staple in Germany, and if carefully prepared, is very tasty indeed.

What
2 rabbits, cut up
1 cup fine, browned bread crumbs
½ tsp. salt
½ tsp. black pepper
⅓ cup melted butter
¾ cup sour cream

Marinade
1 pint wine vinegar
2 cloves garlic, crushed with 1 tsp. salt
8 peppercorns, crushed
1 pint sliced onion
6 cloves
1 bay leaf, crumbled
1 cup celery, sliced thin
1 tsp. tarragon flakes

How
Combine all the marinade ingredients, and put in the rabbit pieces to marinate 8 to 12 hours. Drain and wipe dry, then rub in salt and pepper. Saute in the butter until lightly browned all around. Add 1 cup of strained marinade, cover, and cook until marinade is gone. Add ½ cup of marinade and cover. Cook 10 minutes more. Remove rabbit and keep hot. Stir bread crumbs and sour cream into marinade, and

stir-cook until thickened. Return meat to pan and reheat, turning in the gravy while heating. If you have been a good host in supplying ale and wine while cooking, you may be able to find 4 to 6 guests still in condition to eat. This is often served with oven-browned or casserole potatoes. I tried it with German hot potato salad, and it was very delicious in combination. The dish is sometimes varied by cooking cubes of fresh pork (about 1½ inch) with the rabbit. The flavor of the pork combines with the flavor of the marinated rabbit and the result is a poem of taste to remember.

RABBIT STEW

What
1 rabbit, skinned and cleaned
1 tsp. salt
½ tsp. pepper
½ cup bacon fat or lard
½ cup flour
1–2 can tomatoes
1½ pints beef stock or bouillon
½ tsp. basil
2 tbsp. red wine

How
Wipe rabbit inside and out with wet cloth. Disjoint into serving pieces. Mix salt and pepper into flour. Roll the pieces of meat in the flour and brown all around in the fat. Put in stew pot with balance of ingredients. Bring to boil, turn down to simmer, and cook covered for ½ hour. Serves 4.

CURRIED RABBIT

What
1 rabbit, skinned and cleaned

2 tbsp. bacon fat
½ tart apple, chopped
2 medium onions, chopped
2 tbsp. flour
3 tsp. curry powder
¼ cup raisins
1 tsp. lemon juice
2 cups cooked rice
½ tsp. salt
1½ cups ham or beef stock

How
Cut rabbit into serving-size pieces. Soak 1 hour in salted water. Drain and dry with cloth. Brown lightly all around in the bacon fat, transfer to a casserole. Fry onions until soft. Add salt and curry powder then sprinkle on flour and stir until fat is absorbed. Add stock and raisins and stir-cook 5 minutes. Pour over rabbit pieces, add apple. Cover and cook at 325 degrees 1½ hours. Squeeze on lemon juice, and serve. Serves 4.

HUNTER'S PIE—VENISON OR MOOSE

What
1 lb. ground venison or moose meat
½ lb. sausage meat
1 tsp. salt
½ tsp. oregano flakes
½ tsp. black pepper
1½ cups chopped onion
2 tbsp. tomato sauce
2 eggs, lightly beaten
¼ cup dry sherry
3 cups mashed potatoes

How
Fry out sausage meat until lightly browned. Remove to

drain. Cook onions in fat. Remove. In a mixing bowl, mash the sausage meat with a fork until well separated. Add 2 tbsp. of the fat, ½ cup mashed potatoes, sherry, venison, tomato sauce, and seasonings. Mix thoroughly with the egg and put into a greased loaf pan or casserole. Bake at 350 degrees for 1 hour. Top with balance of potatoes and bake 40 minutes more. Serves 6.

ROAST CANADA OR SNOW GOOSE

What
1 goose, 10 to 14 lb.
10 slices salt pork or bacon
1 tbsp. lemon juice

For stuffing
⅓ cup butter
2 cups raw brown rice
½ cup chopped celery
½ cup chopped onions
2 tbsp. parsley flakes
1½ cups chicken broth or consomme
1 tsp. salt
½ cup sherry
½ tsp. thyme
½ tsp. pepper
1½ cups raw cranberries

How
Stir-cook onions, celery, rice, and seasonings in butter, until rice is well browned. Add chicken broth and wine, cover, and simmer 20 minutes until liquid is absorbed. Add chopped cranberries, stir in, and cook covered 5 minutes more. Set stuffing aside, uncovered, until cool enough to handle. Wipe goose inside and out with damp cloth, and rub with lemon juice. Stuff and sew up or use skewers and lacing, tie legs

and wings. Place in roasting pan with the breast up. Cover with the salt pork or bacon. Bake in a preheated 325 degree oven, uncovered, 25 minutes per pound. Baste every half hour after the first hour.

MULLIGAN SQUIRREL

What
2 squirrels, about 1 lb. each
1 cup corn niblets or fresh corn
1½ cups diced potato
2 cups condensed tomato soup
½ cup smoked bacon, diced
½ cup chopped onion
½ tsp. thyme flakes
½ tsp. bay leaf—crumbled
1 tsp. salt
½ tsp. fresh black pepper
1 cup dry red wine

How
Disjoint skinned and cleaned squirrels. Put in stewpot with 3 cups water and balance of ingredients. Bring to boil, turn down heat, and simmer covered 2 hours.

PARTRIDGES CHAUSSEUR

What
3 partridges, cut up for serving
4 tbsp. butter
1 finely chopped onion
1 tbsp. parsley flakes
3 tbsp. flour
½ tsp. dried thyme

½ cup chopped celery
1½ cups chicken or ham stock or consomme
1½ cups sliced mushrooms
1 tsp. lemon juice
½ cup dry sherry
½ tsp. salt
¼ tsp. black pepper

How
Brown partridge lightly on all sides in butter. Add onion, celery, and seasonings. Stir flour into consomme and wine. Toss mushrooms with lemon juice, stir into flour and wine mixture, and add to pan. Cover and simmer 20 to 30 minutes. Serve with toast fingers or croutons. Serves 3.

BARBECUED TROUT

What
2 trout, 10 to 12 oz. each
6 slices bacon
1 tsp. salt
½ tsp. M.S.G.
2 tbsp. lemon juice
¼ tsp. fresh black pepper

How
Wash and dry each cleaned and scaled trout. Rub inside and out with lemon juice and seasonings. Wrap in bacon, secure with skewers or picks, and grill in basket broiler about 3 inches from coals about 4 minutes on one side and 3 minutes on other side until bacon is crisp. Serves 2.
If somebody insists on sauce, serve lemon butter on the side.
For lemon butter, mix 1 tbsp. lemon juice and a dash of Tabasco in 4 tbsp. melted butter.

18
Salads Selection

Kindly do not just pass up this section with some nasty like, "Rabbit food, hahgh." While you are leaning on your hospitalization insurance, with your tongue in your cheek, those middle-aged rabbits are racking up a score that would heat the bearings on an adding machine. Be honest, now. Have you ever heard of an overweight or an undersexed rabbit? These wonderful raw foods supply vitamins and minerals to fuel you through many happy hours of surreptitious activities. If you learn to eat generously of salads, you will never have to resort to buying vitamins from an anemic salesman. You might also note that advertisers who advertise vitamin-fortified products, are probably apologizing, publicly and at a profit, for the vitamins they have extracted in processing their products.

Salads are not only low in calories, but actually help to burn up calories taken in other foods. Just remember that a fat man lives in a vicious circle, his own belt line!

So, now it is time to get out that old lemonwood salad bowl. Its aroma, faintly redolent of exotic spices, carries nostalgic memories of past delights, and imbues the present creations with the haunting flavor of an exciting past. Wipe off the oil, rub gently with a split clove of garlic, and get ready to enjoy.

Note I have found out that you can cook spinach in 1 minute in a pressure cooker. Big deal. That just means you have to eat the damn stuff 14 minutes sooner.

SALADS SELECTION

Satisfactory salads are based on crisp greens, balanced ingredients, and compatible dressings. To crisp greens, clean and wash well, and put in a bowl in the refrigerator, covered or wrapped in a damp cloth. For crisp cole slaw, put shredded cabbage in ice water for a half hour or so.

Wooden salad bowls should never be washed. Rub thoroughly with absorbent paper, oil lightly, and keep covered when not in use. When ready to use, wipe off oil, rub with split clove of garlic. Many people object to cucumbers because of a gas problem, which with some people is quite severe. For burpless cucumbers, slice them and place in a salt brine made of $\frac{1}{4}$ cup of salt to 1 quart of water. About an hour for slices $\frac{1}{8}$ inch thick will take the trouble element out of them. Wash, soak for 15 minutes in clear water, and drain for use.

To take the heat out of onions, slice them, and salt a slicing board, well. Place the slices on the salted board, then salt them on top. Leave them a half hour, then drain and wash well. You now have mild onions with a good taste and no bite.

Since salad dressings are basic to all salads, I start with a list of popular dressings.

FRENCH DRESSING

Pour into a bottle:

What
6 tbsp. salad oil
1 tsp. salt
$\frac{1}{4}$ tsp. pepper
Dash paprika
6 tbsp. vinegar or lemon juice

How
Cover bottle tightly and shake until thoroughly mixed. For a more flavorful dressing use ground onion or garlic.

ROQUEFORT DRESSING

Mash Roquefort cheese with fork, and gradually work in French dressing until of desired consistency. A tablespoon of sour cream improves the flavor. Nice with fruit salad or any green salad.

RUSSIAN DRESSING

Combine:

What
1 cup mayonnaise
3 tbsp. chili sauce
2 tbsp. lemon juice
3 tbsp. finely chopped green pepper
2 tbsp. finely chopped red sweet or pimento pepper
2 drops Tabasco sauce
1 medium, sour cucumber pickle, finely chopped
½ tsp. grated onion
Usually served over head lettuce.

THOUSAND ISLAND DRESSING

Mix well:

What
1 cup mayonnaise
1 finely chopped pimento

2 tbsp. chopped sweet pickle
⅓ cup chili sauce
⅓ cup whipped cream
1 finely chopped hard-boiled egg

TOMATO FRENCH DRESSING

Combine:

What
1 can (1⅓ cup) tomato soup
¾ cup vinegar
½ cup sugar
1½ cups salad oil
1 tsp. salt
½ tsp. pepper
1 tsp. paprika
2 tbsp. Worcestershire sauce
1 tbsp. prepared mustard (½ tsp. dry mustard)

How
Beat with rotary beater until well blended. Garlic powder
may be added, if you wish.

FRUIT SALAD DRESSING

Cook four minutes:

What
¼ cup orange juice
3 tbsp. lemon juice
¼ cup sugar
Add 2 eggs, beaten, and cook to custard consistency. Chill.
Add ½ cup whipped cream. Happy Lorna Doone to you.

CHIFFONADE DRESSING

Shake together in jar:

What
½ cup salad oil
3 tbsp. vinegar
¼ tsp. salt
¼ tsp. paprika
1 tbsp. hard-cooked egg white
1 tbsp. finely chopped red sweet pepper
1 tbsp. finely chopped green pepper
1 tbsp. finely chopped onion

How
Keep on ice until ready to serve. Shake thoroughly before using. Serve on hearts of lettuce, thinly sliced cabbage, or any green salad.

ITALIAN DRESSING

To French dressing (1½ cups) add 1 tsp. oregano, 2 finely chopped cloves of garlic, and 1 tsp. rosemary. Set aside for a few days, shaking now and then. Shake well before using.

BOILED DRESSING

Heat in saucepan:

What
¾ cup vinegar
¼ cup water
⅓ cup sugar
1 tsp. salt

2 tbsp. cornstarch
1 tsp. dry mustard

How
Cook until thick. Add 1 egg, beaten, and 1 tbsp. butter.
Cook until clear. Cool. Thin with milk when ready to serve.
This dressing will keep in the refrigerator for weeks without
milk added.

Note
If you beat in 4 tbsp. soft peanut butter, it will make this a
delicious fruit salad dressing.

SAVORY DRESSING

What
½ cup minced parsley
½ cup fine cut chow-chow
1 tbsp. onion juice
1 tbsp. salt
1 tsp. white pepper
3 cups olive oil
¾ cup vinegar

How
Put in jar and shake well, also every time it is used.

PINEAPPLE DRESSING

What
1 cup French dressing
½ cup grated pineapple
¼ cup ground nut meats
½ cup cream

1 tsp. salt
½ tsp. pepper
1 tsp. paprika

How
Shake well together, and every time you use it. Good on
bland fish, fruit salad.

SPANISH DRESSING

What
¼ cup lemon juice
½ cup tomato catsup
1½ cups olive oil
1 tbsp. Worcestershire sauce
1 tbsp. sugar
1 tbsp. salt
1 tbsp. dry mustard
1 tsp. paprika

How
Mix seasonings. Add lemon juice and catsup. Beat in oil.
Chill and serve.

TAVERN DRESSING

What
¼ cup dry mustard
¼ cup water
1 pint salad oil
1 tbsp. salt
1 tbsp. sugar
2 tsp. paprika
1 tbsp. Worcestershire sauce
½ cup vinegar

How

Mix mustard and water. Add a little oil at a time, beating with rotary beater. Add vinegar and seasonings. Use on meat or fish salads.

COLE SLAW

What

1 small cabbage, sliced fine
1 green pepper, sliced thin
3 pimentos, sliced thin
10 stuffed olives, sliced

How

Pour on 1½ cups French dressing, and let stand 3 hours before serving.

POTATO SALAD

Potato salad is as temperamental as the people who eat it. It can be good or horrible, depending on the care taken in preparation. Soft, overcooked potatoes, too much vinegar, too much onion, or overseasoning can ruin the best potatoes, and the disposition of the nicest guest. This one is good, if you stick to the rules.

Allowing 1 medium potato for each person, boil peeled potatoes until firmly done (about 25 minutes at sea level). Cool and dice in ½ inch dice. Allowing ½ cup onion to 2 cups potatoes, grate onion into potatoes and toss lightly to mix. For 2½ cups, marinate lightly with about ⅓ cup French dressing. Place in refrigerator until serving time. Then add enough mayonnaise to moisten well and season with salt and pepper, and add 1 tbsp. chopped parsley. Serve in lettuce cups and garnish with tomato wedges and quartered hard-cooked eggs sprinkled with paprika.

GREEN SALAD

Salad greens may be lettuce, endive, watercress, romaine, chicory, escarole, parsley, tender dandelion, or spinach leaves. Take Chinese cabbage, celery cabbage, fennel, and salad chervil. Whatever your selection, wash well, and wrap in waxed paper, cellophane, or paper towel, to crisp, in refrigerator. Fifteen minutes before using, tear greens and marinate lightly in French dressing. Just before serving add the dressing of your choice as a topping.

SPRING TONIC

Sprinkle with water and drain 2 cups finely sliced cabbage. Let stand in refrigerator 15 minutes to crisp. Combine with 1 cup grated raw carrot, 1 cup chopped tart apple, ½ cup chopped green pepper, 1 small onion, grated. Season with salt.

BEET, CABBAGE, AND PINEAPPLE SALAD

2 cups finely sliced cabbage that has been crisped in the refrigerator. Combine with 1 cup drained, diced pineapple, and 1 cup diced cooked beets. Moisten with mayonnaise and season to taste.

PINEAPPLE WALDORF

Combine:

What
1 red apple, diced and unpeeled
1 slice pineapple, diced
2 tbsp. walnut meats

How

Marinate in French dressing, and just before serving moisten with mayonnaise.

EGG AND ONION SALAD

What

½ doz. hard-cooked eggs, diced
½ cup celery, diced
1 small onion, diced
½ tsp. salt
½ tsp. paprika
2 tbsp. French dressing
2 tbsp. mayonnaise
Pinch white pepper

How

Combine all ingredients and chill. May be sprinkled with grated sharp cheese for different flavor.

CHICKEN SALAD

What

3 cups diced chicken
½ cup French dressing
3 cups diced celery
1 tbsp. minced parsley
1 tsp. salt
¼ tsp. pepper
6 hard-cooked eggs
1½ cups mayonnaise
½ cup capers

How

Marinate chicken with French dressing 10 minutes. Combine

with all other stuff except eggs. Slice them and garnish with capers.

CUCUMBER BOATS

What
3 large cucumbers
½ cup French dressing
2 bunches watercress

How
Pare cucumbers and cut lengthwise into halves. Scoop out seeds and pulp. Sprinkle with French dressing and chill ½ hour. Fill with chicken, fish, shrimp, or crabmeat and top with chopped watercress, with French dressing dribbled over top.

CINNAMON APPLE

What
6 apples
1 cup water
1 cup red cinnamon drops
2 cups sugar
Lettuce
Chopped nut meats
Cream cheese (3 oz. pkg.)
Mayonnaise

How
Peel and core apples. Heat water, cinnamon drops, and sugar in a large saucepan until cinnamon drops are melted. Add apples and simmer until tender, turning over in syrup often. Lift apples carefully from syrup and cool. Place on

lettuce. Mix chopped nut meats with cream cheese and place in center of apples. Top with mayonnaise. If cinnamon candies are too hard to find, use 1 tsp. cinnamon and red food coloring.

SUMMER SALAD BOWL

What
2 cups cooked peas
6 cooked-cauliflowerets
2 cups cooked green beans
2 tomatoes, sliced
1 head lettuce
Watercress
1 bunch radishes

How
Marinate all vegetables except lettuce and radishes and watercress. Line a salad bowl with outside lettuce leaves, and place four lettuce cups in center of bowl. Fill cups with marinated vegetables, and garnish with watercress and radish roses.

STUFFED CABBAGE SALAD BOWL

What
1 small head cabbage
1 onion, minced fine
4 tbsp. chopped parsley
6 stuffed olives, sliced
3 pickled beets, cut in strips

How
Wash cabbage and remove outside leaves. Hollow out center, to make a shell. Chop the cabbage removed from center,

finely, and toss with French dressing, along with parsley, onions, beets, and olives. Refill shell with salad and garnish with more slices of olive. Top with Russian dressing.

CHICKEN IN ASPIC

What
1 5 lb. stewing chicken
1 carrot
1 bay leaf
1 tbsp. salt
4 tbsp. unflavored gelatin
½ cup cold water
6 cups chicken stock
½ tbsp. brandy
2 cups drained canned peas

How
Cover chicken with boiling water. Add carrot, bay leaf, and salt. Cook chicken until tender, about 2 to 3 hours. Remove chicken and strain broth, and measure 6 cups. Soften gelatin in cold water 5 minutes, and add to hot broth. Cool broth and add brandy. Remove chicken from bones and skin. Cut into thin slices. Pour about ½ inch of aspic into ring mold, and chill until set firmly. Arrange chicken slices and peas in layers in mold. Fill mold with remaining aspic, and chill until set. Fill center with a mixture of finely chopped green pepper, (3 tbsp.) mayonnaise, and whipped cream.

HAM ASPIC

What
2 tbsp. unflavored gelatin
½ cup cold water

3 cups tomato juice
1 tsp. sugar
½ bay leaf
1 tbsp. chopped onion
3 cups minced baked ham

How
Soften gelatin in cold water. Simmer tomato juice, bay leaf, sugar, salt, and onion 10 minutes. Strain and add gelatin, stir and cool. Add ham, mold, and chill.

MOLDED CUCUMBER SALAD

What
1 large cucumber, peeled and diced
½ tsp. salt
½ sweet pimento, diced
½ tsp. lemon juice
2 tsp. unflavored gelatin
¼ cup cold water
1 cup cream, whipped

How
Combine cucumber, salt, pimento, and lemon juice. Soak gelatin in cold water 5 minutes. Dissolve over hot water, and mix thoroughly with whipped cream. Add cucumber mixture and pour into mold. Chill. Serves 4.

TUNA SALAD IN VEGETABLE RING

What
2 tbsp. unflavored gelatin
¼ cup cold water
¾ cup stock off cooked vegetables

1 cup tomato juice
¼ cup vinegar
1 small onion, chopped
½ tsp. salt
1 7 oz. can tuna
1 cup chopped celery
Lettuce hearts
Mayonnaise

How
Soften gelatin in cold water. Combine vegetable stock, tomato juice, vinegar, onion, and seasoning. Heat to boiling
and simmer 3 minutes. Strain, pour over gelatin, and stir
well until dissolved. Pour into oiled ring mold and chill
until firm. Combine tuna, celery, and mayonnaise to moisten.
Unmold aspic on lettuce, fill center with tuna salad, and
garnish with ripe and stuffed olives. Serves 6.

CRAB FLAKE SALAD

What
2 cups crab flakes
2 tbsp. lemon juice
2 tsp. grated onion
1 cup sliced cucumbers
¼ tsp. salt

How
Combine all ingredients. Add mayonnaise to moisten. Serve
in a bowl garnished with salad greens, or in lettuce cups as
individual servings. Serves 4. Diced celery or green peppers
may be used instead of cucumber.

SHRIMP STUFFED CELERY

What

1 cup cooked shrimp
2 cups grapefruit segments, chilled
3 oz. cream cheese
2 tbsp. mayonnaise
¼ tsp. salt
6 stalks crisp celery
Lettuce leaves

How

Cut shrimp fine. Drain grapefruit. Mash cheese, add mayonnaise, salt, and cream together. Add shrimp and mix well. Pack grooves of celery with mixture, cut into 1-inch lengths. Arrange on lettuce with grapefruit segments. Sprinkle with French dressing. Snack for 6.

TURKEY SALAD

What

2 cups diced turkey meat (mix light and dark if available)
1 cup diced celery
1 tbsp. grated onion
½ cup chopped green pepper
4 tbsp. French dressing
½ tsp. salt
¼ tsp. pepper

How

Mix all ingredients together, and let marinate for an hour. Moisten with mayonnaise, and serve in lettuce cups, sprinkle on top with paprika.

MEXICAN SALAD

What
1/2 cup olive oil
1/2 tsp. minced garlic
1 pint bread cubes, about 1/2 inch
1 cup diced celery
2 cups diced boiled potatoes
1 cup shredded onions
1 cup grated carrot
1 cup cooked green beans
1/4 cup minced green peppers
1/4 cup chopped pimentos
1 1/2 tsp. salt
1 1/2 tsp. chili powder
1/4 cup vinegar

How
Heat 1/2 the olive oil with garlic. Add the bread cubes and brown. Add remaining oil and other ingredients. Mix all together lightly. Remove, chill, and serve in salad bowls lined with lettuce leaves.

CHEESE AND APPLE SALAD

What
1 pint cream cheese
1 cup French dressing
3/4 cup diced celery
1 tsp. salt
1/4 tsp. cayenne pepper
1/4 cup chopped pecans
8 medium-sized apples
1/3 cup currant jelly

How

Mash cream cheese and thin out with half the French dressing. Add celery, salt, cayenne pepper, and pecans. Core and hollow out apples, and stuff with the mixture. Mix currant jelly with remaining French dressing. Serve stuffed apples on crisp lettuce leaves. Pour over the jelly-dressing mixture. Serves 8.

WATERCRESS SALAD

What

6 bunches watercress
1 cup ripe olives
¾ cup minced celery
3 hard-cooked eggs
1 cup mayonnaise
3 tbsp. French mustard

How

Cut stem ends from watercress. Remove any dead leaves. Wash thoroughly and drain well. Remove stones and chop olives. Peel and chop eggs. Toss all ingredients together until well mixed. Chill and serve.

19

Soups, Sauces, and Gravies

A good soup can really turn you on, and a large section of the population cannot make good soup. A good many of the soups in both homes and restaurants taste as though they were made from a stewed catcher's mitt. There is an old adage (ever hear of a new one?) amongst chefs, that a soup can be no better than its stock. Very true. If the stock is made of the proper ingredients, fully flavored, and not scorched in the making, some delightful soup will result. Stock made from leftover bones from roasts, etc., is dark. Clear stock is made from raw bones and meats. Combinations of stocks made from different meats can be much more delightful in taste than a straight stock. In the finest restaurants many types of meats and bones go into the stock pot. They use fish, fowl, ham bones, marrow bones, etc. Every morning they skim the stock pot, and draw off the stock required for the day. Then the pot is charged again, and more bones and garni added. The time-tested flavoring ingredients, onions, carrots, parsley, celery, and tops, add their delightful flavor. After long cooking they should be firmly discarded, as their value is in the stock, and nothing is left in the pulp. Stock should be strained and poured into jars. The fat will rise to the top and form a seal, and prevent souring. Fat-sealed stock will keep for weeks in the fridge without souring. If you use part of a jar, save the fat, and reheat the unused portion with the fat, which will again seal the jar.

Now we come to the subject of basic white sauce. It comes thin, medium, and thick. First you melt the fat, remove from heat, and stir in the flour well. Let stand 5 minutes, then return to heat, and stir in milk slowly, and stir-cook until well cooked and smooth.

WHITE SAUCE

Ingredients	Thin	Medium	Thick
Butter, oil, fat	1 tbsp.	2 tbsp.	4 tbsp.
Flour	1 tbsp.	2 tbsp.	4 tbsp.
Milk	1 cup	1 cup	1 cup

For cheese sauce, add grated cheese and paprika. These basic white sauces are versatile, and can be flavored as you wish. You may add any spice or other ingredient that will not thin the sauce. If you add any other liquid, reduce the amount of milk accordingly.

Making a good gravy is an art, yet simple if you follow the rules. Never use a fat that has been burned, as a good gravy is a balanced blend of flour, potato flour, cornstarch, arrowroot, or other cereal starch, together with fat, butter or oil, flavoring, and browning materials as desired or available. Most of the flavor of meat is in the fat, so that fat off a well-browned roast or fowl makes flavorful gravy. This is especially true if you cool and skim the brown stock, strain and return the exact amount of fat to the pan to balance the amount of flour you wish to use. Fat and flour should be 50-50 as to proportion. Use the brown stock to make the gravy. To make gravy that is fine in texture, melt the fat, remove pan from heat, and stir in flour. Let sit 5 minutes until flour is expanded, and has fully absorbed fat into the granules. Failure to do this will result in a granular, coarse-textured gravy with a raw taste due to the raw flour in the center of the granules. Stir whatever liquid you are using, slowly into the roux in the pan, and stir-cook until thickened. (*Roux* is the term for a fat and flour combination.)

There are many liquids used in making gravy. Some like to add milk, wine, consomme, vegetable juice, or other liquid. For instance, the famous Tennessee red gravy is made with 1 cup ham stock, 1 cup strong coffee, and 1 cup milk as liquid, using ham fat as the fat. It is loved by both Tennesseeans and tourists, who lap it up with Smithfield ham and pour it over corn pone, moaning with delight. The canned gravies are mostly made with incompletely hydrolised vegetable protein hydrolisate as a base. These do not match the flavor of true meat-fat gravy, although the base does have flavor of its own.

Very few people use bacon fat in making gravy, yet it is among the most flavorful of fats. You can strain it and then clarify it by frying a couple of slices of potato in it. It is especially good with fish, used to make a white sauce. The gravy makes the quality of the food, in some cases. A strong fish is nicely balanced with a bacon-fat gravy.

MEAT SAUCE VALENCIA

A goody from sunny Italy. Since meat sauce is a universally popular mixture, everyone gets into the act. The little boys who made mixed-up mud pies grow up into big boys who throw together a bunch of unrelated ingredients into a wild melange, then toss in hot peppers like a crazed Mexican. The result atrophies the taste buds, and turns the guests into fire-breathing dragons. These heartburn specials make no one happy except the nut who perpetrates them. He beams, "Separates the men from the boys, eh Horace?" (and the diner from his stomach lining) .

This meat sauce may not win the Italian equivalent of the

Congressional Medal of Honor, but it lets you keep your cook and makes friends of your guests.

What
½ lb. lean ground beef
¼ lb. lean ground pork
¼ cup ground smoked bacon
½ cup chopped onions
2 cloves garlic, chopped
3 stalks celery, sliced thin
1 green pepper, in strips
1 cup canned tomatoes
1 5 oz. can tomato paste
2 8 oz. cans tomato sauce
1 tsp. brown sugar
¼ tsp. baking soda (if needed)
1 cup sliced mushrooms
1 tsp. oregano flakes
¼ tsp. rosemary (optional)
¼ tsp. black pepper
1 tsp. chili powder
1 tsp. salt
½ cup claret wine
2 tbsp. oil

How
Brown the pork and bacon in the oil. Add the beef, garlic, onion, and green pepper. Stir-fry until beef is gray and onions just tender. Add the celery, tomato sauce, tomato paste, canned tomatoes, sugar, and all the seasonings. Simmer slowly 1 hour. Taste and if slightly acid, stir in the baking soda. Stir until foam subsides. Add mushrooms, and the wine, with 1 tbsp. cornstarch stirred into it. Simmer 10 minutes more. Remove from heat and keep hot until serving. This sauce is even better 1 or 2 days old, as the flavors blend and improve.

CHICKEN SOUP

Use a good strong chicken soup stock, or bouillon. Thicken
with flour, mixed with cold stock or water. Stir in 1 tbsp.
butter per quart of soup, and sprinkle with chopped chives
when serving.

BAKED BEAN SOUP

What
2 cups baked beans
1 quart water
½ cup chopped onion
½ cup diced celery
1½ tbsp. butter
1½ tbsp. flour
1 cup strained, cooked tomatoes
¼ tsp. basil
½ tsp. salt
¼ tsp. pepper

How
Cook the baked beans in the water, with the onion and
celery. When vegetables are tender, rub through sieve, or
run in blender. Melt butter in pan, and add flour. Stir in
tomatoes and seasonings. Cook until thickened, and add
bean puree. Heat and serve.

CREAM OF CABBAGE SOUP

What
1 onion
3 cups chopped cabbage
1 quart water

2 cups medium white sauce
¼ tsp. salt
¼ tsp. pepper
½ tsp. paprika
2 tbsp. dry sherry
¼ tsp. chervil

How

Grind onion and cabbage. Add balance of ingredients except white sauce, and cook 30 minutes, simmering. Add white sauce, and a little more sherry, if you wish. To really appreciate cabbage soup, you should take a drink of sherry, then taste the soup, then another sherry, and taste again. Decide which you like best and concentrate on that one!

ONION SOUP

Saute 1 lb. onions, sliced thin, in 4 tbsp. butter, until browned. Sprinkle with 1 tbsp. flour, and stir in until flour is well blended. Stir into 1½ qt. rich beef stock, preferably dark stock off roast. Stir until smooth and season with salt and pepper. Sprinkle Parmesan cheese on 1 slice of thick French bread, per serving. Toast on top of the onion soup in a hot oven or under the broiler. This soup is better made several hours before serving, then reheating to serve. Serves 8.

CREAM OF ONION SOUP

Saute 4 thinly sliced onions in ¼ cup of fat. When amber color, stir in 2 tbsp. flour. Stir in while cooking 3 pints milk. Simmer 15 to 20 minutes. Add ½ tsp. sugar, 1 tsp. salt, ⅛ tsp. pepper. Serves 6 to 8.

CRÊME VICHYSOISSE

White parts of 6 leeks, sliced fine, 3 stalks celery, sliced fine. Saute in 1/4 lb. butter. Add 2 cups cubed raw potatoes, and one quart strained chicken stock. Cook until all is tender. Put through a sieve or blender. Add 1 pint coffee cream, 1/4 lb. of butter. Season with salt and pepper. Serve hot with chopped mushrooms or chives on top; or reheated in top of double boiler next day is even better. Also serve chilled with whipped cream sprinkled with chopped chives, or sour cream sprinkled with finely chopped cucumber. Serves 8 to 10.

VEGETABLE SOUP

Take the fat off 1 quart of good beef stock or if you like from mixed stock. Add 1 onion, cut fine, 1/2 cup diced celery, 1 cup diced carrot, 1 cup peas, 1 cup lima beans, 1 1/2 cups canned tomatoes, to the stock. Add 2 cups hot water, 1/2 tsp. salt. Cover and cook 20 minutes. Beef bouillon cubes may be used to make the quart of stock.

CREAM OF MUSHROOM SOUP

Saute 1/2 lb. of sliced mushrooms in 1/4 lb. butter. Stir in well 4 tbsp. flour. Add 1/4 tsp. pepper, 2 tsp. salt, and 1 quart strong chicken stock. Heat and add 2 cups whole milk. Let sit an hour before serving. Reheat and add 1 tbsp. dry sherry. Serves 8.

JELLIED TOMATO CONSOMME

What
1 1/2 quarts chicken stock or bouillon

2 cups strained, canned tomatoes
1 medium onion, chopped
½ bay leaf
4 cloves
½ tsp. celery seed
¼ tsp. basil

How
Boil all the foregoing together for 20 minutes. Add a pinch of curry powder, and a pinch of paprika. Strain through a colander, then through cheesecloth. Soften 2 tbsp. gelatin in ¼ cup water, and stir in. Pour into shallow dish, and when firm cut into cubes, and serve in bouillon cups.

CONSOMME MADRILENE

Cook 1 lb. lean beef (shank or shin) in 1 quart water and 1 quart chicken stock. Add 2½ cups canned tomatoes, and cook about 2½ hours, simmering slowly. Strain through fine cloth and season. Stir in 1 tbsp. gelatin, softened in ¼ cup cool water. Add red food coloring to make a rosy color. Serve in cups, hot or iced. Serves 5 or 6.

JELLIED CLAM BOUILLON

1 quart hot liquor from steamed clams, or canned clam juice. Soften 3 tbsp. gelatin in ¼ cup cool water. Stir into hot clam juice, and stir until gelatin is well dissolved. Add 2 tbsp. tomato catsup. Serves 4, hot. To serve cold, pour into shallow dish, chill and cut in cubes, or chop finely. Can be served with garnish of whipped cream with prepared horseradish stirred into it, to taste.

OYSTER OR CLAM BISQUE

Cut fine a 1½-inch cube of salt pork. Fry until brown, stir-

ring and turning. Fry with it near the finish, 1 sliced onion.
Add 1 quart clam juice, and 1 pint of clams or oysters,
chopped or ground. Add 4 cups milk, scalded. Salt and
pepper to taste. Serves 8.

CLAM CONSOMME

Combine:

What
1 can chicken consomme
1 can water
1 cup clam juice
1 cup tomato juice

Then
Add a large sprig of parsley, 1 slice onion, and 2 thin slices
of lemon. Simmer 10–12 minutes. Strain and season to taste.
Float a cracker with a little salted whipped cream on top.
Serves 4 to 6.

CRAB BISQUE

What
¼ cup butter
¼ cup flour
2 quarts milk
4 cups crabmeat
1 tbsp. salt
½ tsp. pepper

How
Blend butter and flour and cook until lightly browned. Do
not burn! Add milk and bring to boiling point. Add finely

chopped crab meat. Add seasonings and serve after 5 minutes simmering. Add 2 tbsp. sherry, if desired. Serve hot with oyster crackers. Serves 10, or 5 hungry ones.

BORSCHT

This is the authentic Russian recipe and if you should find hungry Russians storming out of the steppes in answer to the delightful aroma of this dish, don't blame me. It won't make you a Communist, but it will make you well fed.

What
2 quarts of good strong beef stock, and a hambone or 1 quart of ham stock
2 sliced carrots
2 stalks celery, chopped
2 onions, sliced
2 bay leaves
8 medium beets
½ head of cabbage (small) sliced ½ inch thick
½ tsp. fresh-ground pepper
1 tbsp. vinegar (wine is best)
2 cups canned tomatoes
6 tbsp. butter
1 tbsp. flour
1 tsp. salt
Dairy sour cream

How
Add bay leaves, cabbage, salt, and pepper to stock, and start simmering. Simmer beets, cut in ¼-inch square strips, in vinegar and 4 tbsp. butter. Simmer carrots, onions, and celery in 2 tbsp. butter until lightly brown. Add to soup. Sprinkle beets with flour, stir thoroughly, and add to soup. If you desire to have meat in the soup, dice, flour, and brown in

butter before adding. Serve as is, or top with sour cream, for those who are dyed-in-the-wool borschters.

MOCK TURTLE SOUP

What
4 lb. veal neck bones, with some meat
1 gallon water
2 tsp. salt
2 bay leaves
1 tsp. cloves
¼ tsp. allspice berries
¼ tsp. thyme
¼ tsp. mace
¼ tsp. celery salt
1 cup chopped onions
½ cup diced carrots
¼ cup butter
¼ cup flour
1 tsp. lemon juice
3 hard-boiled eggs

How
Place veal bones in water with all ingredients except butter, flour, lemon juice, and eggs. Cook until nearly done, when meat falls off bones. Remove bones and reduce stock to about 2 quarts. Mix flour and butter, thin with stock, then stir into stock in pot. Add 2 cups of cubed meat, from bones. Add lemon juice. Boil 5 minutes. Serve with fried egg balls made by mixing meat and seasoning with mashed egg, and frying in butter.

THICK DRIED PEA SOUP

What
2¼ cups dried peas

1 gallon of water
1 cup chopped onion
¼ cup butter
3 tbsp. flour
1 pint milk
½ tbsp. salt
½ tsp. celery salt
½ tsp. pepper

How
Soak peas in about a gallon of water overnight. Drain and cover with one gallon of water. Add onions and simmer 1½ hours. Run through sieve or blender; blend butter and flour and stir in the scalded milk. Combine with soup and seasonings. Stir while reheating. Serves 8 to 10.

SAUCES

A good sauce will accent the flavor of most dishes. Sometimes it will even cover up for less-than-perfect preparation. Here they are, the what and how, of the graceful adjuncts. Of course, the list of sauces is endless, and the individuality of the chef is often expressed in the sauce. At times, the fumblefinger gives himself away by marrying ingredients that fight worse than some of our modern psychotic married teams. At any rate, here are the most tasty and popular of the sauces.

BEARNAISE

For steak or other meat. Cook slowly together:

What
3 tbsp. dry white wine
3 tbsp. white wine vinegar
8 white pepper kernels, crushed

2 shallots, chopped
2 sprigs tarragon (or ½ tsp. flakes)
2 sprigs parsley (or ½ tsp. flakes)
1 bay leaf
½ tsp. meat extract

How
Cook mixture until reduced to half original size. Put
through a fine sieve. Add 6 slightly beaten egg yolks, away
from the heat. Stir together until well blended. Remove from
hot water and add slowly 1 lb. melted butter. Beat continually until smooth. Hold at moderate temperature, if not
serving at once. You can make half the quantity, of course.

BECHAMEL SAUCE

Mix in saucepan:

What
2 tbsp. butter
1 tbsp. chopped onion
½ tsp. chopped parsley
½ tsp. thyme
1 bay leaf
Cook slowly till onion is yellow.
Stir in 2 tbsp. flour.

How
Cook ¾ cup milk or chicken stock until thickened. Add a
little of mixture to 1 slightly beaten egg yolk, then stir the
egg mixture into the sauce. Cook for 2 minutes, and serve
hot with meat. This recipe makes about 1 cup sauce.
Bechamel is also good mixed in preparation of croquettes,
also thinned out and served over them.

QUICK SAUCE BRUNE
(Brown Sauce)

What
1 can beef gravy (10 oz.)
4 oz. Burgundy or other red wine
1/8 tsp. celery powder

How
Heat gravy to boiling. Reduce heat and stir in wine and seasonings. If thinner sauce is desired, add more wine. Serve with almost any cooked meat.

SAUCE CHAMPIGNONS
(Mushroom Sauce)

What
1 can (10 oz.) beef gravy
3 oz. Madeira wine
1 4 oz. can mushrooms
Juice from mushrooms
1 tbsp. butter
1 tsp. parsley flakes

How
Heat gravy, add wine, mushroom juice, parsley, sliced mushrooms, and butter. Serve with steaks, rolled roasts, or meat pies.

BEURRE DE CREVETTES
(Shrimp Butter)

What
1/2 cup cooked or canned shrimp

¼ lb. melted butter
1 tbsp. tomato paste
½ tbsp. tarragon flakes

How
Put in blender, and leave ½ minute on medium speed. Keep refrigerated. Serve on canapes, or as garnish on hot or cold fish dishes.

SAUCE AU MADÈRE
(Madeira Sauce)

What
1 can (10 oz.) beef gravy
1½ tbsp. butter
4 oz. Madeira wine
1 pinch cayenne pepper

How
Heat gravy with butter, then stir in wine and pepper. Keeps well, refrigerated. Use on beef, veal, meat loaf, lamb.

SAUCE À LA PROVENÇALE

What
1 can (8 oz.) tomato sauce
½ tsp. garlic powder
½ tbsp. parsley flakes
½ tbsp. chive flakes
1 tsp. grated orange peel
¼ tsp. saffron (optional)

How
Heat all ingredients together but do not boil. Let stand at

least a half hour for flavors to blend. Reheat and serve on meats, spaghetti, barbecued meats, or pastas.

SAUCE AU CURRY

What
1 can condensed cream of chicken soup
½ cup light cream
1 tsp. curry powder

How
Heat all ingredients together. Serve over cooked meats, poultry, vegetables, or fish.

SAUCE MORNAY

What
1 can cheese soup
½ cup light cream
½ tsp. paprika
¼ tsp. white pepper

How
Heat everything together. Do not boil. Serve over broccoli or other vegetables, with turkey or fish. Brown lightly under broiler. Do not blacken the top, as cheese and cream will darken very quickly.

CUMBERLAND SAUCE

For duck, tongue, ham, game.

What
2 tbsp. slivered orange peel
⅓ cup cold water

10 oz. currant jelly
1/4 cup port, or medium sherry
1/4 cup orange juice
1 tsp. cornstarch
1 tsp. dry mustard
1/4 tsp. ground ginger
1 tbsp. lemon juice
Dash of Tabasco

How
Bring orange peel to a boil in water. Drain and set aside.
Melt jelly, add wine, and orange juice. Mix cornstarch and
spices with lemon juice to a smooth paste. Stir into wine-jelly
mixture. Bring to boil, reduce heat, and stir-cook until
clear and thickened. Add orange peel. Serve hot or cold, as
desired.

HORSERADISH NUT SAUCE

The German chefs recommend this highly on fish.

What
2 tbsp. butter
1/4 cup ground almonds
2 tsp. cornstarch
2 tsp. sugar
1 cup hot coffee cream
1 tbsp. drained horseradish
1/4 tsp. salt
1 tbsp. lemon juice

How
Cream butter and nuts together until fluffy. Mix cornstarch
and sugar together. Add enough cream to make a smooth
paste. Stir nut-butter mixture into hot cream, then stir in

cornstarch paste. Stir-cook slowly until thick and smooth. Remove from heat and stir in horseradish, lemon juice, and salt. If reheating to serve, do not boil. Makes 1 cup.

SWEET-SOUR LEMON SAUCE

For almost any seafood.

What
2 tbsp. salad oil
1 tsp. instant onion, or flakes
1 tsp. green pepper flakes
1/3 cup brown sugar
1 tbsp. cornstarch
1/2 tsp. dry mustard
1/2 cup lemon juice
1 tbsp. soy sauce
1/2 tsp. garlic salt

How
Soak onion flakes, garlic salt, and green pepper flakes in the oil. Mix mustard, sugar, and cornstarch together. Stir in soy sauce and lemon juice to a smooth texture. Stir-cook until smooth and thick. Add green pepper mixture, and stir-cook 2 minutes more. Makes 2/3 cup.

CREAMY COCKTAIL SAUCE

A quick and tasty cold sauce for seafood.

What
2 tbsp. prepared horseradish, drained
1/2 tsp. dry mustard
1 tbsp. tomato paste

½ tsp. Worcestershire sauce
½ tsp. salt
Dash of Tabasco sauce (optional)
½ cup whipping cream

How
Combine smoothly all ingredients except whipping cream.
Whip cream and fold into balance of ingredients. Makes
about 1¼ cups.

HOT COCKTAIL SAUCE

A zingy dipping sauce.

What
½ cup ketchup
½ cup chili sauce
2 tbsp. drained horseradish
2 tsp. grated onion
2 tbsp. lemon juice
1 tbsp. white sugar
1 tsp. Worcestershire sauce
¼ tsp. salt
3 dashes Tabasco

How
Combine all ingredients well. Let stand a few hours to
develop flavor. Makes 1½ cups.

NUT SAUCE

For Swiss chard, cauliflower, beet greens, or turnip.

What
½ cup crushed or ground almonds or pecans
1 tbsp. butter

1 egg, beaten
2 tbsp. white sugar
2 tbsp. brown sugar
1 tsp. dry mustard
2 tsp. cornstarch
¼ cup cider vinegar
½ cup whipping cream
¼ tsp. salt

How
Combine egg, sugar, and butter. Blend mustard, cornstarch, and vinegar into a smooth paste, and add to egg mixture, mixing well. Add salt and stir-cook until thickening begins. Add cream and stir-cook until smooth and thick. Stir in nuts and serve hot over vegetable.

WINE SAUCE

Especially good with beets.

What
½ cup port wine
½ cup juice from beets
2 tsp. cornstarch
1 tbsp. white sugar
1 tbsp. butter
1 tsp. grated orange peel
¼ tsp. salt
⅛ tsp. fresh black pepper

How
Heat beet liquid and wine. Mix sugar and cornstarch with enough beet liquid to make a smooth paste. Stir into hot liquid, and stir-cook until clear and thickened. Remove from heat and stir in butter, orange peel, and seasonings. Makes 1 cup.

CHEESE SAUCE

For vegetables and boiled fish. Stir 1 cup grated cheese into 2 cups medium white sauce.

CUCUMBER SAUCE

For salmon and other cold fish.

Combine:
1 cup heavy cream, whipped
¼ tsp. salt
Pinch of pepper and cayenne
2 tbsp. vinegar
1 tbsp. sugar
1 cucumber, peeled and chopped finely.
Makes 1 cup.

SAUCE DIABLÉE

For steaks, lamb chops, boiled fish.

Mix well:
½ cup melted butter
½ cup coffee cream
1 tsp. prepared mustard
2 tbsp. Worcestershire sauce
4 tbsp. HP sauce or A-1 Sauce
Dash Tabasco
¼ tsp. salt
1 tbsp. vinegar
1 tbsp. mint sauce
1 tsp. sugar
Makes 1½ cups.

BERCY SAUCE

This is a butter sauce, good on anything, for people who like the taste of garlic butter.

What
1¾ cups butter
½ tsp. white pepper
4 tbsp. minced chives
3 tbsp. minced parsley
¼ tsp. garlic juice, or grated garlic

How
Cut butter into pieces and let soften at room temperature. Cream well, and mix in the balance of ingredients.

BORDELAISE

Good on steak or fish.

What
¼ cup finely minced onions
1 tsp. minced garlic
½ cup butter
1 tbsp. finely minced parsley
1 tbsp. lemon juice
¼ cup flour
1 tsp. tomato puree (condensed tomato soup will do)
1 cup strong stock (mixture of veal and ham is best)
¼ tsp. thyme
1 bay leaf

How
Saute onions and garlic in butter 5 minutes. Stir in flour well, add stock, stirring. Add bay leaf and cook 5 minutes;

remove bay leaf, add the balance of ingredients, simmer slowly another 5 minutes. If sauce is becoming too thick, add enough stock to bring to desired consistency.

EGG SAUCE

For fish or vegetables.

What
1 hard-boiled egg
1 cup medium white sauce
½ tsp. prepared mustard
¼ tsp. paprika

How
Stir the last three ingredients well together, and add chopped or sliced hard boiled egg. If desired 1 tbsp. lemon juice may be added for fish.

HOLLANDAISE

For green vegetables, fish, chicken.

Place about 1 inch of water in bottom of double boiler. Water must NOT touch top section.
Cream over the hot water in the top of the boiler ¼ cup of butter. Add 4 egg yolks, one at a time, beating each in thoroughly with a rotary beater or wire whisk before adding the next. Add ¼ tsp. salt, pinch of cayenne, and very slowly, beating, ½ cup boiling water. Cook until thick. (If you get anxious for speed, and the sauce curdles, beat in slowly 1 tbsp. cream, which will reblend the sauce). Add juice of 1 lemon, beating in slowly. Serve hot on vegetables or cold on salads.

HORSERADISH SAUCE

For roast or pot roast or cold beef.

To one cup medium white sauce, add
4 tbsp. prepared horseradish, and blend in well.

MAÎTRE D'HOTEL

For potatoes, steak, fish.

Cream 6 tbsp. butter, add 10 drops lemon juice, ½ tsp. salt,
¼ tsp. pepper, 1 tsp. finely chopped parsley. Makes about
½ cup.

MINT SAUCE

For lamb.

Wash, shake dry, and chop finely enough mint leaves to
make ¼ cup. Add 1 tbsp. wine vinegar, 2 tsp. sugar, ¾ cup
currant or tart apple jelly, grated rind of 1 orange. Let stand
a few hours to develop flavor before using. Keeps well and
improves in flavor (refrigerated).

MUSTARD SAUCE

For broiled fish, tripe, steak, hamburger.

Saute until tender 1 tbsp. minced onion, in 3 tbsp. butter.
Add 2 tbsp. wine vinegar, and simmer for 5 minutes. Mix
2 tbsp. dry mustard with 1 tbsp. water, and add to vinegar
mixture. Blend with 1 cup brown gravy, and simmer 2
minutes. Makes 1¼ cups.

RAISIN SAUCE

For ham.

Boil 1 cup water and 1 cup sugar. Add 1 cup seedless raisins, 2 tbsp. butter, 2 tbsp. vinegar, 1/4 tsp. clove, 1/4 tsp. cinnamon, 1/2 tsp. salt, 1 glass (6 oz.) apple jelly, 1 tsp. cornstarch, mixed with a little cold water into thin paste. Stir over low heat until raisins are plump and sauce slightly thickened. Serve hot over hot ham.

RAREBIT SAUCE

For baked fish.

Melt over hot water in top of double boiler, 2 tbsp. butter. Blend in 1 tbsp. flour, 1/2 tsp. salt, 1/4 tsp. prepared mustard. Add slowly, 1 cup milk. Stir-cook until thickened. Blend in 1 cup grated cheese and stir until melted. Add 1 egg, lightly beaten. Cook a few minutes more, pour over fish, and sprinkle with paprika.

TARTAR SAUCE

What
4 tbsp. mayonnaise
2 tbsp. chopped gherkins
2 tbsp. chopped olives
2 tbsp. chopped onion
2 tbsp. chopped parsley
1/2 tbsp. chopped capers

How
Mix all the foregoing to make 3/4 cup sauce.

So, now you have all the sauces for gracefully accenting your master cheffing. Stick to the rules as laid out. An underdone sauce containing flour can taste almost as good as stale wallpaper paste.

For those who wish to take short-cuts to taste sauces, there are many new products at the supermarkets. You can save a lot of time when you are rushed, tired, or just a little lazy, yet want to add a tempting sauce to zing up that TV dinner, or other quick route to eating. Here are some of the available makes of gravy, sauce, and seasoning mixes. The product name is first, followed by the maker.

À la King Sauce Mix	Durkee
Barbecue Sauce	Kraft, Durkee, McCormick
Cream Sauce Mix	Durkee, McCormick, French's
Cream of Mushroom Sauce Mix	Durkee
Curry Sauce Mix	McCormick, Gourmet
Hollandaise Sauce Mix	Gourmet, Durkee, French's
Horseradish Sauce Mix	Gourmet, Durkee, French's McCormick
Orange Sauce Mix	McCormick, Gourmet
Sour Cream Sauce Mix	McCormick, Gourmet, Durkee, French's
Spaghetti Sauce Mix	McCormick, Gourmet, Durkee, French's
Stroganoff Sauce Mix	Lawry's
Tartar Sauce Mix	Lawry's
Tuna Casserole Sauce Mix	McCormick
Veal Scallopini Mix	McCormick
White Sauce Mix	Durkee
Brown Gravy Mix	Durkee, French's, Pillsbury, Lawry's
Chicken Gravy Mix	McCormick, Durkee, French's, Lawry's
Herb Gravy Mix	McCormick
Home Style Gravy Mix	Pillsbury
Mushroom Gravy Mix	McCormick, Durkee, French's
Onion Gravy Mix	McCormick, Durkee, French's

Caesar Dip & Seasoning Mix   Lawry's
Chili Seasoning Mix   Durkee, French's, Lawry's
                                  McCormick

Green Onion Seasoning Mix   Lawry's
Hamburger & Meat Loaf
    Seasoning   McCormick
Italian Dressing Mix   Four Seasons, Lawry's
Spicy Onion Dip Mix   Lawry's
Spanish Rice Seasoning Mix   Lawry's

CANNED WHITE SAUCES AND GRAVIES

Beef Gravy   Franco-American
Chicken Gravy   Franco-American
Mushroom Gravy   Franco-American
White Sauce   Aunt Penny's

All of you chefs-in-a-hurry must remember that many of the canned condensed soups are very handy for making sauces. With a little imagination, some very nice sauces are possible with combinations of canned soups and other ingredients.

20

Desserts and Dessert Sauces

If I can't keep you away from desserts, I will at least make sure that you enjoy them to the full extent of your belt. Here's the list of waistline expanders. Tie a knot in your guilt complex, and away we go.

BUTTERED RUM SAUCE

Mostly for baba au rhum.

Boil together for two minutes 2 cups sugar and 1 cup cold water. Remove from heat and stir in 1 tbsp. butter and ⅓ cup rum. I prefer light rum, but let your preference be your guide. This sauce is also good on fruit cake and plum pudding. I am aware that you will probably fudge a bit, and buy sponge cakes, etc., for the various desserts. Good sauce covers a little sinning in this department, and can save your reputation as a discerning host-chef.

BUTTERSCOTCH SAUCE

Use with white cake or ice cream.

What
1¼ cups white sugar

2 cups brown sugar
½ cup light corn syrup
1¼ cups boiling water

How
Boil all ingredients together to 225 degrees on thermometer.
This is the thread forming stage, if you have no thermometer.
Add 3 tbsp. butter, and take off heat. Cool a bit and serve.

CHOCOLATE SAUCE

Melt together ¼ cup butter and ¼ cup shaved baker's chocolate. When smooth, stir in ¼ cup cocoa, ½ cup coffee
cream, and ¾ cup sugar, a pinch of salt and 1 tsp. vanilla.
Bring to just under boil.

CLARET WINE SAUCE

Boil together for 6 minutes ½ cup water and ½ cup sugar.
Cool a bit and stir in ½ cup claret. Serve cold on pudding
or ice cream.

CINNAMON SAUCE

For toast, pancakes, or waffles.

Cream 3 tbsp. butter and work in ½ cup powdered sugar
and 1 scant teaspoon cinnamon. Melt together over heat,
and let cool. Spread on toast or pancakes.

CUSTARD SAUCE

Heat 1 cup milk in top of double boiler over boiling water.

Beat the yolks of 2 eggs, and add 1 tbsp. cornstarch well mixed with ½ cup sugar. Pour hot milk slowly into egg mixture, stirring well. Return to double boiler and cook 10 to 12 minutes. Cool slightly and stir in 1 tsp. vanilla. Serve cold.

HARD SAUCE

Cream ⅓ cup butter well until soft. Work in 1 tbsp. cream, and 1 cup powdered sugar. Add 1 tsp. almond extract, or rum, with or without ¼ tsp. cinnamon, according to taste. Beat mixture until fluffy. This is an infinitely elastic sauce as to ingredients. For the tablespoon of cream and the teaspoon of almond extract, you can substitute the same amount of strong coffee, maraschino juice, brandy, ginger syrup, mashed banana, or fresh fruits such as strawberries and raspberries. Let your adventurous spirit be your guide.

PUDDING SAUCE

For apple cakes and puddings.

Boil 1 minute together ½ cup pineapple juice, ⅔ cup sugar, juice and grated rind of one lemon. Add to 3 well-beaten egg yolks. Cook in top of double boiler until thick. Cool and fold in 1 cup whipped cream.

ORANGE SAUCE

For bread pudding or other bland pudding.

Stir into 2 well-beaten egg yolks the juice and grated rind of 1 orange. Add ½ cup powdered sugar and stir well until fully dissolved. Just before serving add 1 cup whipped cream. **Serve cold.**

HAPPY DAY SAUCE

For all steamed puddings.

Beat ¼ cup sugar well into 1 egg yolk. Beat 1 egg white until stiff and add ¼ cup sugar. Fold into egg yolk mixture. Add 1 teaspoon rum or brandy. Just before serving fold in ⅔ cup stiffly whipped cream.

TROPICAL SAUCE

For plain puddings and cakes.

Beat lightly 3 egg yolks. Add ¼ cup sugar and ¼ tsp. salt. Add 2 cups scalded milk and cook the mixture in the top of a double boiler until mixture will coat a spoon. Chill the sauce. Add 1 cup whipped cream and 4 tbsp. finely chopped candied fruits.

VANILLA SAUCE

Cook together 2 minutes, 2 tbsp. melted butter, 1 tbsp. cornstarch. Stir in gradually ½ cup milk and stir until mixture boils. Simmer 5 minutes and add 2 eggs beaten with 1 cup sugar. Add the eggs gradually, stirring in well. Put mixture in a bowl standing in hot water. Beat till frothy. Add ½ tsp. vanilla.

LEMON SAUCE

What
Juice of 1 lemon
1 tbsp. thin lemon peel

2 tbsp. cornstarch
½ cup sugar
Dash of salt, nutmeg
2 tbsp. butter

How
Blend on high speed 20 seconds. Stir-cook until thickened
and clear.

ORANGE SAUCE

What
1 cup orange juice
Thin rind from ½ orange
¼ tsp. salt
½ cup sugar
2 tbsp. cornstarch

How
Blend on high speed 20 seconds. Stir-cook until thickened.
Makes 1 cup.

FAST CHOCOLATE SAUCE

What
1 pkg. (6 oz.) semi-sweet chocolate
¼ cup hot coffee

How
Blend on high speed 20 seconds.

AMBER PUDDING

Mix 4 tbsp. tapioca with 1 cup brown sugar and pinch of

salt. Add to 2 cups cold water. Cook 10 minutes, or until clear and soft. Add ½ tsp. vanilla, after cooling. Top with whipped cream or peaches. Serves 4.

ROSY APPLES

Mix 1 cup sugar, 1 cup red cinnamon candies, and 1 cup water. Boil slowly until candies are dissolved, then add 8 cored and peeled apples and cook until just tender. Cool and fill centers with whipped cream. Top with chopped nuts.

BUTTERSCOTCH PUDDING

Put to soak 4 slices bread in ¼ cup whole milk. Cream 1 cup dark brown sugar with ½ cup butter. Add 2 cups hot milk and hold over low heat for 5 minutes. Mix in slowly 2 beaten eggs and 1 tsp. vanilla. Pour over the bread in the baking dish and bake for 45 minutes at 325 degrees. Top with whipped cream when serving. For those who like sour cream, top with sour cream and chopped nuts. Serves 4.

SCOTCH PUDDING

What
2 cups bread crumbs
Peel of 1 orange, pared off so as to have only the thin outside orange peel
1 cup sugar
½ cup water
2 apples, sliced thin
½ cup water mixed with 1 tsp. lemon juice

How
Boil water and sugar together until fairly thick. Add orange

peel and continue cooking until syrup is brown. Put 1 cup crumbs in the bottom of a baking dish. Lay in the 1 sliced apple, and pour over half the syrup. Sprinkle on half the remaining crumbs, and add the rest of the sliced apple, then more syrup. Top with the rest of the crumbs and any remaining syrup. Add the cup of lemon water and bake at 350 degrees until apples are soft (covered). Remove cover and bake until top is brown and crisp. Serves 5 to 6.

This may be served with whipped cream or hard sauce.

COCONUT CUSTARD

Mix into ½ cup bread crumbs, ½ cup shredded coconut and 2 cups milk. Beat 1 egg until light and frothy. Add ½ tbsp. melted butter, 3 tbsp. sugar, and ¼ tsp. salt. Add to coconut and crumbs, and mix. Pour into a greased baking dish or individual ramekins. Set in pan of hot water in oven, and bake at 325 degrees for 25 to 40 minutes, until a silver knife comes out clean. Serves 4.

CHOCOLATE MOUSSE

What
½ cup semisweet chocolate chips
3 egg yolks
1 tsp. vanilla, rum, or brandy
3 egg whites

How
Melt the chocolate in a mixing bowl over hot water. Beat the yolks well and stir slowly and well into chocolate. Add vanilla or other flavoring. Beat egg whites until stiff but not dry. Fold into chocolate. Spoon into sherbet glasses and chill well. Serve topped with ice cream or cream and a maraschino cherry.

CHOCOLATE SOUFFLÉ

Just for the helluvit, here's one with plenty of calories.
Don't say I didn't warn you!

In the top of a double boiler, blend 3 tbsp. butter with
3 tbsp. flour. Cool a little and add 1 cup milk. Return to
heat and cook until thick. Melt in 1 square of semisweet
chocolate, and stir well. Beat the yolks of three eggs, add
¼ tsp. salt and ⅓ cup sugar. Mix well, then pour the chocolate mixture over the egg mixture. Mix well and cool to
under 90 degrees. Add 1 tsp. vanilla. Beat the egg whites
stiff, and fold in. Put in a lightly greased baking dish, and
bake at 350 degrees for 30 minutes. Serve at once with
Happy Day Sauce to 6 who have no fear of calories.

FRUIT COBBLER

In the bottom of greased custard cups, put some of your
favorite canned fruit (about 1 heaping tbsp. per cup). On
the fruit, drop a heaping tablespoon of biscuit dough. Bake
at 500 degrees in preheated oven for 15 minutes. Turn out
and serve topped with whipped cream, mixed with chopped
nuts, or chopped fruit.

ORANGE SPONGE PUDDING

Heat in top of double boiler 1 pint milk. Add 2 cups bread
crumbs. When crumbs are soft stir in 2 tbsp. melted butter,
or melt in and stir until melted and mixed. Add the juice
and the grated rind of a medium orange, ¼ cup sugar, and
¼ tsp. salt. Fold in 3 stiffly beaten egg whites. Put into a
lightly buttered baking dish, and bake at 325 degrees for
30 minutes, or until firm. Serve hot with orange sauce.

PRUNE WHIP

I don't know what the inoffensive prune did to deserve this treatment. Just desserts, maybe?

Mix 2 egg whites, 1 tsp. grated lemon rind, and 2 tsp. lemon juice. Melt in ⅓ cup sugar, and cook in the top of double boiler. Beat steadily until mixture is fluffy and will hold its shape. Fold in ½ cup finely chopped, drained, well-cooked prunes. Serve with custard sauce or orange sauce. Serves 4.

This can be made with any other strained fruit that suits your fancy.

SHREDDED WHEAT PUDDING

This gets rid of the old shredded wheat nobody wants, or any other shredded cereal of like excitement and appeal.

Crumble 2 shredded wheat biscuits into a baking dish. Mix in a bowl 2 cups milk, 1 tsp. cinnamon, ¾ cup dark molasses, ¼ tsp. salt, and 2 lightly beaten eggs. Stir well until blended and pour into buttered baking dish, over the shredded wheat. Bake at 350 degrees about 45 minutes. Stir every few minutes during baking. Serve hot to 6.

TAPIOCA CREAM

Beat 1 egg white, foamy, and add 2 tbsp. sugar. Beat until mixture holds a peak. Now, in a saucepan beat 1 egg yolk into ½ cup milk. Add 3 tbsp. minute tapioca, ⅛ tsp. salt, and 2 tbsp. sugar, with 1½ cups milk. Bring to a boil over low heat, stirring constantly. Remove from heat, cool slightly, and fold into egg white. Add 1 tsp. vanilla. Cool for 20 minutes, then stir lightly. Chill and serve with any topping that makes you happy, such as soft ice cream or heavy cream. This pudding is pretty elastic as to additives. You can fold in cubed fruit gelatins of various flavors, chocolate bits, or chopped nuts. Just wing it and the adventure will be your own private creation. 2 or 3 colors of fruit gelatin make a very colorful dish, maybe attractive to the other colorful dishes you are able to attract to your den of devilish dining!

CUSTARD CREAM PUFFS

What
1 doz. small cream puffs, custard filled
1 cup lump sugar
½ cup water
1 tbsp. corn syrup

How
Combine syrup, sugar, and water in saucepan. Cook at medium heat until sugar melts. Turn up heat and cook until light brown color. Put cream puffs in aluminum foil. Cool caramel to about 100 degrees, then pour on each puff. Let cool until caramel is set, then keep cool until serving. Serves 6.

CRÊPES SUZETTES JUBILEE

What
1 cup pitted black cherries, drained
4 tbsp. red currant jelly
4 tbsp. orange marmalade
2 tbsp. cherry juice
2 tbsp. brandy
2 pkg. (5 each) frozen cherry blintzes

How

Heat blintzes as directed on package. Heat the 2 tbsp. cherry juice, and stir in marmalade and jelly. Stir until melted. Add brandy and cherries. Warm and pour over blintzes. Serve hot to 5.

CHOCOLATE BAVARIAN CREAM

What

2 envelopes plain gelatin
½ cup hot, strong coffee
¼ cup cold water
6 oz. semisweet chocolate bits
2 egg yolks
1 cup coffee cream
1 cup crushed ice

How

Put coffee and water in blender. Add gelatin and blend on high 20 seconds. Add chocolate and blend 10 seconds. Add egg yolks and cream and blend 10 seconds. Add crushed ice and blend on low until ice is melted. Pour into small individual molds or one 4 cup mold. Chill until set. Serve with whipped cream with 1 chocolate Maple Bud on top. Serves 6.

STRAWBERRY BAVARIAN

What

1 pkg. frozen strawberries, defrosted
½ cup of juice from strawberries
¼ cup milk
2 envelopes plain gelatin
¼ cup sugar
2 egg yolks

1 cup cream
1 heaping cup crushed ice

How
Heat strawberry juice. Put milk in blender, then gelatin, then start blender on low speed. Pour in hot strawberry juice. Blend on high speed 10 seconds. Add sugar, strawberries, and egg yolks. Blend on high speed 20 seconds. Add cream and ice and blend on low 20 seconds, then on high speed 10 seconds. Pour into molds of your choice and chill until set. Serves 6 adults, or two children who are alone with the dessert.

MAPLE CUSTARD

What
3 tbsp. maple syrup
¾ cup milk
1 egg
2 tbsp. sugar
½ tsp. vanilla
⅛ tsp. salt

How
Coat the inside of 3 custard cups with maple syrup. Blend balance of ingredients on high speed 4 seconds. Pour into custard cups. Set cups in 1 inch of hot water in baking dish. Bake at 325 degrees 20 to 30 minutes, until set. Serves 3. Double recipe for 6.

APPLE CRISP

What
1 quart sliced apples

1 tsp. cinnamon
½ tsp. nutmeg
1 cup brown sugar
6 slices bread
1 cup diced sharp cheddar
2 tbsp. butter

How
Crumb bread in blender on low speed. Add cheese and blend on low speed until well mixed. Mix in bowl with balance of ingredients except butter. Put in buttered baking dish, dot with butter, and bake at 350 degrees about 40 minutes until top is crisp and brown. Serve with thick cream or soft ice cream. Serves 6.

FROZEN FRUIT CREAM
(Strawberry, Raspberry, Peach)

What
1 pkg. frozen fruit, cut in chunks
1 tsp. lemon juice
⅔ cups evaporated milk

How
Put in blender. Cover and blend on high speed 30 seconds, or until smooth. Makes 1 pint.

QUICK CHEESE PIE

What
1 crumb crust in 8-inch pie plate
2 envelopes plain gelatin
Juice of ½ lemon
A few slivers of lemon peel

¼ cup sugar
2 eggs
½ cup hot milk
8 oz. soft cream cheese
1 heaping cup crushed ice
1 cup whipping cream

How
Blend milk, gelatin, lemon juice, and lemon peel on high
speed 30 seconds. Shut off. Add sugar, eggs, and cream
cheese. Blend on low 10 seconds and on high speed 10 seconds. Add ice and cream and blend on high speed 20 seconds.
Pour into pie shell and it's ready to serve in 10 minutes.

ZABAGLIONI (Zabaioni)

The Italians are very high on this as a dessert. It is a sort of
custard with wine, and takes time and attention. If you pay
strict attention to the rules, the result is worth the trouble.

What
5 egg yolks
1 whole egg
2 tbsp. sugar
4 ozs. Marsala wine

How
Combine egg yolks, egg, and sugar in top of double boiler
over simmering water. Beat with wire whisk or rotary beater
until pale yellow and fluffy. Gradually beat in Marsala and
keep on beating until thick enough to hold soft peaks. This
may take 10 to 12 minutes more. Serve hot in compote dishes
or stemmed glasses. Serves 4.

ZIPPOLAY

Take 1 cup crushed arrowroot biscuits (or graham crackers).

Grind and mix with ½ cup of the crumbs, ¾ cup pitted dates, ½ lb. small marshmallows, 1 cup nutmeats (any kind you like), and ½ cup thin cream or evaporated milk. Mix thoroughly, and shape into a roll. Roll in the balance of crumbs and chill, for a few hours in refrigerator. Slice and serve with whipped cream, or, if your laziness is showing, one of the commercial whipped toppings. Serves 6 to 8.

Now, as was inevitable, we come to the low calorie desserts. You just take off a calorie here and a calorie there, and before you know it you'll be your old sylph again!

This one is called, for no discernible reason that we can find:

SPANISH CREAM

What
2 cups skim milk
1 envelope of unflavored gelatin (1 tbsp.)
2 eggs, separated
⅛ tsp. salt
8 tsp. sugar, or equivalent in noncalorie sweeteners
1 tsp. vanilla

How
Soften the gelatin in ½ cup of the milk. Beat egg yolks, salt, and balance of milk together. Heat in top of double boiler, then stir in milk and gelatin mixture. Cook, stirring until gelatin is dissolved, for 5 to 6 minutes. Remove from heat and cool slightly. Stir in vanilla. Chill to consistency of unbeaten egg whites. Beat egg whites until stiff, and fold into the gelatin mixture. Remove to single or individual molds, and chill until firm. Serve to about 8 frightened people, who live in the shadow of an inflated waistline.

LEMON SNOW

What
1½ cups water (no calories there)
1 envelope unflavored gelatin
16 tsp. sugar (so use the noncalorics if you must)
¼ cup lemon juice
2 tsp. grated lemon rind
1 egg white

How
Soften gelatin in ½ cup of the water. Add sweetener. Heat gently until gelatin is dissolved. Remove from heat and stir in remaining water, lemon juice, and rind. Chill until slightly thickened. Add unbeaten egg white and beat until fluffy. Serves 6.

COFFEE WHIP

Mix 1 envelope of unflavored gelatin and ⅓ cup sugar, then add ½ cup strong coffee. Stir over low heat until gelatin is thoroughly dissolved. Add 1 cup strong coffee and 1 tsp. of the vanilla. Chill until thickened to consistency of unbeaten egg white, or slightly thicker is even better. Beat until light and fluffy, and mixture will hold firm peaks. Chill in dessert dishes.

CHOCOLATE CHIFFON

What
½ cup sugar
⅛ tsp. salt
⅓ cup cocoa
1½ cups milk

3 eggs. separated
1 tsp. vanilla

How

Mix gelatin, ¼ cup of the sugar, salt, and cocoa in top of double boiler. Beat the egg yolks and milk together and add, stirring well. Stir-cook over boiling water 6 minutes, making sure gelatin is well dissolved. Remove from heat, cool for 10 minutes and add vanilla. Beat egg whites until stiff, then beat in remaining sugar. Fold in chocolate gelatin mixture; chill in single or individual molds. Serves 6 to 8.

WALDORF SALAD

Here's a low calorie that the ladies like. I am not quite sure if it is a salad or a dessert, but it is a pretty good anti-ballooning snack.

Mix in saucepan, 1 envelope of unflavored gelatin, ⅓ cup sugar, and ¼ tsp. malt. Add ½ cup water. Stir over low heat until gelatin is well dissolved. Stir in 1 cup water, ¼ cup vinegar or lemon juice, and remove from heat. Chill to un-beaten egg white consistency. Fold in 2 cups unpeeled, diced, tart apples, ½ cup finely diced celery, and ¼ cup chopped nuts of your choice. Turn into mold, or molds, and chill. Serves 6.

This ends the low-calorie desserts. They are guaranteed to be nonfattening, and certainly non-habit-forming, if my experience is any criterion!

21

Notes on Wine Serving

Wine is served according to tradition only by those who are hide-bound sticklers for the ancient traditions. There are no hard and fast rules as to what wines to serve with what food, time of day, or occasion.

As a general rule, dry wines should be served before meals and with meals, while the sweeter wines should be served with desserts and with coffee. Again, this is largely a matter of individual taste. Women tend to like rosé wines, which are generally a blend of white and red wines, except in the case of the very expensive types.

The following chart is supplied only as a guide, and is not to be considered a Bible of wine bibbing. Let the tastes of you and your guests be your guide in selection of what wine and with what food.

WINE CHART

CLASS	TYPE	WHEN, and With WHAT
APPETIZER WINES	Sherry Vermouth Flavored wines	Serve chilled, alone or with hors d'oeuvres, nuts or cheese

WHITE TABLE	*Sauterne* Semillon Sauvignon Blanc *Chablis* Chenin Blanc Pinot Blanc *Rhine Wine* Reisling Sylvaner Traminer	Serve with snacks and lighter dishes, also chilled with omelettes, chicken, fish or any of the white meats.
RED TABLE WINES	*Burgundy* Gamay Red Pinot Pinot Noir *Chianti* *Claret* Grignolino Cabernet Zinfandel	For heavier dining. Serve chilled to about 60 degrees, with game, roasts, chops, cheese dishes, meat pies and spaghetti and other pasta type dishes.
ROSÉ WINES	Various Blends	Goes with almost any food, according to the individual taste. Rosé is a favorite of women.
DESSERT WINES	Muscatel Angelica Cream Sherry Tokay Port	Serve cool or chilled with fruits, cookies, cheese snacks, cake, or nuts.
SPARKLING WINES	*Champagne* Brut (Very dry) Sec (Semi-dry) Doux (Sweet) Pink Champagne Sparkling Burgundy	For those who like the sparkling wines. Serve well chilled. Widely used in various party punches.

22

Helpful Hints

Should you burn some of the contents of a pan to the bottom, place the pan in cold water immediately. This will set the burned stuff (yeuch!) and you can pour off the rest of the contents without having the burned taste in the product. You can then remove the guck with a pot cleaner, steel wool, or a passing wire-haired terrier.

It is great to be able to make all your homemade soups and sauces. However, a stock of the various types of canned soups gives you a sense of comfort and confidence in an emergency, where you have no time for the long route. Canned soups can form the bases for quick sauces, dips or potages.

Laugh and the world laughs with you. Peel onions and you weep alone. Soak the onions for ten minutes in warm water with a little vinegar, and they'll peel tearlessly.

Orange peels will come off clean, with the white parts adhering to the skin if you put them in boiling water for four or five minutes before peeling.

A damp cloth under the mixing bowl keeps it steady and prevents it slipping on a smooth surface.

Vinegar or lemon juice rubbed on the hands will help remove onion or garlic odour.

Warm rolls and muffins taste twice as good. They're easy

to warm wrapped in foil in the oven, in top of a double boiler or in your electric frypan.

Add 1 tablespoon cooking oil or soft butter per layer when whipping up a cake for extra lightness, moistness, and keeping qualities.

To keep macaroni, noodles, and spaghetti separated during cooking and also to keep the water from boiling over, add a tablespoon of cooking oil for every quart of boiling water.

Most fresh fruits and vegetables need refrigeration, but some keep better when stored outside the refrigerator. For instance bananas darken in the refrigerator and unripe melons, pineapples, and tomatoes ripen better in a cool room (65 degrees F.) than at refrigerator temperatures; after ripening, all except bananas can be held for a short time in the refrigerator.

Cook most foods at low to medium temperatures. If the heat is too high meats will shrink excessively, fats break down and smoke. Milk can acquire a scorched flavor, and eggs and cheese become rubbery. High temperatures also speed the destruction of thiamine and vitamin C.

If you cook food in a large amount of liquid and then discard the liquid, you are throwing away not only some flavor but also valuable water-soluble vitamins and minerals. Save the juices to add to meat stock for delicious soups and gravies.

Do not discard juices from canned fruits; add them to desserts and sauces for flavor and nutritive value.

For braising, boiling, or simmering choose pans with tight-fitting lids. A well-fitting lid holds in most of the steam and so shortens the cooking time. Escaping steam carries with it some of the flavor and too long cooking destroys some of the vitamins.

Don't fool with the mixmaster. This is a delicate and versatile mechanism that may get temperamental if tinkered with. In fact, he's our bartender.

Teach your nose to recognise the smell of properly seasoned food; otherwise you can taste on about two hundred calories per meal.

Don't make the mistake of using too much of hot spices in preparing chili or meat sauce. They not only submerge the flavor, but will get you—in the end.

Remember that a great variety of small and larger aluminum dishes for one-time use are available. Saves buying dishes, as well as washing them, when making individual meat pies, baked, or chilled dishes.

When a recipe calls for part of a cup of solid fat of any kind, fill a measuring cup partly full of water, then add the desired amount of fat, and pour off the water.

SUGGESTIONS

1. Read recipes through completely before you begin working.
2. Assemble utensils needed.
3. If the oven is required, set the temperature control so that the correct heat will be reached by the time you have mixed all the ingredients.
4. Start every meal by assembling all the ingredients needed. It is more efficient to start work on the dish that will take the longest time to prepare and cook.
5. Plan your cooking so that hot foods are served piping hot and chilled foods remain icy cold.
6. Prepare and chill foods which may be readied in advance: for example, vegetables for the salad, the salad dressing, cold desserts, relishes, and nibbles, as well as cold sauces.
7. Generally the last minute tasks are cooking the vegetables and making a pan-gravy.

CHEF'S DICTIONARY OF COOKING TERMS

BAKE: To cook in an oven. Covered or uncovered containers can be used. When meats are cooked in an uncovered pan the method is generally called roasting.

BARBECUE: To roast slowly on a gridiron, spit, over coals. Usually the food is basted with a well-seasoned sauce. Sometimes the term is popularly applied to foods cooked in or served with barbecue sauce.

BASTE: To moisten meat and other foods while cooking to add flavor and to prevent drying of the surface. The liquid is melted fat, meat drippings, fruit juice, or sauce.

BEAT: To make a mixture smooth or to introduce air by using a brisk regular motion that lifts the mixture over and over.

BLANCH: To precook or preheat in boiling water or steam. Blanching is used for two purposes. Before canning, freezing or drying the boiling water inactivates enzymes and shrinks the food. The usual method is to blanch vegetables in boiling water, while fruits are blanched in boiling fruit juice, syrup, water, or steam. Blanching is also used to facilitate the removal of skins from such nuts as almonds, such fruits as peaches, as well as from some vegetables such as tomatoes.

BLEND: To mix thoroughly but gently two or more ingredients.

BOIL: To cook in water or flavored liquid in which bubbles rise continually and break on the surface. The boiling temperature of water at sea level is 212 degrees F.

BRAISE: To cook slowly in a small amount of liquid or steam using a covered utensil. (The meat is generally browned in a small amount of fat before braising. This seals in the juices and gives a better appearance.)

BREAD: To coat with dry bread crumbs. Sometimes the food is first dipped in milk or egg and then rolled in crumbs.

BROIL: To cook under or by direct heat.

CANDY: When applied to small fruits, fruit peel, or ginger it means that the food has been cooked in a heavy syrup until plump and transparent. It is then drained and dried. Sometimes known as crystallized fruit. When applied to sweet potatoes, yams, and carrots the term means to cook with a small amount of sugar or syrup until the vegetable is glazed.

CARAMELIZE: To heat sugar or foods containing sugar slowly until a brown color and characteristic flavor develops.

CHOP: To cut into small even pieces with a sharp knife.

CREAM: To work together one or more foods, usually fat and sugar, until soft and creamy. Creaming is done with a mixer, a spoon, or a paddle.

CUT: To divide food using either a knife or scissors.

CUT IN: To distribute fat into dry ingredients using knives or a pastry blender until the mixture is evenly divided and looks like crumbs.

DICE: Cut into cubes.

DREDGE: To sprinkle or coat with flour or other fine dry substances such as granulated or icing sugar, cinnamon and sugar, or cornmeal.

FOLD: To combine two mixtures by using two motions: first cutting vertically through the mixture, then turning over and over by sliding the spatula across the bottom of the mixing bowl with each turn.

FRICASSEE: To cook by braising such meats as fowl, rabbit, or veal. The dish is usually finished with a cream sauce.

FRY: To cook in fat. When a small amount of fat is used the method is called saute or pan-fry. When a deep layer of fat is used, it is called deep-frying.

GLAZE: To coat with a thin sugar syrup cooked to the crack stage. When applied to single crust pies the method is called glazing, and mixture is not cooked to such a high temperature but it may contain thickening. Occasionally a glaze is uncooked, for example, melted apricot or currant jam to glaze a fruit tart or cheesecake.

GRILL: *See* Broil.

GRIND: To reduce to particles by cutting, crushing, or grinding.

KNEAD: To manipulate with a pressing motion accompanied by folding and stretching. The kneading helps develop the gluten in a yeast dough.

LARD: To insert strips of fat called lardoons into meat which would otherwise be dry and free from fat. Pieces of fat may also be tied onto the top of lean uncooked meat. The adding of fat gives additional flavor and prevents the surface from drying.

MARINATE: To let food stand in an oil-acid mixture, such as French dressing, to add flavor and to help tenderize.

MASK: To cover a cooked food completely. This usually means coating cooked meat or fish with mayonnaise or seasoned jelly.

MELT: To liquefy.

MINCE: To cut or chop into very small pieces.

MIX: To combine ingredients.

PAN-BROIL: To cook uncovered on a hot surface using a heavy frying pan. The fat is poured off as it accumulates.

PAN-FRY: To cook in a small amount of fat. *See* Fry *and* Saute.

PARBOIL: To boil until partially cooked. The cooking is usually completed by another method.

PARCH: To brown by means of dry heat. Usually applied to grains such as corn.

PARE: To cut off the outside covering or to remove the skin.

PASTEURIZE: To preserve food by heating sufficiently to destroy certain microorganisms and arrest fermentation. The temperature used varies with the food but commonly ranges from 140 to 180 degrees F.

PEEL: To strip off the outside covering.

POACH: To cook gently in hot liquid.

POT ROAST: Used when referring to larger cuts of meat cooked by braising. *See* Braise.

RENDER: To free fat from connective tissue at low heat.

ROAST: To cook, uncovered, by dry heat. Usually done in an oven but occasionally in ashes, under coals, or on heated stones and metals. The term is usually applied to meats but may refer to other foods such as potatoes, corn, or chestnuts.

SAUTE: To brown or cook in a small amount of fat. *See* Fry.

SCALD: Generally to heat milk to just below the boiling point, but it can also mean to dip food in boiling water. *See* Blanch.

SCALLOP: To bake food and the sauce mixed together or arranged in alternate layers in a baking dish. The top may or may not be covered with crumbs.

SEAR: To brown the surface of meat with a short application of intense heat.

SIMMER: To cook in a liquid just below the boiling point at a temperature of from 185 to 210 degrees F. Bubbles will form slowly and then collapse below the surface.

STEAM: Steam is applied directly to the food as in a steamer. Or the food is cooked in steam under pressure as with the pressure cooker. Or food may be wrapped in foil or put between two plates and placed over a container of boiling water.

STEEP: To allow a substance to stand in liquid just below the boiling point to extract flavor, color, or other qualities.

STERILIZE: To destroy microorganisms. For culinary purposes this is most often done at a high temperature with steam, dry heat, or by boiling in a liquid.

STEW: To simmer in a small quantity of liquid.

STIR: To mix food materials with a circular motion for the purpose of blending or securing a uniform consistency.

TOAST: To brown by means of dry heat.

WHIP: To beat rapidly to produce expansion due to the incorporation of air in the mixture. Generally applied to cream, eggs, and some gelatin dishes.

SUBSTITUTIONS

If recipe calls for this ingredient	*You can use this one*
¾ cup molasses	1 cup brown sugar
1 tsp. baking powder	⅓ tsp. baking soda and ½ tsp. cream of tartar
1 tbsp. cornstarch	1¾ tbsp. flour
⅓ cup cocoa	1 oz. chocolate and ½ tbsp. shortening.
¾ cup cracker crumbs	1 cup bread crumbs
1 cup butter	⅘ cup clarified bacon fat, or ⅞ cup chicken fat, or ⅞ cup lard, or ⅞ cup vegetable oil, or ½ cup suet

EQUIVALENTS

Dash	⅛ teaspoon
3 teaspoons	1 tablespoon
4 tablespoons	¼ cup
5 tablespoons plus 1 teaspoon	⅓ cup
8 tablespoons	½ cup
16 tablespoons	1 cup
1 cup	8 fluid ounces
2 cups	1 pint
2 pints	1 quart
4 quarts	1 gallon (liquid)
16 ounces	1 pound

For accurate measuring, use standard measuring spoons and a standard measuring sup. All measurements are level. To level, scrape across the top of the measure with a spatula.

23

Use Your Seasoning Skills

One of the great things that separates the rank amateur from the skillful gourmet cook is the use of seasoning. Skillful use of herbs and spices delicately accents but does not submerge the true flavor of the food. The volatile aromatic oils that contain the flavor in spices and herbs are lost in too-long or too high temperature cooking. Except in closed dishes such as a meat pie or casseroles, spices should be added in the last twenty minutes of cooking. This is especially true of skillet and stew-type dishes, where the flavors can easily escape. Curry powders should be slowly heated in melted or clarified butter, to develop the full flavor, before adding to the main dish.

Learn to gauge the strength of spices by rolling them between your fingers until crushed lightly. Then, inhale the aroma and determine the strength. You can also taste them with the tip of your tongue, when the strength will be evident. Underseasoning is better than overseasoning.

Keep spices in a cool dark place, well sealed to protect color and flavor.

As an additional dividend to taste, the aroma of an artfully spiced dish may generate certain excitement beyond the palate. Depending on the sex and attitude of your guest, this chain excitement may be channeled toward some interesting diversions. This alarming result should not deter you from further spicing.

HERB DIRECTORY	POULTRY & GAME	VEGETABLES	SALADS	SAUCES	DESSERTS
BASIL	Venison Duck	tomato eggplant onions	tomato green seafood	spaghetti orange fish butter sauces	fruit compote
BAY LEAF	stew pie	carrots potatoes tomatoes	seafood aspic	marinades Espagnole champagne	
CHERVIL	chicken butter sauce		green salad	Madeira Bearnaise Vinaigrette	
MARJORAM	chicken goose dressings	carrots peas spinach	chicken green	brown sauce sour cream sauce	
OREGANO	stuffing marinades pheasant guinea hen	tomatoes cabbage broccoli lentils	seafood aspic	Spaghetti tomato	
PARSLEY	bouquet garni stuffing	potatoes carrots peas tomatoes	potato fish green	beurre noir Bordelaise Tartare	

HERB DIRECTORY	POULTRY & GAME	VEGETABLES	SALADS	SAUCES	DESSERTS
MINT		carrots new potatoes zucchini	fruit cole slaw green	mint	frostings fruit ices
ROSEMARY	capon duck partridge rabbit	peas spinach	fruit		fruit
SAGE	all stuffings	lima beans eggplant onions tomatoes			
SAVORY	chicken stuffings	beans, rice sauerkraut	green Russian	fish sauce horseradish	pear compote
TARRAGON	duck, chicken squab	salsify celery root mushrooms	green fish chicken	Bearnaise tartare mustard	
THYME	all stuffings	onions carrots beets	pickled beets aspics	Creole Espagnole garni	

HERB DIRECTORY	APPETIZERS	SOUPS	FISH	EGGS & CHEESE	MEATS
BASIL	Vegetable juices seafood cocktail tomato	Minestrone Turtle Tomato	shrimp sole broiled fish	rarebit scrambled eggs	lamb liver sausage
BAY LEAF	tomato juice aspic	stock bouquet garni	court bouillon fish kabob	egg dishes cream cheese	stews pot roasts marinades
CHERVIL	garnish	spinach	fish butter sauces	egg dishes cream cheese	veal beef
MARJORAM	mushrooms patés	clam turtle onion	broiled baked	omelets scrambled	pork, veal lamb, beef
OREGANO	tomato	tomato bean minestroni	stuffing		pork, lamb sausage meat sauce
PARSLEY	garnish canapes	garnish bouquet garni chowder	all fish court bouillon	omelets scrambled	lamb veal steak stews
MINT	fruit cup fruit juice	pea		cream cheese	lamb veal

HERB DIRECTORY	APPETIZERS	SOUPS	FISH	EGGS & CHEESE	MEATS
ROSEMARY	fruit cup	turtle pea, spinach chicken	salmon stuffing	omelet scrambled eggs	lambs ragouts meat sauce beef stew ham loaf
SAGE	cottage & cheddar cheese	chowders cream soup stuffing	stuffings	cottage & cheddar	pork sausage stews stuffings
SAVORY	Vegetable juice	fish consomme bean	broiled baked	deviled & scrambled eggs	pork, veal
TARRAGON	fruit tomato seafood	tomato consomme turtle chicken mushroom	frog legs broiled lobster & fish	all eggs	sweetbreads veal Yorkshire pudding
THYME	seafood tomato	borscht gumbo chowders vegetable	broiled baked	shirred eggs cottage cheese	mutton veal

Index

Fondues

VEGETABLES